D0065195

REAL LEADERSHIP

REAL LEADERSHIP
Helping People and Organizations Face Their Toughest Challenges

Dean Williams

BERRETT-KOEHLER PUBLISHERS, INC.
San Francisco

Berrett-Koehler Publishers, Inc.
235 Montgomery Street, Suite 650
San Francisco, CA 94104-2916
Tel: (415) 288-0260   Fax: (415) 362-2512   www.bkconnection.com

Ordering Information

Quantity sales. Special discounts are available on quantity purchases by corporations, associations, and others. For details, contact the "Special Sales Department" at the Berrett-Koehler address above.

Individual sales. Berrett-Koehler publications are available through most bookstores. They can also be ordered directly from Berrett-Koehler: Tel: (800) 929-2929; Fax:(802) 864-7626; www.bkconnection.com

Orders for college textbook/course adoption use. Please contact Berrett-Koehler: Tel: (800) 929-2929; Fax: (802) 864-7626.

Orders by U.S. trade bookstores and wholesalers. Please contact Publishers Group West, 1700 Fourth Street, Berkeley, CA 94710. Tel: (510) 528-1444; Fax (510) 528-3444.

Production Management: Michael Bass Associates

Berrett-Koehler and the BK logo are registered trademarks of Berrett-Koehler Publishers, Inc.

Printed in the United States of America

Berrett-Koehler books are printed on long-lasting acid-free paper. When it is available, we choose paper that has been manufactured by environmentally responsible processes. These may include using trees grown in sustainable forests, incorporating recycled paper, minimizing chlorine in bleaching, or recycling the energy produced at the paper mill.

Library of Congress Cataloging-in-Publication Data
Williams, Dean, date–
    Real leadership: helping people and organizations face their toughest
challenges / by Dean Williams.
      p. cm.
    Includes index.
    ISBN-10: 1-57675-343-3; ISBN-13: 978-1-57675-343-9
    1. Leadership. I. Title.
HM1261.W55 2005
158´.4—dc22

2005045219

First Edition
10 09 08 07 06 05   10 9 8 7 6 5 4 3 2 1

To Rosie

Contents

Introduction

This is a book for those who are serious about improving the human condition. It is about real leadership—the kind of leadership that helps organizations, communities, and nations face their toughest challenges and have their best shot at success.

Real leadership is lacking in the world today. Much of what passes for leadership, I suggest, is actually counterfeit leadership, even though it might have the appearance of being effective leadership because people are following the leader or buying into his or her agenda. This book defines real leadership and explains why it is desperately needed, and it provides a well-developed model for how to exercise real and responsible leadership for some of the most demanding challenges organizations, communities, and nations face.

Fundamentally, real leadership gets people to confront reality and change values, habits, practices, and priorities in order to deal with the *real threat* or the *real opportunity* the people face. It facilitates improvements in the human condition. Counterfeit leadership, on the other hand, provides false solutions and allows the group to bypass reality.

Certainly, exercising leadership successfully in a complex world is a formidable task. Few people do it well. Their knowledge of how to act in complex, problematic situations is often incomplete and inadequate. They make mistakes, do foolish things, and, at times, misjudge the dynamics of the situation before them, and thereby perpetuate the very problems that they wish they could resolve.

Part of the problem is that many of the popular notions of leadership are inadequate for the challenges we face today. They do not address the complexity and diversity of the problems, threats, and opportunities that groups and institutions must confront if they are to progress. They focus primarily on leading in unsophisticated environments and unduly emphasize the role of the leader in "having convictions," "articulating a vision," "showing the way," and generating "loyal followers."

Real leadership is not about having strong convictions and imposing them on the group. Nor is it about amassing followers and showing the way forward. Even when the exercise of leadership grows from sincere moral or ethical considerations, that leadership may be wholly irresponsible if its effect is to damage the long-term viability and well-being of the group or larger system. One can be "right" in regard to the problem and what a group should do but be terribly "wrong" and ineffective in the exercise of leadership. The world is rife with examples of so-called moral leaders acting irresponsibly and of committed, intelligent men and women whose stubborn pursuit of a particular strategy weakens the group or enterprise to which they should be responsible.

Rather than teach people how to be visionaries or motivators, this book addresses the demanding task of mobilizing people to confront their predicament and solve their most pressing problems. The focus is not on getting people to follow but on getting people to face reality and think and act responsibly, thereby enabling their organizations and communities to address their toughest challenges and make meaningful progress.

The subject of real leadership is critical for corporate managers, school superintendents, nonprofit directors, senior government officials, and politicians. Anyone concerned about leadership must distinguish more carefully between those acts of power that create value and prosperity and those that destroy value and thwart prosperity. How people conceive of the use of power has serious repercussions. If people with power do not learn how leadership can advance the well-being of the collective, corporations will continue to be plagued by productivity problems, schools will always be leaving children behind, and the nations of the world will lose much of their accumulated gains in unnecessary wars, chicanery, and blunders.

If those seeking power and authority can learn the strategies and practices of real leadership and operate with greater insight and self-awareness, then they can enhance their chances of success. If leaders can diagnose their challenges with greater clarity, design and execute smarter interventions, and improve their ability to reflect and learn while they are in the midst of action, then they will have a greater hope of generating and sustaining progress.

This book provides a framework for how to exercise real leadership in different contexts. It will help the leader

- analyze the specific nature of the most critical challenge the group or organization faces at a given time (this is the principal challenge that must be attended to if the group is to advance);
- understand the kind of leadership strategies needed to address that challenge;
- recognize how real leadership, as an interactive art, can be manifest in different ways to assist people to face the reality of their predicament, attend to their problems, and be given their best shot at success; and

- appreciate the ways in which power, when used irresponsibly, can wreak havoc on all it touches—therefore the need to be responsible with one's power and exercise real leadership.

We need people who can provide real leadership in multiple and diverse contexts

When I ask my students who they think were responsible leaders worth emulating—leaders who did something positive—invariably the responses include the names of Gandhi, Martin Luther King, and Winston Churchill. I point out that even these people, as great as they were, failed basic principles of real leadership in some contexts in which they attempted to exercise their power. For example, Churchill provided brilliant leadership in mobilizing his country in the face of a formidable threat posed by Hitler's Germany.[1] However, at the end of the war, when he proceeded to do what he had always done, he was not reelected because so few people had confidence in him to provide the economic and developmental leadership needed to rebuild Britain. Earlier in his career, he also had failed miserably as First Lord of the Admiralty during World War I, when he sent thousands of Australian and Allied troops to their deaths at Gallipoli.[2] For that fiasco, he was fired from the cabinet. While Churchill provides a decidedly mixed model of leadership, his life highlights the incredible difficulty of exercising consistently successful leadership across the sectors and eras of a life.

Sometimes a tough and demanding authority figure finds himself in a set of circumstances where his style brings great leadership acclaim. Indeed, this happened with New York mayor Rudolf Giuliani. As mayor, he was often under attack for his insensitive and domineering approach, irrespective of the fact that it was, at times, very effective. His personal life was the subject of daily ridicule in the newspapers and on talk radio. Nevertheless, following the events of September 11, 2001, Giuliani came to symbolize the aspirations and resolve of New Yorkers and many Americans more generally to move forward with courage. This crisis produced a very different context in which Giuliani's characteristics and strategies of operating suddenly provided what New Yorkers needed for them to deal with and manage the aftermath of that horrific event.

Unfortunately, too many powerful people have recognized too late that the mode of operating that led to past success was inadequate for the demands of a new and different context. The person who, based on his or her natural tendencies and inclinations, keeps using the same approach to leadership has a diminished chance of success and will eventually fail. For example, the war hero who becomes president or the social activist who attains formal authority as an elected official rarely performs as well in the new context, because the person cannot see how his or her natural tendencies and inclinations are actually dysfunctional in the different context. They think that leadership is a set of traits or characteristics that are applicable in any setting. I disagree. Different contexts call for different leadership strategies if the people are to productively address the problems they face and open up pathways to progress.

More than ever, we need men and women who can succeed in multiple contexts. Nowhere is this more true than in the field of education. Even straightforward tasks such as teaching children the basic skills of reading, writing, and arithmetic require a broad array of leadership strategies to get the complete system functioning in the service of children. There are more than fourteen thousand school superintendents in the United States, all struggling to address the complex educational challenges of their respective communities. In large urban districts where social and economic problems exacerbate the demands of reform, the average tenure of a superintendent is less than three years. For many of these men and women, the problems are so overwhelming and the politics so vicious that they find it almost impossible to make lasting progress. Given the demands of the job, many school boards throughout the country look for candidates outside the field of education so that they can get a different kind of individual to lead their districts. In recent years, a number of businessmen and military generals have been appointed with the hope that they have this "leadership thing" figured out and can fix the system. These individuals, like their predecessors, struggle bravely to get something meaningful accomplished and generally do no better.

And this point is true for business as well. According to a recent report of CEO turnover at the world's 2,500 largest publicly traded corporations, most companies are setting higher standards of performance for chief executive officers than ever before, and CEOs are falling short in record numbers.[3] The report notes, "This phenomenon is now fully global, even in regions not burdened by governance scandals. CEOs are being replaced at a faster rate in Europe than the United States, and CEO turnover has skyrocketed in Asia, where chief executives of major corporations had been relatively protected from market forces."[4]

Rakesh Khurana of Harvard Business School has documented how and why boards of directors have become enamored with charismatic, superstar CEOs who they hope will be a corporate savior and guide the company to the market equivalent of the "promised land."[5] Most do a mediocre job, and many fall short. The excessive reliance on their charisma and visionary outlook that may have worked in a past setting is often insufficient to produce real and sustainable progress. Khurana points out that many of these CEOs have an inadequate appreciation of the role of context in determining what the best approach to leadership should be.

Leadership must be approached as an interactive art

To increase the chances of success, real leadership must be approached as an interactive art. It is an art in that it requires creativity and imagination, rather than a singular set of well-honed practices; and it is interactive in that one must be willing to "dance" with the reality of the context so that the best solutions can emerge. It cannot be treated as a hard science with prescriptive approaches such as "Do X and you will produce Y." On the contrary, as an art, real leadership requires the capacity to improvise, be imaginative, and make ongoing corrections according to the specific challenge the people face, the discoveries of the group as they tackle the challenge, and the shifting dynamics of the context. Therefore, strong diagnostic skills and considerable flexibility in one's intervention style are essential if one is to lead effectively in multiple contexts on multiple challenges.

Of course, I am not the first to make this observation on the situational demands of leadership. The social psychologist Victor Vroom has written extensively on the subject.[6] But what is missing from these writings, by Vroom and others, is a way to categorize the specific nature of the challenge the people face and explain what real leadership should look like in different settings. In this book, I present a model to assist in the diagnosis of the context to ascertain the group's principal challenge. I also put forward a set of leadership principles and intervention strategies to get the people to do the requisite problem-solving work to address that challenge.

For nearly two decades, I have been involved in the teaching and study of leadership and authority around the world, working with men and women in business, government, schools, and community organizations. In recent years, as research for this book, I have interviewed more than a dozen current or former presidents and prime ministers of nations to gain insight into the leadership challenges they have faced. I have interacted with many educational administrators at the local, state, and national levels to explore the demands of educational reform. I have been an adviser to many executives in corporations, community groups, and governments, as they have undertaken reform initiatives to revitalize their institutions.

I have also had a unique chance to examine power, authority, and social change at the most primal and traditional level—with the nomadic Penan people in the rain forest of Borneo. I have observed the Penan tribe deal with the huge adaptive challenge of cultural survival caused by the creeping forces of modernization and an eroding habitat due to the shady practices of logging companies and the misguided strategies of politicians.

Perhaps my most valuable resource in the study of leadership has been my students at the Kennedy School of Government at Harvard University. They have challenged my thinking and given me an amazing array of personal case studies that have helped me explore and develop the notion of real leadership in different contexts.

Of particular importance in my understanding of leadership has been my relationship with Ronald Heifetz and Riley Sinder. Heifetz was my professor and mentor at Harvard in the mid- to late 1980s when I was a doctoral student. Today I am honored to be his colleague at the Kennedy School, and together we teach and consult on leadership. Sinder is also a valued colleague, and, over the past few years, we have spent many an hour in rich and imaginative discussion about the challenges of leading in diverse settings. His contribution and support have enriched my knowledge and helped, in no small way, to shape the ideas in this book.

Heifetz and Sinder distinguished (1) leadership from authority and (2) technical challenges from adaptive challenges.[7] This book is primarily about exercising leadership with authority, although at various points I discuss the demands of leading when one has little or no authority. But I am mostly referring to people in authority positions who have a special opportunity to exercise real leadership—an opportunity that is often neglected or squandered. The book is about helping leaders sense what those opportunities might be.

The opportunities of real leadership are primarily in addressing demanding adaptive challenges. A *technical* challenge requires the straightforward application of expertise to solve the problem, whereas an *adaptive* challenge is more complex in that it necessitates changing people's values, habits, practices, and priorities. Leadership for an adaptive challenge requires orchestrating a process of getting the various factions and entities who own a piece of the problem to do *adaptive work*. In the following chapters, I present my discoveries about real leadership and adaptive work. I give examples of people who tried to lead and failed, while illustrating where they went wrong. I also write about individuals who *were* able to treat leadership as an interactive art and understood the notion of doing adaptive work, and thereby succeeded in helping people face their most crucial challenges and advance.

In Part I, I describe the concept of real leadership—its features and characteristics—and distinguish it from counterfeit leadership. *Counterfeit leadership* is a set of actions and strategies used by an authority figure that thwarts progress, whereas *real leadership* is a set of actions and strategies that facilitates progress. The first step in exercising real leadership is to diagnose correctly the principal challenge the group *really* faces—be it an organization, a school system, a community, or a nation. I describe six distinct adaptive challenges that can befall a group and threaten the health and survival of the system. Each challenge requires a specific leadership approach.

Part II addresses the six domains of adaptive challenge and provides an intervention framework for how to lead effectively and responsibly in these different but extremely critical problem contexts. The six domains are: an activist challenge, a development challenge, a transition challenge, a maintenance challenge, a creative challenge, and a crisis challenge. Each chapter in Part II presents cases and examples that illustrate leadership successes and leadership failures for these six respective challenges. I also provide practical tools and specific strategies for helping committed men and woman use their power to exercise real leadership and get the people to address the principal challenge and varied tasks needed to produce genuine and sustainable progress for their enterprise or community.

In Part III, I look at real leadership in the context of multiple challenges. Using the case of Lawrence of Arabia, I address the question, How does one transition between challenges, modify one's role and provide context-appropriate leadership—and succeed? Leadership for multiple challenges requires enormous flexibility, creativity, and sensitivity. In this section I also consider the personal work of being a real leader and discuss what it means to take responsibility for oneself as an instrument of power. All leaders have personal preferences, idiosyncrasies, and natural predilections. Such stylistic predispositions can either help or hinder the adaptive work of progress. Learning how to discover the effect one's interventions have on others in their problem-solving endeavors and make adjustments according to situational needs, is essential if one is to successfully lead in diverse contexts.

We desperately need women and men who can provide real leadership for the full array of problematic challenges we face in this complex and interdependent world. "What is real leadership, and how does one employ power to exercise it?" are crucial and central questions for the operation of business, government, and the full array of our civic and social institutions. I believe that real leadership can make the difference between success and failure in all aspects of human activity—between developed states and failed states; between great schools and poor schools; between mediocre companies and extraordinary companies; even between war and peace. And that is why the study of real leadership—the kind of leadership that gets people to face reality, be responsible for their predicament, and deal with their toughest challenges—is of paramount concern.

Acknowledgments

I would like to thank the many people who helped me with this book. They include Rosie Lim Williams for her tireless support, endless encouragement, and brilliant input; Riley Sinder for his generosity of time and intellect in helping me in this project; Tom Champion for his talented editorial assistance; Ronald Heifetz for his ongoing encouragement, recommendations, and friendship; Barbara Kellerman for reading the manuscript in its earliest version and giving me some very useful and practical advice; and Hugh O'Doherty for his suggestions and friendship. I also want to thank those people who read either part or all of the manuscript and gave me helpful editorial feedback or suggestions on the content: Paul Porteous, Werner Erhard, Margaret Richardson, Sharon Daloz Parks, Marshall Carter, David Chamberlain, Bruce Gilles, Chris Lee, Karen Manz, Todd Manza, and Warren Fernandez. And thanks to my assistant Samir Randolph. At Berrett-Koehler, Steve Piersanti, Jeevan Subramaniam, and the entire team have been just tremendous. I am especially appreciative to my family, Marie Lin, Kristal Li, and Shona Mei for their wisdom and lessons on life. And thanks to Mum, Dad, Jon, Calvin, and Jedda.

PART I

Real Leadership
The Engine of Progress

CHAPTER 1

Odin, Enron, and the Apes

Distinguishing Real Leadership
from Counterfeit Leadership

I sat with the prime minister of East Timor to discuss his options. Five days earlier, a mob of angry protestors burned his home down and wreaked havoc by destroying government buildings, businesses, and houses. They were angry because change wasn't happening fast enough. During the melee, poorly trained police fired on the protestors, killing one young man and wounding others. The prime minister had been in his job for less than a year. Furthermore, he was East Timor's first local leader, as the country had been under colonial rule for the previous four hundred years, by Portugal and then Indonesia. Under the Indonesians, a tenth of the population was killed. The prime minister had a seemingly impossible task: to create an honest and effective government and to build a nation from the ashes (not to mention his own home, which itself was also in ashes). The country was a powder keg, ready to explode. He knew he had to be exceptionally astute and responsible in how he used his power in this demanding and precarious predicament. All eyes were on him to see what he would do.

Prime Minister Mari Alkatiri faced, at a more extreme level, the leadership challenge many men and women confront every day: attempting to employ power to add or protect value and ensure that their organization, community, or nation not only can survive but is in a position to thrive. The prime minister had to consider a number of serious questions, such as, What challenge do the people *really* face? What strategies will give the people their best chance of success? What values should be promoted at this time? How will my behavior impact the people's perception of those values? In essence, he was considering, "Given this problem, what would real leadership look like?"

3

Ultimately, Alkatiri handled the crisis well. He chose not to lash out, take revenge, or engage in wasteful politics. He realized that the social contract between the state and the people was fragile and would take time to strengthen—after all, this was a country that had been denied self-rule for centuries. He stood before the people and reiterated his commitment to democratic practices, reminded them of what was at stake, and personally sought out marginalized and discontented factions to assure them that they would be listened to and included in the nation-building process. These choices ensured that East Timor would not descend into civil war and would continue to develop the capacity for democratic self-governance.

The Features of Real Leadership

The question "What is real leadership—the kind of leadership that keeps our world from falling apart and improves the human condition?" is one that philosophers, politicians, poets, and prophets have wrestled with since the beginning of time. Today, depending on whom you ask, you will probably get a different answer. When I asked the chairman of a Fortune 500 company, he explained that real leadership was about developing a unique corporate strategy and creating a sophisticated incentive system to entice managers and staff to focus on financial goals. Mullah Omar, the former head of the Taliban in Afghanistan, understood real leadership to be the implementation and enforcement of his interpretation of the Koran. A general in the U.S. Army recently told me that real leadership was manifest in the "art of motivation" to get soldiers to do what you want them to do. A former prime minister explained that for him real leadership was "all about persuasion" to ensure that the people would buy into his government's agenda. The head of a church community described real leadership as simply "being an example." A politician explained that, for him, real leadership was about "being committed to something," and "when you're out in front and you look behind you and your people are still with you, you're probably a real leader."

These notions are different variants on the same theme—"showing the way" and "getting people to follow." These notions of leadership prevail in the modern marketplace. Basically, the goal is to get the people to do what you want them to do. To show the way and get people to follow, this model suggests that leaders must craft a vision, motivate people through persuasive communication, be an example, and employ a system of punishments and incentives to sustain action.

This perspective is insufficient for dealing with the complexity of the challenges institutions and communities face in the age of globalization. What if the leader's direction is wrong? What if the vision is the product of delusional thinking? What if the leader seeks to manipulate the people for his own nefarious purposes? What if the people become unhealthily dependent on the leader and fail to develop their own capabilities? What if the people yearn for easy answers and painless solutions, and reward charismatic, answer-giving demagogues with power? Given these possibilities, I believe that we need a new notion of what it means to be a real and responsible leader—one that does not emphasize the dynamic of *leader-follower and goal* but the dynamic of *leadership-group and reality*.

Real Leadership Gets People to Face Reality

"Showing the way" and generating "masses of followers" might be the primary measure of success for an authority figure or politician who seeks to gain power and get their way, but it should not be the measure of success in the realm of real leadership. Leadership that targets authentic progress must gauge success by the degree to which people are engaging the *real* problem versus symptoms, decoy concerns, or false tasks. That is, are the people facing reality or avoiding reality? Answers to tough problems are rarely obvious, and real solutions are elusive precisely because they require due regard for the ingrained values and habits of the group, which members of the group protect with daily striving and sacrifice.

Therefore, real leadership demands that the people make adjustments in their values, thinking, and priorities to deal with threats, accommodate new realities, and take advantage of emerging opportunities. At its essence, real leadership orchestrates social learning in regard to complex problems and demanding challenges. People must learn why they are in a particular condition in order to invent pathways forward that produce genuine progress, as opposed to hollow and temporary gains. If the people refuse to face hard truths, are weak at learning, or learn the wrong things, then their problem-solving capacity will suffer, and their group or enterprise may eventually wither and die.

When Carlos Ghosn became president of Nissan Motor Corporation in 1999, he had to get management and employees to face some hard truths—the company was deteriorating rapidly, and if it was to be turned around, the Japanese business practices that had existed in the company for generations would have to be revolutionized. This was a message that the traditionalists did not like to hear. It meant that there would be plant closures and massive layoffs, and the dismantling of the Nissan *keiretsu*—the network of suppliers and affiliated companies that underlies Japan's blue chip corporations.[1]

One reason the company was close to bankruptcy was due to the negligent behavior of management. They were avoiding reality in regard to the condition of the company and the nature of the competitive threats. Ghosn spent time wandering the halls, showrooms, and factory floors of Nissan, questioning and listening. He wrote of his discovery:

> To tell the truth, I never met anyone in Nissan who could give me an exhaustive analysis of what had happened to it. I never went to a single place where one could speak about the company articulately. No one was able to offer me a summary of the problems listed in order of importance. Management was in complete and obvious chaos. This was, I believed, the primary cause of Nissan's difficulties.[2]

In putting reality in front of people, Ghosn faced opposition or criticism from many quarters—employees, suppliers, unions, even Japanese business associations. Few people wanted to acknowledge that the condition of Nissan was so bad, and few people were willing to accept the "medicine" that Ghosn was offering. Besides, the tradition had always been that if a company was in trouble, the government would bail it out. Given that Japan was in the midst of financial crisis, that option was impossible. The problem could not be resolved through a technical fix such as simply throwing money at it. It would require superior leadership. Remarkably, even though he was a foreigner (or perhaps because he was a foreigner), Ghosn was able to challenge the system and turn it around. He succeeded in getting people to face reality and make the necessary sacrifices and take the essential steps to transform Nissan from a sick and ailing entity with a $5.6 billion loss in 2000 to the most profitable large automotive manufacturer in the world by 2004.

Real Leadership Engages the Group to Do Adaptive Work

Through the exercise of real leadership, the conditions are created to give the people (or the organization) their best shot at success in the context of the particular challenge that the group faces. Success, however, should not be narrowly defined. It is not simply achieving a goal, although it certainly includes achieving goals. Fundamentally, it is about ensuring that whatever gets generated is *inclusive*, not exclusive; is *moral*, not immoral; is *constructive*, not destructive; is *substantive*, not delusional.

We need to think of real leadership as a normative activity that adds real value to a group (in contrast to hollow or superficial gains that cannot be sustained). When I use the term *group*, I mean a social system of some sort, such as a company, school, community, or nation. By *value*, I mean the knowledge, relationships, capacity, and goods that produce sustained well-being, authentic satisfaction, and higher levels of performance in the group. Accordingly, real leadership must deal with the moral and ethical components of human affairs. Without concern for the moral and ethical elements of problem solving and collective effort, group value could be lost overnight.

To ensure that the people have their best shot at success and add value to their enterprise, the leader must get the people to address their adaptive challenges. An *adaptive challenge* is a problem that does *not* subside even when management applies the best-known methods and procedures to solve the problem. Generally, the resolution of an adaptive challenge requires a shift in values and mind-sets. For example, at least two competing values might shift to resolve a budget crisis in a company. On the one hand, the problem could be resolved if the employees shifted their values to take less pay and still be satisfied. On the other hand, the problem might be resolved if management shifted the values and mind-sets in the organization to direct the business to new profitable markets, perhaps global markets.[3]

The work the people must do to progress in the face of an adaptive challenge is simply called *adaptive work*. Adaptive work is the effort that produces the organizational or systemic learning required to tackle tough problems. These problems often require an evolution of values, the development of new practices, and the revision of priorities. Leadership for adaptive work requires getting the various factions of the system addressing the conflicts in their values and priorities and refashioning those values and priorities to deal with the threat or take advantage of the opportunity.

Real Leadership Involves the Pursuit of Insight and Wisdom

Real leadership is not easy. It requires considerable wisdom to be a real leader on multiple adaptive challenges and succeed. The work of real leadership is often to defend or promote particular values and practices, while discouraging or phasing out other values and practices that impede progress, even though some people hold dearly to the impeding values and practices. Therefore, whoever exercises real leadership must discern which values to promote and protect, and which values need to be challenged or changed. It takes a degree of wisdom, not simply experience or intelligence, to know what to promote and how to promote it so a group can do the adaptive work.

Unfortunately, outside the realms of religion and folklore, the concept of wisdom seems to be on the decline. We talk easily about intelligence, information, and knowledge, but wisdom seems to be a quaint, antiquated, outdated notion. We may think of Maimonides, Ben Franklin, Chaucer's Wife of Bath, or Tolkien's Gandalf as wise, but when was the last time you heard anyone say they admired a corporate CEO, a manager, or a politician because of her or his wisdom? Wisdom remains outside the standard requirements for CEOs, managers, and politicians. Such people might be praised as smart, capable, or savvy—but wise, rarely.

As metaphor for the quest for insight and wisdom in regard to how to use one's power in a responsible manner to help organizations and communities prosper, I use the Norse god Odin. The mythological Odin was deeply concerned with the issue of real and responsible leadership. Odin was god of the gods—the chairman of the board—a powerful authority figure who could use his power to create or destroy.[4] He was also known as the god of magic, poetry, wisdom, and battle. You have heard indirectly of Odin through the days of the week. Wednesday is named after Odin (Wodin's day). But what makes Odin an especially compelling and relevant mythological figure is that unlike many other deities, Odin was not omniscient or omnipotent. He was a flawed god. He knew his knowledge was incomplete, and therefore he actively sought to learn more about the world so that he could do a better job of being head god. Indeed, he was so hungry for knowledge that he put himself through terrible ordeals, including willingly sacrificing his eye, to acquire sufficient wisdom to lead.

Metaphorically, Odin represents all authority figures—bosses, managers, politicians, and CEOs. He is a powerful god, yet he never sees himself as having all the answers. In spite of his sincere quest for wisdom, there are times when his personal hungers and foibles lead him to commit many errors and to engage in wasteful activities that have more to do with self-interest and personal gain than with the real work of progress. His power is both a burden and a boon—and his challenge is to learn how to use it in a responsible and effective manner.

Odin's quest for insight led him to the World Tree (Yggdrasil), the center of creation. The World Tree represented the physical and moral laws of the world.[5] Odin was informed that in order to gain enough wisdom to actually help people, he would have to hang on the World Tree for nine days and nights. In the epic twelfth-century collection of poems known as the *Elder Edda*, Odin recounts his experience:

> I know I hung on the wind-swept tree nine entire nights in all.
> Wounded by a spear dedicated to Odin, given myself to myself,
> On the tree of which nobody knows from which root it grows
> With nothing to eat and nothing to drink I bent my head down
> and groaning, took the runes up, and fell down thereafter.
> . . . Then I began to thrive and be wise, and grow and prosper.[6]

Must an aspiring leader go to Odin-like extremes in order to gain enough wisdom to use power responsibly and exercise real leadership? Perhaps not—although I am sure that many people would take great satisfaction in seeing their bosses hung on a tree for nine days of torment in order to be transformed into a wiser, more humane leader. But I suggest that taking responsibility for a group with a serious problematic challenge, be it a school, corporation, or nation, will at times feel like one is hanging alone on the World Tree. The responsibility that comes with the exercise of real leadership can be a heavy burden.

Wisdom, as it pertains to real leadership, does not mean having all the answers. It requires pursuing the truth with fervor and passion, being sensitive to the context in which the problem resides, and holding the question in each context, "What will make our work worthwhile—to our lives and the lives of others?" Even if one is accustomed to top-down management, one needs to understand the relationship between wisdom, power, and real leadership. For example, upon hearing that Dwight D. Eisenhower had been elected president of the United States, Harry S. Truman famously remarked, "He'll sit here, and he'll say, 'Do this! Do that!' And nothing will happen. Poor Ike—it won't be a bit like the Army. He'll find it very frustrating."[7] This is because in complex political and organizational systems where power is diffuse, leaders need considerable wisdom to navigate the terrain of thorny and complicated group dynamics, and to activate processes that get the people focusing on, not fleeing from, their most pressing problems. A leader cannot rely on deference, discipline, or dominance conditioning to achieve worthwhile and sustainable results.

The wisdom to lead does not come by being isolated from the people in one's office or castle, or being excessively preoccupied with formulating strategies and plans. Wisdom derives from the interactive and reflective process of figuring out with the group how the various strands of a problematic reality are connected to the people's values and priorities, and then determining what values to promote in order to give the people their best shot at success. Fundamentally, wisdom is a deeper form of insight into why the system works the way that it does.

To accumulate wisdom and avoid the distorted reality that can come with authority, the great Odin learned to travel in disguise. He wanted to see the world as it was. This approach enabled him to ask questions of the people and bargain with them to see what they might be willing to give up in order to gain something of significant value. Ancient images of Odin show him as a wandering pilgrim. (The *Lord of the Rings* author J. R. R. Tolkien drew the character of Gandalf the wizard directly from the Odin myth.)

The social psychologist Robert Sternberg has done considerable research on the subject of wisdom and leadership. He suggests that wisdom is about working for the "common good" while "balancing various self-interests . . . with the interests of others and of other aspects of the context in which one lives, such as one's city or country or environment or even God."[8] He adds that leadership wisdom "also involves creativity, in that a wise solution to a problem may be far from obvious."[9]

I agree that wisdom, as it pertains to real leadership, is required to balance the multiple interests and expectations of individuals and groups in any complex social system—be it a business, school, community, or nation. I also believe that creativity is essential in addressing demanding problematic concerns. But no one is wise enough to know what to do, or creative enough to know how to do it, all the time. Therefore, we should not look at wisdom as an "arrived state of being" but as an ongoing process of continuous learning and discovery—for the one leading and also the people.

Real Leadership Is the Willingness to Be Responsible

Because of his sacrifice, Odin was granted insight into the hidden mechanics of how people conduct themselves—as individuals, in groups, and in communities. One of the hidden mechanics of human behavior that Odin soon discovered (which was one of Sigmund Freud's most important insights) was that humans will go to great lengths to avoid facing their real problems. As individuals and in groups, people tend to shy away from addressing tough, complex, painful problems that are caused, perpetuated, or protected by their own values, habits, and priorities. Rather than look at the reality of the predicament they are in, they often distort what they see, put the problem outside themselves, scapegoat others, and create distractions—all as a way of distancing themselves from responsibility for the real issue.

Given this natural human predilection, a prime duty of real leadership is to help people face the reality of their problematic condition, no matter how painful or disturbing, and do the requisite problem-solving work of bringing resolution to the their unresolved concerns and take advantage of the unique opportunities before them so that progress can unfold. Fundamentally, real leadership is about being responsible for one's world and helping others be responsible.

The word *responsible* means "being the cause, agent, or source of something."[10] It also denotes the "ability to act without guidance or superior position," including to make "moral decisions" as well as "showing good judgment or sound thinking."[11] The word *Odin*, according to the mythologist Jacob Grimm, in ancient times literally meant the "source of movement."[12] Thus, Odin becomes the creator god, the source of all movement in the world. I assert that our institutions, communities, and the larger global condition can only improve to the degree that someone takes responsibility for being a source of movement to help people face the reality of their predicament and deal sensibly with their problems and challenges. In the absence of real and responsible leadership, groups perpetuate the dysfunctions embedded in the status quo, which, in turn, can easily precipitate the loss of the organizational and social value accumulated through the efforts of committed and hardworking people over many years.

Hitler's Germany illustrates the horrific and incomprehensible consequences flowing from the absence of responsibility and real leadership. Hermann Goering, Hitler's right-hand man, provides a particularly potent example of the disasters of irresponsibility. During the Nuremberg trials, Goering discussed his role in the Third Reich's operations with American psychiatrist Leon Goldensohn. Goldensohn wanted to understand Goering's mind and to learn how such an educated and "cultured" man of Goering's status could allow, even *encourage*, the extermination of six million men, women, and children. Goering told him:

> For myself I feel quite free of responsibility for the mass murders. Certainly, as second man in the state under Hitler, I heard rumors about mass killings of Jews, but I could do nothing about it and I knew that it was useless to investigate these rumors and to find

out about them accurately, which would not have been too hard, but I was busy with other things, and if I had found out what was going on regarding the mass murders, it would simply have made me feel bad and I could do very little to prevent it anyway.[13]

While Goering is an extreme example, his pathetic excuses that he "was too busy doing other things," "it simply would have made me feel bad," and "I could do very little to prevent it anyway" echo the reasoning people use all the time when confronted with messy adaptive challenges. These excuses allow people to distance themselves from responsibility to produce a shift in people's values, beliefs, and practices and tackle the adaptive work needed to advance. Rather than engage in real and responsible leadership, Goering chose inaction and neglect, thus colluding in the evil acts of the Third Reich. Or, he was lying altogether, which is another form of irresponsible behavior.

Fundamentally, real leadership is a choice—a choice to respond to the problems, dysfunctions, and tremendous opportunities that emerge in our organizations and communities. It is a willingness to be responsible for what goes on in the world and take the necessary stands and make the necessary interventions. It requires thoughtful, creative, strategic, and courageous action to mobilize enough people to confront reality, tackle their problems, and generate solutions that produce morally based progress.

Specifically, in exercising real leadership to get the people facing their adaptive challenges, a leader must be responsible for the following:

1. Be responsible for the *diagnostic process*. This will enable the person exercising leadership to determine the precise nature of the challenge that the people or enterprise face and ascertain the people's readiness level to confront the challenge. That means discovering what aspect of reality the people are avoiding, understanding the nature of the threat to the group, and determining the resources needed to deal with the challenge. Diagnosis is not a one-off activity but must be ongoing so that midcourse corrections can be made according to what the people learn and their capacity to accommodate new realities and make adjustments in their values and behavior.

2. Be responsible for managing the *problem-solving processes* in the group, organization, or community. The work of the people is to interrogate reality, work through conflicts in values and priorities, and embrace new practices that bring resolution to situations of irresolution and open up pathways for genuine progress. The problem-solving

process cannot be left to a small group of "wise-heads" who determine what the solution is and then impose it on the group. Problem solving must be viewed as a sense-making activity that includes all factions affected by the prevailing reality.

3. Be responsible for oneself as an *instrument of power*. A leader's awareness of how his or her power—authority, presence, and interventions—affects the thinking and actions of others as they tackle their challenges is essential to success. Ultimately, one's power and authority must be used *not* to get people to follow but to get the people to confront reality and do the necessary adaptive work. In taking responsibility for oneself as an instrument of power, the leader must ensure that his or her "personal case"—one's natural predilections and habitual ways of operating—are an asset rather than a liability in the exercise of leadership.

In the following chapters, each of these components will be addressed in more detail. At this stage it is important to appreciate that the exercise of real leadership helps people face their challenges; see with clarity the nature of the problem or opportunity before them; and, if necessary, make adjustments in their values, thinking, and priorities to ensure that the group or organization is given its best shot at success.

Although I focus predominantly on the task of leading with authority, real leadership can be exercised by anyone, with or without authority—of course, in varying degrees. Each person has at least some power that can be used to affect the behavior of others. Hence, each person can mobilize a few people, at least, to begin tackling the problematic realities that impede the organization's capacity to advance. A person who desires to lead might consider the following question: "How can I wisely use the power I have to start a process that gets enough people to engage realistically with the problems and opportunities that we face?" The answer will depend on the particular challenge confronting the group, one's leadership ability, and the nature and extent of one's power.

Counterfeit Leadership: How a Group Is Given a False Set of Tasks

To exercise real leadership, one must understand how easy it is to be unwise and irresponsible with one's power and engage in *counterfeit leadership*.

Counterfeit leadership is not necessarily deceitful leadership but the kind of actions, irrespective of one's intentions, that result in putting a false set of tasks before the people. False tasks include any activity pursued by a group that has nothing to do with progress. It could be a false strategy, a false goal, political game playing, interdivisional rivalries, tolerance of counterproductive meetings where people skirt around the real problem, the scapegoating of another person or group, or the refusal to confront error and learn. If the people are addressing a false set of tasks, then they will be wasting time and valuable resources and putting the group or organization in a precarious state. For example, in 1692 the town leaders of Salem, Massachusetts, put a false set of tasks before the people. They assumed that by devoting valuable resources to weeding out sorcery and witchcraft, the town would be in a better position to progress. That was a costly and mistaken view. But even modern organizations waste time and valuable resources attending to their own superstitions and spurious beliefs, and end up putting a false set of tasks before the people that have nothing to do with making the organization more humane, fair, productive, and profitable.

Consider the counterfeit leadership provided by Enron's chairman and CEO, Kenneth Lay, in 2001. Here was a man with considerable knowledge and expertise, who was the head of one of the world's most successful and profitable companies. The pundits at *Fortune* magazine had described Enron as one of the best places to work in America. Enron at the end of 1999 had a market capitalization of more than $65 billion and a share price of $82. Lay was hailed as an extraordinary leader. One year later, however, Enron's share price had dropped to $0.65, thousands of employees had lost their retirement investment, and, almost overnight, the world woke up to a tale of corporate greed, malfeasance, and financial chicanery of Shakespearean proportions. Once the epitome of the New Economy's pride and power, Enron had become a symbol of corporate America's irresponsibility.

To appreciate what it was like to be the boss of the Enron kingdom, with all that Odin-like power, imagine for a moment that you are Kenneth Lay and how, when the opportunity presented itself, you might have exercised real leadership to divert the impending disaster. The following scenario is based on the available documentation of what happened.

• • •

Clearly, Kenneth Lay failed to exercise real and responsible leadership to resolve the crisis. (Lay himself has argued differently, of course.) It is possible that nothing he could have done at that stage would have

SCENARIO

Kenneth Lay, Enron, August to December 2001

You have been asked to return to Enron as CEO, after doing other things for a number of years. During your first few days back at the helm, you feel the pressure of people looking to you for direction. You decide to make a speech to your core employees, assuring them that you are committed to the aggressive business practices that have made the company so successful in the past and that you also want greater employee input—*and* that you intend to pay attention to the suggestions and complaints that people put in the comment box.

A few days after that meeting, an anonymous note left in the comment box expresses concern that many of Enron's "assets" are fictitious accounting entries. The note's author goes on to say, "I am incredibly nervous that we will implode in a wave of accounting scandals."

At a meeting the next morning with a group of senior managers, you decide not to refer to the issues raised by the anonymous note. You unveil a business plan as if everything were normal.

Soon after that meeting, a senior executive, Sherron Watkins, asks to talk with you about some serious concerns. She comes to your office and tells you about what she calls "phony Enron partnerships" to which Enron debts were sold as "fictitious assets" registering large, but illusory, "profits" on the Enron balance sheet. She gives you a seven-page memo, including an attachment with a marked-up copy of the documentation for one of the fake partnerships. She has circled one section of the partnership document and has written in the margin, "There it is! This is the smoking gun. You cannot do this!"

You tell Watkins that you plan to give the documents to Enron's outside law firm so that they can conduct an investigation. Watkins disagrees, suggesting that you, Kenneth Lay, personally must make an inquiry and intervene to save the company from disaster. In her view, that is how serious the situation has become. After all, the outside law firm has reaped a bonanza in litigation fees. What incentive will they have to bite the hand that feeds them?

As CEO, you weigh your options and decide to proceed as if all business functions remained normal. When you talk to Enron's outside law firm, you do not say explicitly that you are looking for ways to fire Watkins, but you hint that you are displeased with her. The attorneys sense your anger at Watkins and follow up on your hint: Two days later, one lawyer writes a memo to you that begins, "Per your request, the following are some bullet thoughts on how to manage the case with the employee who made the sensitive report." The memo offers some legal justifications for punishing and firing "corporate whistle-blowers."

In the ensuing weeks, several opportunities arise for addressing the accounting problems that Watkins revealed to you. But a month later, you exercise your personal stock options while the value of the stock is still high, netting you an additional $1.5 million. Shortly after that, you make an upbeat address to Enron employees, telling them, "Our financial liquidity has never been stronger," even though you have evidence that Enron is in deep trouble. You hope to boost the confidence of the employees, Wall Street analysts, and the market, perhaps buying the time needed to work out the company's problems. Only one month later, however, your accountants announce a $1.2 billion write-off resulting from losses in partnerships similar to the "smoking gun" arrangement described to you by Watkins. Within two months, Enron's vendors, customers, and investors lose confidence, forcing the company into bankruptcy. Enron's stock drops from the January 1 value of over $75 to the December 31 value of less than a dollar. You are despondent.

changed the final outcome. Yet, despite that possibility, his failure to exercise responsible leadership and seek knowledge about the problem when it was offered to him should not be excused. Watkins offered Lay a golden opportunity to learn important truths about his organization—truths that affected the company's ability to survive. If he already knew these truths and was covering them up, then his behavior was deceptive, even criminal. If he did not, then he failed in one of the cardinal duties of real leadership: to seek the knowledge and wisdom that he needed to protect and enhance the value of the organization. Indeed, he was so incurious, so fearful of knowledge, so irresponsible that he even took steps to punish an employee who brought important information to his attention. Lay's behavior is illustrative of counterfeit leadership—the using of power to avoid reality.

However, while it is easy to target Enron's management for the ruin of the company—and, indeed, they should be held accountable—this scenario seems disturbingly common and very human. After all, many people at different levels of the organization, as well as academics, journalists, and management consultants, fueled and perpetuated the organization's delusional belief that it could do no wrong. In different ways, all of these factions contributed to the emperor's belief that he was in fact wearing fine new clothes, when in reality he was naked. This led Lay, as we all do at times, to become distracted, to ignore vital information, and to promote the wrong values over the right values, or at least the values that would have given the organization its best chance at success.

The leadership failure was a product not only of Lay's arrogance but also of the fear that accompanied disappointing people with bad news that could lead to the loss of their respect and admiration. Think how difficult it would have been for Lay to upset everyone's inflated expectations of Enron's success. How do you puncture such a dream bubble?

We see this pattern time and again—what begins as a noble and thrilling venture of building a great company, upon success, produces a hubris in management that results in extremely irresponsible choices and behavior. Management might become complacent and fail to spend adequate time assessing the competition and developing the capacity of employees to respond to threats and opportunities. When errors or problems emerge in such a predicament, they are often covered up, and the myth that everything is going well is perpetuated—thus creating the conditions that make it even harder to face reality and attend to the organization's toughest challenges.

The point is, no matter how good you think you are, it is very easy to engage in irresponsible acts that undermine all the value that has been generated in a group, organization, or community. Irresponsibility is not a fixed feature of a human being, but it is fluid behavior that is generally dependent on the dynamics of the context. It is a product of counterfeit leadership and leads to the toleration and perpetuation of corrosive values and practices and a false set of tasks being put before the people. The prevailing values and practices in Enron's corporate culture of "let the good times roll" fueled the unhealthy competitive and deceitful dynamics that led management to pursue a false set of tasks, destroying the abundant wealth and resources of the company that had been garnered over many years.

As we examine what happened at Enron and other cases, a pattern begins to emerge that can provide vital signals that one is in the "danger zone" and might be providing counterfeit leadership. These primary indicators are

- a preoccupation with dominance,
- a failure to engage the group and its various subfactions in figuring out and facing the real work of progress,
- an unwillingness to explore beyond one's comfort zone to find a solution, and
- the conviction that you alone have "the truth."

A Preoccupation with Dominance

A common feature of counterfeit leadership is the propensity to dominate others, maintain excessive control, and get one's way. This is not so for all people, but it is true for many who seek power and enjoy positions of significant authority. We often refer to the dominant individual in a group as "the leader." I suggest that to the degree that any dominant individual acts in ways that reduces the capacity of a group or organization to function at peak effectiveness, he or she is providing counterfeit leadership, not real leadership. Therefore, it is not particularly instructive to call the dominant figure "the leader." Kenneth Lay and his partner at Enron, Jeffrey Skilling, had mastered the skills of maintaining dominance, but not real leadership. To get people to face their challenges purposefully and productively, the exercise of real leadership requires imagination, creativity, and resourcefulness. Dominance is often used to suppress the truth, thwart creativity, and demand compliance—all in the name of maintaining power and getting people to follow. This has been a common phenomenon since the beginning of time.

We can learn a lot about dominance—the need to control the group, maintain status, and get one's way—by examining primate communities. After all, we share 98 percent of our DNA with chimpanzees.

Primates live in hierarchical groups with dominant males and females overseeing the community. The alpha male's role is to protect the group and maintain the current order. Significant perks come with being the alpha, and as such it is a position that others covet. Alpha males have first pick of the food, enjoy the best nesting area, and mate with whomever they choose.[14] Given the status and benefits of being alpha, there is constant testing as subordinate members jockey for position in an attempt to rise in the social hierarchy. This testing includes provocation and direct challenges as junior males attempt to find vulnerabilities and weaknesses in the more dominant ones. Sometimes these tests lead to violent displays of power and aggression, often leaving a member wounded and occasionally dead. Younger males in particular are more aggressively competitive than the older adult males.[15]

Occasionally chimp communities experience coup d'états. Jane Goodall, renowned for her study of chimpanzees in the Gombe region, witnessed several such takeovers.[16] Generally, the coup leader in such a competition is not the biggest or the strongest but ascends to power by getting the other males to submit to him through a mix of tricks, favors, and intimidating displays. The coup leader and his allies then become the new alpha coalition.

As with primate groups, humans have dominance needs and often seek to gain power and status by rising in the hierarchy or creating coalitions that can advance factional interests and intimidate others into submission.[17] Of course, in politics and international affairs we see such behavior time and again, but it can also be seen in the everyday workplace. For example, we commonly observe authoritarian bosses or aggressive managers vie for attention in meetings by hogging the airtime, cutting off competitors, and ingratiating themselves to their superiors. In business it is not unusual for coalitions to be formed and territorial battles to take place that pit employees or departments against one another in order to control valuable resources or gain recognition and status. Such behaviors have nothing to do with the work of progress but serve as a frustrating, even entertaining, form of diversion.

Of course, some people seek dominance more than others. This penchant for dominance is known as a *social dominance orientation*. According to the research by Pratto and Sidanius and their team at Stanford University, such people seek out hierarchy-enhancing professional roles and favor hierarchy-enhancing ideologies and policies.[18] In other words, they are highly competitive within the confines of hierarchy, they value status and the chance to grow in status, and they are inclined to be rigid in their thinking and beliefs. The rigidity of their thinking ironically serves to demonstrate loyalty and commitment to their "in-group." Their belief that their in-group is superior leads them to discriminate against "out-groups" that they perceive to be inferior. And, according to the research, they show less concern for the values of empathy, tolerance, communality, and altruism. That is, they are not particularly good listeners, they are intolerant of differences, and they pursue self-interest to the detriment of the well-being of the larger system.

Of course, seeking power and having a social-dominance orientation is not a bad thing in and of itself. Psychologist David McClelland has shown how the power motive is a major unconscious drive for many managers, even the most successful managers.[19] The fact that an individual enjoys influencing and controlling others often leads that person to pursue positions of authority in order to make a genuine contribution to the organization or in politics. The problem arises, however, when a craving for status and control leads to excessive dominance and a preoccupation with gaining and maintaining power and status without offering people any valuable service in return. If such a person has power, status, and authority and does not provide a valuable service to the group, he or she is likely to end up putting a false set of tasks before the group. Either this person personally becomes a distraction, or he or she generates activities that become a distraction, thus taking the people away from the adaptive work of progress.

I once consulted to the management of the botanical gardens in a large tropical city. I was called in by the board of advisers because they felt that the director was "out of control." He was so preoccupied with being the alpha in his garden park that he ignored the board, demanded complete compliance of his staff, and refused to entertain recommendations from anyone. The garden was his territory, but it was in a state of decay as the collaborative work needed to make it a success was not happening. The community volunteers and all other potential contributors had been alienated. I asked the director why he was so authoritarian and whether he knew how his behavior was affecting others. He responded, "This is not my problem. They hired me to be the boss, and that's exactly what I am doing—being the boss!"

Dominance dynamics are not always manifest like a silverback gorilla thumping its chest and roaring, "I'm the boss! You better follow me, or else." Often the dynamics are subtle, even unconscious. They get played out in the social interactions that form corporate politics and the organization's culture. In one company I consulted to, the politics in the ten-member senior management team was so vicious that it poisoned the larger organizational culture. The characteristics of that culture included a lack of trust, the cover-up of errors, the distortion of data in the service of one's narrow interests, and the subtle subversion of the projects and initiatives of other divisions. The dominance dynamics led managers and divisions to compete for positions and resources while undermining each other, thus pursuing a false set of tasks that had nothing to do with corporate productivity. As a result, the company's performance was mediocre.

The only female member of that team, the vice president for information technology, repeatedly described how difficult it was for her to operate in a group where the men were constantly vying to be the "alpha chimp." She was particularly frustrated by the way they treated her, not as a senior colleague or equal but as a subordinate. The decision-making dynamics in the team were competitive and dysfunctional. When she tried to raise her concerns, she would generally be ignored, cut off, or told, "That's not important."

While dominance can be used to get attention, unify people, and maintain order, it can also displace the energy, responsibility, and commitment of people as they grapple with the reality of their condition. If one truly seeks to provide real and responsible leadership, it is essential that one become cognizant of how one's power might be used, intentionally or inadvertently, to perpetuate dominance–submission dynamics that have nothing to do with the real work of progress.

Failure to Fully Engage the Group and Its Many Factions

Progress is ultimately dependent on the people's capacity to do the requisite problem-solving and opportunity-enhancing work. If the people are resistant, and the leader does not appreciate the nature of that resistance, no amount of pushing, tugging, demanding, or pleading will produce success. A group, in some ways, is like a five-ton elephant. If it does not want to move, it won't. But, unlike a five-ton elephant, a group is not a singular entity with one brain but a complex system with multiple brains. That is, in any group—a company or a community—there are subgroups or factions that coalesce around a particular narrative of the problem, share common values, and resonate to specific concerns in a consistent manner. The leader, therefore, must consider and engage the group—the entire system—in the work of progress. Failure to fully engage the group and orchestrate a learning process for each of the factions will compromise the foundations of even the most important work. The appearance of progress might exist for a while, but it will soon evaporate when people become overwhelmed by the complexity and difficulty of the adaptive work.

The superintendent of Philadelphia's school system, David Hornbeck, fell into such a trap.[20] An honorable man with honorable intent, Hornbeck was on a mission. In many respects, he was probably one of the finest and most knowledgeable educational administrators in the country. But when it came to leading change, he could only get so far. He aspired to improve an ailing school system where more than half of the students failed statewide exams. In 1994, when Hornbeck became superintendent, the Philadelphia School District was a system in a state of decay inside a city in a state of decay. The city had high unemployment, high crime, and considerable social problems. Mayor Ed Rendell described the educational context by saying, "We get kids coming in beaten. We get kids coming in hungry. We get kids coming in sick. And the average teacher will tell you here they spend more than 50 percent of their time as a social worker, cutting dramatically into what they can do as an educator."[21]

Hornbeck had a vision and a plan to achieve his vision. It was called Children Achieving. It consisted of ten principles that would serve as guidelines to rejuvenate schools and ensure that each child developed proficiency in reading, math, and basic computer skills. It also prescribed teacher accountability for student learning and decentralization of administrative functions so that schools could have more autonomy and flexibility.

This was going to be a daunting challenge as there were 257 public schools and more than 270,000 students in the district. But Hornbeck was optimistic and confident in his plan. He visited churches, synagogues, mosques, and civic groups to enroll the community in his vision. "It is we, not somebody else who are called to lead our children out of bondage," he told one church group. "Leave no child behind. Somebody is calling your name, and yours and yours, throughout this land. We must not permit another season of bondage for our children."[22]

Indeed, there was a "buzz" throughout the city that this former preacher turned superintendent just might be able to do what he was promising. The teachers, however, remained skeptical. They had heard this kind of talk before. As one of them said, "Everyone pretty much assumes they will in fact wait out the new superintendent and they will wait out the flavor of the month educational reform."[23]

Hornbeck plowed ahead with his reform agenda and possessed the zeal, focus, and fanaticism of a medieval crusader. Five years later, however, when the results of Hornbeck's efforts were supposed to be evident, he had little to show. The system had not been transformed. What's more, it had decayed further. Frustrated with the lack of support, David Hornbeck resigned. In 2002, the state government took control of the Philadelphia School District and appointed a special commission to determine its fate.

What went wrong? According to the evaluators of Children Achieving, the key factor was that Hornbeck had not adequately worked with the various stakeholders to get them on board and help with the facilitation of change. There was little ownership in the system. The evaluators noted, "In its six years of implementation, [the plan] never became a civic undertaking—that is, an effort widely understood and championed by the business, civic, and government elites, and frontline educators who would work tirelessly for its success."[24] What's more, Hornbeck had failed to get the support of the teachers' union, which was a thorn in his side from the day he began.

Although the business community initially supported Hornbeck, when the promised results were not forthcoming, they lost faith in his vision. They were also disappointed with, and embarrassed by, Hornbeck's constant bickering with the state legislators. At one point, when the funding that he wanted for the district was not forthcoming, he called the legislators "racist." This was a bold and provocative intervention, but it alienated the constituents that he needed to enact his agenda.

Hornbeck also tried to push too much reform on the system before building an adequate foundation.[25] The urgency of doing it all at once placed an excessive burden on the teachers, principals, and central office staff. The central office administrators, who were charged with the task of rolling out the reform agenda, would dictate to schools what needed to be done and then move on to the next priority. Given the amount of things that had to be done, they rarely had enough time to work with the schools on implementation and address the concerns of principals and teachers, and take feedback. For these reasons, Hornbeck and his team were not able to learn when and where they were off course and make the necessary midcourse corrections.[26] The program evaluators observed, "The reform plan created fatigue and resistance among teachers and disempowered principals. Initial support from the business community evaporated and civic leaders became exasperated with the intractability of the reform plan and its leader. *Children Achieving* raised hopes in Philadelphia, but left the city confused and anxious."[27]

A disappointed Hornbeck quit after a courageous five-year effort to fix a broken system. The leadership that he provided, though principled and based on sound ideas, was inadequate for the scope of the complex political challenge that he faced. He could not mobilize the entire system to do the adaptive work. Real leadership requires mobilizing all factions to shoulder their share of the work of modifying values, habits, practices, and priorities, so that progress can slowly evolve. Adaptive work takes time and must be paced so the people can adjust to new realities. Hornbeck bypassed or alienated key actors and failed to orchestrate a collective discovery process to ascertain the best solution for the system.

A more measured approach of action, feedback, learning, and corrective action might have produced a successful outcome.

An Unwillingness to Look for Solutions beyond One's Comfort Zone or the Prevailing Paradigm

While curiosity may have killed the cat, the lack of curiosity has killed many a counterfeit leader. It certainly destroyed Kenneth Lay, given his lack of curiosity in regard to the information offered him by Sherron Watkins. Real leadership necessitates a curious disposition in pursuit of the rigorous exploration and testing of alternatives that generate the best and most appropriate pathway forward for the group. A rigidity of thought or action limits the available options and may put the group in a state of volatility and danger. The unwillingness to test prevailing assumptions and creatively explore alternatives, due to stubbornness or simple ignorance, is irresponsible and foolhardy. To illustrate this point, consider the story of the Australian explorers Burke and Wills.

In August 1860, Robert O'Hara Burke and William Wills, along with sixteen others, tried to do something that had never been done before (by white men, at least): cross Australia from the south to north, traversing through the central desert—the outback. Burke, Wills, and two others—John King and Charlie Gray—halfway into the journey, left the rest of the team at a place they named Cooper's Creek, to make a dash to the Northern Gulf. On the return, Gray died of dysentery. When Burke, Wills, and King arrived back at Cooper's Creek after two months, the rest of the exploring team had departed, leaving few supplies. The confused men wandered in circles for a month. Burke and Wills eventually died of starvation, but King survived.

A rescue party eventually found King living with a group of Aborigines and discovered the dismembered bodies of Burke and Wills, which they brought back to Melbourne. Although Burke and Wills had died in their adventure, they were hailed as heroes, and more than one hundred thousand people stood in line to walk by their caskets and honor them at their state funeral.

A royal commission was set up to investigate the tragedy. In regard to Burke, the leader of the expedition, they concluded, "We cannot too deeply deplore the lamentable result of an expedition undertaken at so great a cost to the Colony; but while we regret the absence of a systematic plan of operations on the part of the leader, we desire to express our admiration of his gallantry and daring."[28] But in the realm of leadership, gallantry and daring can only get you so far. Gallantry and daring did not produce success. So what went wrong?

Although the explorers perished from hunger, food and water were in abundance in the area had they known how to access it. It remained invisible to them. The Aborigines knew where it was, as they and their ancestors had inhabited this land for many millennia. The Aborigines knew not only how to find food but also how to find their way in the austere environment. This territory was as familiar to them as our own neighborhoods are to us today. They were the custodians of the land and could have easily guided Burke and Wills through the confusing terrain.

But for most of the journey, the explorers intentionally avoided dealing with the Aborigines, whom they considered savages. They had a few brief encounters, but none were meaningful. The Aborigines generally kept a distance from the Europeans, while monitoring them carefully. After all, foreign creatures who carried strange weapons, wore bizarre outfits, and spoke a mysterious tongue were invading their territory and sacred ground. Naturally, the Aborigines were suspicious, afraid, and, of course, somewhat curious.

In regard to one encounter with an old Aborigine, Burke wrote, "The old fellow at King's Creek who stuck his speak into the ground and threw dust into the air, when I fired off my pistol, ran off in the most undignified manner."[29] Burke's actions and his words in recording the experience reveal his attitude toward the Aborigines. He considered them for naught. Wills provided more insight in his journal into his perception of the desert nomads. At one point the Aborigines approached the explorers and invited them to participate in a ritual dance. Wills noted:

> A large tribe of blacks came pestering us to go to their camp and have a dance, which we declined. They were troublesome and nothing but the threat to shoot will keep them away; they are however, easily frightened, and although fine-looking men, decidedly not of a war-like disposition. . . . From the little we saw of them, they appear to be mean spirited and contemptible in every respect.[30]

When the explorers finally realized that they were lost, they made an attempt to connect with Aborigines. The members of the Yandruwandha tribe gave the explorers some food, but given the white men's patronizing attitudes, they soon wearied of helping them. The situation came to a head when a young aboriginal man tried to take a piece of oilcloth from Burke. In anger, Burke fired his gun over the head of the young man to scare him and send a warning message to the tribe. Another member of the tribe came up to John King, put his boomerang on King's shoulder, and threatened to kill him. He did not follow through with this scare, but it was a warning, similar to Burke's.

In the evening, some of the tribe came back to the explorers' camp and attempted to reestablish a relationship. They gave some fish nets and food to the men. Burke, in a fit of rage, knocked the items to the ground and fired again at the Aborigines.[31] The Yandruwandha finally had had enough and left the white men to fend for themselves.

Burke, Wills, and King roamed around the outback in a state of confusion and despair, barely able to find any food. The heat was overwhelming, and death was fast approaching. In his journal entry of June 24, 1861, Wills scribbled: "A fearful night . . . King went out for nardoo . . . but he himself is terribly cut up. He says that he can no longer keep up the work, and as he and Mr. Burke are both getting rapidly weaker, we have but a slight chance of anything but starvation, unless we can get hold of some blacks."[32]

But it was too late. A few days later both Burke and Wills perished. John King was eventually taken in by the Yandruwandha people. Three months later he was found by a rescue team that had been dispatched from Melbourne to find the explorers. It is from King's account and Will's diary that we are able to get a sense of what those remaining days were like.

Clearly Burke failed to exercise real leadership. He lacked curiosity, even as his resources dwindled and his demise approached. He assessed the Aborigines as unworthy of either consultation or interaction. In exercising real leadership, one must be open to new ideas and novel information. One must be willing to test deeply held assumptions and question prevailing truths. Too often managers in organizations write off people they dislike and refuse to entertain ideas that don't agree with their particular paradigm or sense of the way things should be. Essentially, one must be willing to learn and explore beyond one's comfort zone, even if that means reaching across boundaries to connect with strangers and opponents. Burke and his team were lacking in all these areas.

There is no denying that Burke and Wills courageously put themselves in unfamiliar space, but their mind-sets remained unchanged in their European bodies. In practice, had they truly been explorers, they might have explored their prevailing paradigm and sought to push the boundaries of their thinking so that a pathway through the desert could have been created, a respectful relationship with the Aboriginal people established, and the journey considered a real success.[33]

The Conviction That You Have the "Truth" and "Know" the Way Forward

It is easy to be self-righteous about one's values and goals, and fail to realize that the work of progress always resides with the people—in their values, habits, practices, and priorities. When a solution is imposed by force or the threat of punishment, or if the people willingly buy into the leader's solution because of the leader's charisma or persuasive capacities, there is always the danger that a false set of tasks is put before the people. Moreover, the people may resort to attacking tangential or irrelevant problems rather than the fundamental barriers that are impeding progress.

Consider the case of Mao Tse-tung, a brilliant strategist who liberated his people from feudalism and warlordism and unified China. Mao went on to jeopardize much of the goodwill and value that had been amassed over the years as he pursued the infamous Cultural Revolution. Why? Because Mao believed that the Chinese people required ideological purification in pursuit of national progress. He held this belief not as a hypothesis to be tested but as the truth.

The "revolution" started in 1962 as Mao looked for a way to curb creeping capitalist and self-interested tendencies on the part of many party activists, workers, and government bureaucrats. Mao believed that the peasants were becoming too attached to material incentives and losing their revolutionary spirit. Over the next three years, he launched an indoctrination program to address these problems. Known as the Socialist Education Movement, the campaign became increasingly fanaticized as Mao and his diehard supporters attacked a wide variety of intellectuals and public figures. By mid-1966, the "purification" campaign became a national movement known as the Great Proletarian Cultural Revolution.

The foot soldiers of the Cultural Revolution were high school and university students, called the Red Guard. They traveled the country to attend and observe party meetings, and to speak with workers and peasants. They became a "shock force" of criticism against anyone who did not display sufficient revolutionary zeal or were too "bourgeois" in their thinking or lifestyle. Harsh criticism in meetings, however, soon turned to public shaming. People were forced to parade through the streets with dunce hats or carry signs saying that they were capitalist liars, pigs, and thieves. Homes were ransacked, and works of art and literature destroyed; thousands of people were beaten, tortured, imprisoned, and killed; and hundreds of thousands of students, teachers, and intellectuals were sent to the countryside to work on farms or in factories as a way of reeducating them and ridding them of their "lazy" Western instincts and habits.

For nearly three years, the country was essentially shut down, and anger, rage, and violence brought the nation to the verge of civil war. Seeing that China was about to implode, Mao called his Red Guards off. However, the atmosphere of paranoia and suspicion—along with occasional purges—continued until Mao's death in 1976.

Whatever progress China had achieved since 1949 came to an abrupt halt during the Cultural Revolution. Indeed, by any human or economic measure, the country regressed. Today China is still paying the price for this catastrophic misadventure, which pulled an entire generation out of schools and universities, denying them the opportunity to be fully educated and productive contributors to the development of their country. The breakdown in social relations led to mistrust and suspicion of neighbors, teachers, government officials, and even relatives. The Cultural Revolution significantly damaged the fabric of a healthy and viable society.[34]

The solution provided by a "great man" might give the appearance of wise and insightful leadership, but, as the Cultural Revolution shows, it may very well be delusional and ultimately destructive. The reality was, Mao used his power to put a false set of tasks before the people, and many people bought into it. These were not the right tasks to bring resolution to the multiple problems facing the country. Economic realities demanded enhanced creativity of the Chinese people and developing a technologically proficient workforce that could contribute quality goods and services in the global economy. Social realities required paying more attention, not less, to the material welfare of the Chinese people, so that they had a stake in supporting a government that gave them a better way of life. Corruption, both ideological and financial, could be purged only by strengthening the institutions of law and regulation and developing a strong moral compass for the nation, not by scapegoating and persecuting others for lack of fanaticism. The real work of progress had less to do with ideological zeal than with feeding and educating the people, and creating the conditions that could improve the quality of life of all people. In other words, the people needed to face reality and figure out the real problems and opportunities that need to be engaged in order to produce sustainable progress.

Conclusion

Let me summarize the ways that Enron, Mao, Burke, and dominance-obsessed primate societies help define what real leadership *is not*:

- Real leadership is not about dominance and control.
- Real leadership is not about putting a false set of tasks before the people and getting them to follow you.
- Real leadership is not about "getting one's way" and trying to get the people to buy into something they are not ready to embrace—even if it is born of strong convictions and moral beliefs.
- Real leadership is not about staying in your comfort zone and doggedly holding onto the world you know, even as the "ship is sinking."

I do not wish to completely denigrate these functions. Sometimes a group *does* need a dominant authority figure and *does* need to be controlled. Sometimes the task *is* to get people to follow, and a fantasy might be what the people need momentarily until they have the maturity to face reality. Certainly, motivating people through the power of one's convictions to do what they are reluctant to do *is* at times an important skill for any manager. But suggesting that such actions are unconditionally real leadership reduces the larger meaning, function, and value of real leadership. By being clear on what real leadership is not, we are in a better position to learn what might make a difference in generating sustainable progress in all domains of human activity—in our corporations, schools, communities, and governments.

The title of this chapter, "Odin, Enron, and the Apes," represents the dangers and opportunities of real leadership. Odin is a metaphor for the pursuit of the insight and wisdom to be responsible with one's power so that one can exercise the leadership that helps people face their toughest challenges. Enron reminds us that even successful companies can rapidly deteriorate in the absence of real leadership. The apes embody the actions and strategies that are the antithesis of real leadership—namely, counterfeit leadership, which includes the excessive preoccupation with getting people to follow, the reliance on dominance as a control measure, and the competitive dynamics of brute politics to protect one's interests, rise in a hierarchy, and maintain one's power. In the absence of real leadership, counterfeit leadership can easily emerge as the mechanism for allocating attention, time, and resources, resulting in organizations and communities getting caught up in a false set of tasks that have nothing to do with progress but are potentially destructive distractions.

Fundamentally, real leadership must focus people on tackling their toughest adaptive challenges—not false tasks. To do that work successfully, leaders need a diagnostic process to discover the real threats and real opportunities the people face. They must have an intervention strategy to draw attention to the problem and the promise. And, they must be able to mobilize the various actors in the social system to do the necessary sense-making and problem-solving work that will give the people their best shot at success. It can be difficult and demanding work, but no other work is more important for our collective well-being and shared prosperity. In the following chapters, the features and processes of real leadership will be presented in greater detail.

THE REAL LEADER

- Gets people to face reality as it pertains to their condition, threats, and opportunities
- Mobilizes the group to do adaptive work and adjust their values, habits, practices, and priorities
- Pursues the needed insight and wisdom to lead
- Takes responsibility for being the source of movement

THE COUNTERFEIT LEADER

- Places an excessive emphasis on getting people to follow
- Is preoccupied with dominance as a control mechanism
- Fails to fully engage the group and its many factions
- Is unwilling to look for solutions beyond one's comfort zone and the prevailing group paradigm
- Holds the conviction that the leader alone has the truth and knows the way forward

---

CHAPTER 2

Diagnostic Work
Determining the Principal Challenge

E ven the wise god Odin knew the importance of diagnostic work. From his throne in the holy city of Asgard, Odin every morning sent his two special ravens, Huginn and Muninn, out to look upon the world that he made and see how his children were faring and whether they needed his providential care. They would fly over the kingdom and return in the evening bringing Odin news of many things. Odin would often follow up on this intelligence by wandering in disguise among the people to see for himself what was happening. He was constantly asking himself, "What challenge do the people face?" Without valid and reliable data, it would be impossible for him to know the people's problems, recognize threats in the environment, and provide appropriate leadership that could attend to the well-being of the community.

"What challenge do the people face?" is an important question all leaders must ask and take the time to pursue. A leader might feel overwhelmed by the process of diagnosis as he or she could easily be beleaguered with information and data about the people's condition and the threats in the environment. But diagnostic work is too critical to ignore or conduct in a slipshod manner. Certainly any group or organization faces many serious problems demanding attention. But the leader must learn how, like Odin's ravens, to take a bird's-eye view of the terrain and generate a more complete picture of the bits and pieces that are presented by the individuals and various factions. Every faction has a piece of the problem and the solution, and they express it in their own way according to their values and aspirations. The leader's diagnostic work is to put the pieces together, like a jigsaw puzzle. Ultimately, the leader needs to ascertain what really is unresolved in the group that if allowed

31

to remain unresolved could destroy the group or impede progress. Or, said in another way, "What challenge do the people face?"

A well-made leadership diagnosis results in a more complete understanding of the condition of the social system—be it a school, corporation, or country—and the interplay between resources of the group, the people's capacities and values, and the terrain over which the people must travel on the road to progress. The diagnosis should lead to knowledge of the threats to the group and the opportunities or promises that are available if the people can muster the will and resources to do the necessary adaptive work. A useful diagnosis can produce a plan of action that can adjust according to what the people confront or avoid. The people may be fast learners, or the people may be slow learners. Either way, the diagnostic process must take into consideration the state and condition of the people if the most productive course of action is to be determined.

For example, imagine that you are a tribal chieftain whose people have been told by their shaman that they can escape a precarious and difficult existence by crossing a mountain range to find a world of promise and plenty that awaits them on the other side. If you are given the responsibility of leading that journey, your first task might be to examine the assumption that promise really does lie in the unseen, far-off land. If the data suggest that there is real promise, then you might diagnose the terrain from the point of view of those who must make the journey. In some situations, your people could make the journey safely and successfully by developing their ability for rock climbing and exertion in thin mountain air. In other circumstances, it may be that the tribe, given its limited resources, will have a slim chance of success in making such an arduous journey and must learn to accept that disappointing reality and make the most of its current existence, however difficult. Each of these possible scenarios requires leadership, but the type of leadership must be tailored to the specific set of challenges. When it comes to crossing a mountain range, even the most adaptable and loyal group of nomadic horsemen are going to have attitudes and capabilities very different from a group of Himalayan Sherpas.

Having observed many powerful men and women in different settings, I have found that they usually have a "sense" of what needs to be done but often cannot articulate the general theory or strategy underlying their analysis or course of action. Much of what they do is intuitive, ad hoc, and emerges out of a limited understanding and a limited set of capabilities. Given their positional power, they might be able to get away with an ad hoc approach to diagnosis and intervention, especially in static conditions that essentially replay the situations under which they have achieved and exercised power in the past. They run into trouble, however, when confronted with a new or novel predicament for which their habitual way of operating is insufficient. Counterfeit leaders, in particular, when they get into trouble, rather than try to understand how their initial diagnosis was incomplete or fundamentally flawed, are inclined to blame the group or some external factor, as Mao blamed the Chinese people for their lack of revolutionary spirit.

In the context of the Cultural Revolution, Mao made an invalid diagnosis. He took no account of the real threats and opportunities confronting China or the ingrained values, beliefs, and preferences of his people. He paid little attention to the "terrain" that must be traversed if useful change was to unfold. That terrain included the fragility of the nation's economy and its civic institutions, and the capacity of working people to cope with severe disruptions in their lives and daily routines. Had Mao thought more about the nature of these terrain issues, and had he engaged diverse and even dissident voices in the process to maximize the production of valid data, he might have reframed the challenge and adopted a very different strategy—possibly even a successful strategy.

In the following pages I will describe the general features of a systematic framework for diagnosing the principal challenge the people face, appreciating the terrain that must be traversed, and determining what actions the leader should take. I will draw on actual cases of a variety of people attempting leadership in different settings.

Six Domains for Leadership Challenges

Every leadership challenge is unique in some way, but there are basic types of terrain, or domains, that recur with such frequency that they constitute identifiable categories. Through many years of teaching, research, and consulting, I have identified six of the most common domains of leadership challenge. Each one of them poses a distinct set of problems for the leader and the group. Each requires a different and distinct approach to leadership. To achieve progress, a useful diagnostic framework must help the leader determine which of these basic domains is the one in which she or he must operate—and what type of leadership will offer the best chance for advancement.

I do not assert that all leadership challenges can be parsed neatly into these six categories. I remain open to the idea that better classification schemes can be constructed. In the meantime, however, these six contexts for leadership challenge are distinct enough, and coherent enough, that they permit useful analysis of past and current leadership initiatives and the development of general observations about the type of leadership technique needed to cope with emerging challenges. They therefore can form the basis for a practical diagnostic framework that can increase the chances of success in getting people to face their problematic realities and do the adaptive work that adds and protects value.

The six domains for leadership challenge are as follows:

The activist challenge

The development challenge

The transition challenge

The maintenance challenge

The creative challenge

The crisis challenge

In the *activist challenge*, the group or a faction of the group refuses to face some element of reality that actually might improve the people's quality of life or institutional performance. To meet the *activist challenge*, the leadership work includes provoking the group or key decision makers to reconsider and modify their assumptions, values, and priorities so that new realities and new ideas can be embraced, or at least entertained. This is often dangerous work. Think of Martin Luther who, in 1517, tried to get the church to face the reality that its behavior was not consistent with the values that it espoused. At great risk, he nailed his objections and concerns to the door of the main chapel in his town in order to provoke debate and begin a process of reform. From a leadership perspective, he faced an activist challenge.

In the *development challenge*, the group can make significant improvements to its quality of life or organizational performance if latent abilities become effective. Therefore, to meet the development challenge, the leader must generate a process that brings the group's latent abilities to full fruition. David Hornbeck, as mentioned in the previous chapter, faced a development challenge in building new capabilities in the Philadelphia school system. He had to get the entire system functioning at a higher level of performance if it was to deliver on the aspiration of providing a quality education for all of Philadelphia's children.

In the *transition challenge*, there is the possibility of great gains if the group can transition its current value set to a new value set. Therefore, to meet the transition challenge the leader must orchestrate a culture change process that includes refashioning the loyalties, mind-sets, and priorities of the people, to the extent necessary, to cope with a new reality. An example of shepherding a transition is Nelson Mandela taking black and white South Africans through the Truth and Reconciliation process that laid the nation's history of violence and racism to rest in order to permit future coexistence and cooperation.

In the *maintenance challenge*, the terrain is such that the group cannot improve its lot even if it develops the full extent of its latent abilities. Various hindrances to improvement may be lack of investment capital, enslavement to a foreign power, or a severe downturn in business. During times of peril, the leadership work is to get the people to protect what value they have amassed and ensure that the essential resources are preserved until the threat passes. The people need to be strategically defensive and incredibly determined if they are to weather the storm. An orderly withdrawal may give up ground gained in battle, but it may save the army to fight another day. An example of a maintenance challenge is when the 1914 Shackleton Expedition's ship became trapped in Antarctic ice, the crew immediately abandoned all hope of exploration and focused instead on surviving and returning home.

In the *creative challenge*, a combination of events presents an unusual opportunity that, if the group can break from routine activity long enough to exploit it, might lead to a major and permanent new benefit. The task is to do something that has never been done before. For example, a great breakthrough is feasible if enough people can muster the time and resources to think beyond their prevailing beliefs and shared assumptions. The task might be to create a new business—as with an entrepreneur—or bring into existence a new solution, an innovative product, or a novel strategy that might benefit the organization or community. A special kind of leadership is needed to ignite the imagination of people and instill the energy, attentiveness, and curiosity to create what needs to be created so that the group can transcend their prevailing paradigm and make a useful discovery.

In the *crisis challenge*, the group faces a potentially explosive situation that could threaten the life of the group or some aspect of the prevailing order. The predicament is extremely serious, potentially dangerous, and time-critical. Given that something unexpected and potentially destructive has happened, the people are anxious, bewildered, and in a highly vulnerable state. To meet the crisis challenge, the leadership task is to a generate a process that first dissipates the explosiveness in the situation and then gets the group to work on any underlying unresolved challenges that may contribute to a reappearance of the crisis in the future.

While most groups and institutions face at least one of these leadership challenges, all groups face many subchallenges or *tasks* that must be attended to if they are to advance. For example, an organization must continuously attend to the requisite *development tasks* if the organization is to remain a functioning and viable entity. If the development tasks in the corporation are insufficient to produce what the corporation needs, or if the routine activities of development are neglected, then a major problem likely will emerge, thus generating a *development challenge*. As a principal challenge, it will require extraordinary attention and resource levels.

An analogy with the health of your body may help. Normally, your circulatory system of heart and arteries provide what your body needs without your paying extraordinary attention to them. Nevertheless, you will have regular tasks to keep your circulatory system healthy, such as exercise and good diet. If your regular tasks do not provide what your body needs, your doctor may say one day, "My friend, you are overweight, your diet is bad, and you need more exercise." Then you have a *principal challenge* in that improving your health will require extraordinary attention and resource levels.

I use Lou Gerstner's introduction to IBM as an example of framing the principal challenge. Gerstner joined the troubled company as CEO in 1993. No one quite knew what to do with the business. It had failed to keep pace with the smaller entrepreneurial companies over the previous decade and was now paying the price. When Gerstner first looked at IBM, he realized he faced a *maintenance challenge* because the company was losing money and on the verge of bankruptcy, and he needed to exercise leadership to either hold the company together or sell off parts of the company for as much as he could get to preserve shareholder value.[1]

After stopping the hemorrhaging, Gerstner listened to the customers, employees, and even competitors to detect what the next challenge might be. He assessed the capacity of the organization and reframed IBM's predicament as a *transition challenge* because he could see that there was a possibility of transforming the culture of the company to take new advantage of changes in the market environment and compete with the smaller, more focused competitors. Specifically, he focused the culture of IBM on the provision of integrated services targeted specifically to customer need. The competencies to make the transition were already in the organization, but the values were lacking.

Before Gerstner took over as CEO, had the ongoing leadership tasks in IBM been providing what the corporation needed, the normal course of business should already have detected this ticking time bomb of a change in the market conditions and would have adapted IBM's operations to keep the company profitable with minimal disruption. But leadership for these tasks was neglected. In the real leadership framework, the ongoing development and maintenance tasks of a corporation will keep people looking for ticking time bombs before they become critical. Ticking time bombs would include emerging competitors, new technologies, changing markets, shifts in customer expectations, and changes in workplace values, habits, and priorities. Because these leadership tasks were not adequately addressed for more than a decade, Gerstner had to lead a transition challenge, which required dedicated resources, considerable time and energy, and a focused leadership strategy.

Knowing what kind of challenge the group faces helps the leader determine the nature of the interventions that need to be provided to bring resolution to a problem or take advantage of an opportunity. Too often those who seek to lead misread the context and fail to provide context-appropriate leadership interventions, or, even if they read the problem correctly, they fail to adjust their interventions to sufficiently address the overriding challenge and make midcourse corrections as new data emerge. If the leader misreads the essence of the challenge, then he or she is in danger of misleading the group, and the problem will remain unresolved. If the problem remains unresolved, it might eat away at the health and well-being of the enterprise and, like a ticking time bomb, eventually explode and jeopardize all the value and gains accrued by the people through years of hard work and dedicated effort.

To illustrate the principles of diagnostic work in determining what challenge the people face and the kinds of interventions that are needed to bring resolution to a demanding and problematic adaptive challenge, let us turn to a case drawn from the career of one of the English-speaking world's most notorious and controversial figures—William Bligh.

Governor William Bligh and the Rum Problem

Bligh is best remembered as the captain whose men and officers mutinied against him in 1789 aboard the HMS *Bounty*. But his career also included service with Captain Cook on his third great voyage of discovery of the Pacific in 1776 and a term as governor of Britain's fledgling colony in New South Wales, Australia, from August 1806 to January 1808. It was in New South Wales that Governor Bligh faced a leadership challenge even more daunting than keeping his ship and crew many years earlier. This leadership challenge would call for every bit of skill, experience, and wisdom that Bligh could muster if he were to succeed.

The colony was established as a penal settlement in 1788 to ease the overcrowding of English prisons. It was populated by about eight thousand convicts working on government road projects, land clearing, port building, or some other form of hard labor. There was also a combination of emigrants from England, soldiers, and officials of the British government, many emancipated convicts who chose to remain in the colony after completing their sentences, and aboriginal tribes who were scattered along the coast, in the forests, and deep in the interior. The total population of the colony was about twenty thousand people.

For the most part, faraway London showed little interest in the affairs of Australia, as England was preoccupied with the wars against Napoleon. Bligh's superiors essentially told Bligh to use his judgment in managing the affairs of the colony—which would include helping the settlers get established, maintaining order in the community, keeping the aboriginals at bay, and overseeing the prison system. Bligh was satisfied with this arrangement because he was confident that his understanding of people, his managerial ability, and his knowledge of the process of governance would serve him, and the colony, well.

Upon arrival in New South Wales, Bligh noticed that rum was a defining characteristic of community life. His predecessor had warned him of this, noting, "It was lamentable to behold the excess to which drunkenness was carried out. It was not an uncommon occurrence for men to sit around a bucket of spirits and drink it with quart pots until they were unable to move."[2] As a naval officer, Bligh was inured to the hard-drinking habits of his time, but this situation went well beyond anything he had seen before. What's more, in a cash-poor society, rum had steadily replaced the English pound as the currency for all trading and was used for buying food, supplies, and even land.

Bligh was particularly disturbed to see the local settlers establishing stills and brewing their own rum for distribution and sale—and some of these men had become quite wealthy from the trade. He was even more disturbed to see soldiers in the New South Wales militia participating in the distribution of rum and profiting from the business.

Bligh decided that the rum trade had gone far enough, as it was actually corrupting the colony's civil authorities and damaging its capacity to develop socially and economically. He recorded in his journal:

I have considered this spirit business in all its bearings, and am
come to a determination to prohibit the barter being carried
on any way whatever. It is absolutely necessary to be done to
bring labor to a due value and support the farming interest. . . .
I am aware that prohibiting the barter of spirits will meet with
marked opposition of those few who have so naturally enriched
themselves by it.[3]

Bligh's Misdiagnosis

Bligh diagnosed the rum problem as a legal issue, a technical problem,
rather than as an adaptive challenge. His first intervention was to issue a
formal edict declaring the trading of rum a criminal offense. As royal
governor, unencumbered by a legislative body, he had the prerogative to
impose any law that he deemed essential for maintaining order in the
colony. Bligh was accustomed to meting out harsh discipline to ensure
order and compliance, and his new edict carried the promise of heavy
punishment for violators of every rank and social station. For convicts
currently serving their sentence, the penalty was one hundred lashes and
twelve months of hard labor. For ex-convicts, it was three months of imprisonment, a twenty-pound fine, and loss of any government benefits;
for free settlers, conviction for rum trafficking resulted in the loss of all
privileges and benefits, and a fine of fifty pounds.[4]

The new rum law provoked widespread anger and resentment, but
Bligh expected this reaction. He reiterated to the community that disor-
derly conduct and blatant corruption undermined the well-being of the
colony—and therefore had to be dealt with harshly. His men made hundreds of arrests and destroyed dozens of stills. The violators were publicly flogged and jailed, sending a strong message that he was serious in
his resolve to wipe out the rum trade. Feeling satisfied with his accomplishments, Bligh wrote to his patron in England, Sir Joseph Banks,
"This sink of iniquity Sydney, is improving in its manners and its concerns. Government is securing a substantive dignity and producing in
good effects on the whole."[5]

But, in spite of his firm hand and willingness to inflict harsh punishments, the rum traffic continued. Bligh was certain that some members
of the community were intentionally challenging his authority and attempting to subvert his effort to put the colony on a more solid moral

and economic footing. His most potent opposition came from two groups: the New South Wales militia (the government army) and the merchant community. The militia was made up of volunteers—many of whom were former convicts—leavened by a sprinkling of professional soldiers from undistinguished regiments. For more than a decade, they had engaged in rum trading as a way to augment their meager wages. They regarded Bligh's campaign as a direct assault on their livelihoods—and they had close allies among the local merchants who interpreted the rum embargo as interference with the principle of free trade.

Bligh's intelligence sources reported that his key opponent—and greatest scofflaw—was none other than John Macarthur, a popular farmer and successful merchant who had been a thorn in his side from the day Bligh arrived. The entrepreneurial Macarthur had been in the colony for ten years and amassed a substantial fortune raising sheep—and selling rum. He became the major power broker among the business and political interests of the free settlers. He was also well-known to the convicts, the soldiers, and government officers and was highly regarded by most. Bligh knew that going after Macarthur would stir things up in the colony, but he was adamant that no one should be above the law, particularly the wealthy. Rules were rules, and Bligh felt that he needed to teach Macarthur and his supporters a painful but essential lesson.

The Rum Rebellion

Bligh worked hard to build a case against Macarthur for making and distributing rum, but his officers could never catch him in the act. Eventually, they got a tip that a merchant ship had just arrived in the harbor carrying two stills, and both of them, Bligh was told, were destined for John Macarthur. He immediately arrested Macarthur and had him tried by the colony's chief justice for the "importation of stills without permission of the governor." But during the trial the judge determined that Macarthur was not at fault, because at the time that he contracted for the stills, it was not illegal for him to do so.

One month later Bligh got another chance. A ship in Sydney harbor, procured by Macarthur for business purposes, was found to have an escaped convict on board. The ship was immediately seized, and Macarthur was arrested for "harboring a fugitive." Bligh now had his man.

As the trial began, people from all over Sydney came to witness the proceedings. The courtroom was filled with more than a thousand people, and many more were gathered in the streets. During the hearing, the packed crowd became loud and disruptive. They clearly did not want to see Macarthur convicted. After a particularly noisy outburst, the judge shouted to the mob, "Get out of my court!" The head of the militia assigned to protect the judge and maintain order responded, "Sir, they are the court!" The judge decided to suspend proceedings until calmer times and quickly fled the courtroom. Macarthur was locked in a holding cell for the night.

The next day, January 26, 1808, the militia freed Macarthur. But their work was not yet finished. With the band playing the "Grenadiers March," they made their way to the governor's mansion.

Bligh was terrified. He couldn't believe that government soldiers had turned against him and taken sides with the renegade Macarthur. He weighed up his dwindling options. He could try to negotiate with the troops. He could stand and fight. He could run. Or he could hide under his bed. Confronting overwhelming evidence that events had slipped completely out of his control, Bligh took the fourth option: He fled to his sleeping quarters and hid under his bed.

A mob of soldiers entered the house, apprehended the terrified Bligh, and placed him in Macarthur's cell. That evening, all across Sydney town—as Bligh later recalled—there were "bonfires, burning effigies, roasting sheep and all manner of riotous dissipation."[6] As one historian noted, "Rum fired the rebellion; in rum it was celebrated."[7]

For the next fourteen months, Bligh languished in confinement—first in a Sydney prison and later under house arrest—as he waited for troops from England to free him and restore him to his rightful place as the king's representative in the colony. Eventually a ship arrived, not to restore his authority but to take him back to London. Once on board the ship, Bligh demanded that the captain fire his cannons on Sydney as a departing "gesture." The captain ignored the order.

On his return to England, an official hearing was held, and it was determined that Bligh acted appropriately and honorably, although the authorities were deeply concerned about his leadership ability—after all, he once lost his ship, and now he lost a colony!

Diagnostic Principles

As a master navigator, William Bligh would never have charted a course by line of sight alone; he would want to know the wind, the tide, the sea depth, and whatever information he could gain from a lookout stationed aloft. He would weigh all these factors before choosing a course and trimming his sails. Once under way, he would also remain alert and flexible. If the seaman taking soundings reported a sudden loss of depth, he would adjust; and if the wind changed, he would readjust. As a sailor, Bligh knew these lessons; as a governor, however, he showed far less diagnostic skill and no flexibility at all. He did not fully appreciate what challenge the people faced and how that challenge was embedded in the people's values, habits, practices, and priorities. He treated the predicament as a bureaucratic functionary, making and enforcing laws without consideration for the context and the realities that would govern public reaction.

From the mistakes of Bligh and others, we can draw a number of important lessons about how to diagnose the terrain and assess the context for leadership problems. Here are five of those lessons.

Set aside your convictions to see what's there

Whoever takes responsibility for advancing a group or organization might have a personal idea of what problems the people face and what needs to happen to resolve those problems. But for difficult adaptive challenges that require a shift of values to bring resolution to the problem, that personal idea is probably not enough. Leaders, therefore, must put their personal ideas—their convictions and notions of "the truth"—temporarily to the side and learn more about the problem, how it is perceived by others, and the values and aspirations of the people that allow the problem to persist in its current form.

Governor Bligh did not set aside his convictions to learn more about the problem and the possible courses of action he might take. Setting aside his convictions would have meant truly listening to the local factions to know their concerns and the values underlying them. Bligh never bothered. He equated leadership with *not* surrendering his convictions. He believed, as do many powerful people who rely on dominance to get their way, that his knowledge of what was right, combined with the power of his position, would be sufficient to maintain order and bring resolution to the problem.

Every group has a story about who they are and who they are not, where they have come from and where they are not from, and where they hope to go and where they do not want to go. The story is a history, a mythology, a narrative that captures their fears, concerns, hopes, and aspirations. The story also reveals how the factions interpret the values and behavior of other factions that have some bearing on the problematic reality that the people are struggling with. Therefore, in the realm of leadership, appreciating the narrative of a group is important work if one is to discover what might be missing for the people.

In examining the people's story, one is listening to hear "what drumbeat people are marching to." By *drumbeat* I mean the loyalties, values, and priorities that shape what people do and the direction they move. Are the people marching to the same drum or different drums? If they are marching to different drums, then there will be stress points in the system. If they are marching to the same drum, then who is the drummer, and in what direction are they marching?

There are stress points in most communities and enterprises due to lack of clarity around purpose and competing notions of reality. In other words, people are marching in different directions. Sometimes one faction's purpose does not take into consideration the current reality of the system as a whole. In addition, as interpretations of reality and the delusional hopes of the various actors clash, the friction produces further stress in the system that generates counterproductive work avoidance dynamics.

This inability or unwillingness to set one's convictions to the side in order to listen to the story of the "other" and see the problem with greater clarity was a problem for the decision makers in the United States government during the Vietnam War. Robert McNamara, former secretary of defense under Presidents Kennedy and Johnson, undertook a period of honest reflection and deep soul searching as he tried to understand how he, and those he worked with, might better have addressed the problems posed by that long and tragic war. In his view, American thinking about the Vietnamese people and their struggle for self-determination was shaped and colored by a larger U.S. preoccupation with containing a monolithic communist menace controlled with single-minded efficiency from the Kremlin.

There was a small nugget of truth in this perception, but it was far outweighed by the larger reality that drove the actions of the Vietnamese. Recognizing the injustices of Vietnam's colonial past—injustices committed by the Chinese, the French, and the Japanese long before the United States became involved—would have helped American officials see the Viet Cong and North Vietnamese Army not simply as Marxist aggressors but also as idealistic nationalists determined to combat external intervention and control their own destiny.

In the 1990s, McNamara and his Vietnamese counterparts had more than seven meetings where they shared perspectives, explored underlying assumptions behind their strategies, and delved quite forthrightly into the errors of judgment that escalated the war. What follows is an interaction in one of the meetings between McNamara and the former Vietnamese foreign minister, Nguyen Co Thach:[8]

> **McNamara:** Before discussing the U.S. mindset, I want to state . . . that if I had been a Vietnamese communist in January 1961, when the Kennedy administration came to office, I might well have believed, as I judge they did, that the United States' goal in Southeast Asia was to destroy the Hanoi government and its ally, the National Liberation Front—the U.S. was an implacable enemy whose goal, in some fashion, was victory over their country.
>
> However, if I had been a Vietnamese communist and had held those views, I would have been totally mistaken. We in the Kennedy administration had no such intention. . . . On the contrary, we believed our interests were being attacked all over the world by a highly organized, unified communist movement, led by Moscow and Beijing, of which we believed, and I now think incorrectly, the government of Ho Chi Minh was a pawn.
>
> **Nguyen Co Thach:** In my way of thinking, the principal problem in the evolution of these mindsets was that the U.S. seemed to want to become the world's policeman. Mr. McNamara correctly quotes President Kennedy's Inaugural Address as evidence of a certain anti-communist mindset. . . . It seemed to us he was asserting that the U.S. wished to become something like the "master of the world." In this way, the U.S. would replace the British and the French, who had previously based their policies on such a wish. In our part of the world, this "fear of falling dominoes" was joined to the "threat of the yellow skin"—so those were two reasons why the U.S. felt justified in taking over as the new imperialists.

The conversation reveals the thinking of both sides in regard to the reasons for the war. They were very different perspectives and born of totally different worldviews. With both sides misdiagnosing the intent of the other, layer upon layer of faulty assumptions built an intractable wall that made clear communication almost impossible and war seemingly inevitable.

Reflecting on these meetings with the Vietnamese, McNamara wrote:

> What a tragedy! We believed that the North Vietnamese were merely doing the bidding of the Soviets and the Chinese, obsessed with spreading communism over all Southeast Asia. So we

discounted their nationalism and completely missed the point of the war, as they saw it, which was to unify their country under Vietnamese leadership—not French, not Japanese, not Chinese, and certainly not American leadership. They, on the other hand, concluded that our aims were those of these colonial powers and went to war to throw us out when, in reality, we didn't want to be there in the first place, except to prevent them from spreading communism. There was approximately zero empathy on each side, no understanding in Washington and Hanoi of the values and assumptions that were driving the policies of their adversaries.[9]

According to McNamara, failing to understand the true reality and aspirations of the Vietnamese led to numerous missed opportunities to end the war earlier and reduce the number of casualties on both sides. At the cost of many lives—a cost for which he is still vilified—he learned that, unless a leader can listen to and sense the reality of the various actors and factions, the results may well be disastrous for all concerned.

By setting aside one's convictions, a leader can increase his or her capacity to hear the people's story unfiltered by personal preferences and biases. In listening to the people's story, the leader hopes to ascertain

- how the people define their purpose,
- how they explain how they got to their current state,
- what their aspirations are,
- what they see as the impediments to the fulfillment of their aspirations,
- what their deepest fears are, and
- what conflicts exist among them—within their group and with other groups.

When people are not listened to or feel that the boss or the chief authority does not appreciate the reality of their predicament, they can easily resist the finest initiatives that might well be in their best interest. The assumption that the leader "knows best" is generally a flawed assumption, particularly when it leads to the imposition of a solution on the group without due consideration of their narrative and peculiar condition.

Diagnose factional dynamics, not personalities

Bligh may have been correct in the view that the role of rum in the community should be reduced. But even in pushing the community in the right direction, he did not take responsibility for the progress of the whole social system because his diagnosis did not consider the opposition that he would get from various factions, and how that opposition would impact the problem-solving process and adaptive work of the entire community. He needed to appreciate how painful and challenging it would be for certain sectors of the community to give up their dependency on alcohol—as a form of power, as a form of barter, and as a form of solace. The shift away from rum would require people to make significant adjustments in their lifestyle, working habits, and moral values.

Bligh made Macarthur a target, believing that by getting rid of him, the problem would be resolved or at least diminished. But Macarthur was acting out a systemic problem—a problem connected to the values of various factions in the system.

In taking responsibility for the progress of the whole social system, Bligh should have taken the time to analyze the factional dynamics, understand the competing values in the community, consider the various interests that were emerging, and challenge the people to discover what losses they would be willing to sustain in order to advance the colony in the direction of sustainable and equitable prosperity. All the factions, in varying degrees, needed to make adjustments in their values and priorities to accommodate a changing predicament.

The factions Bligh had to deal with included the following: The free settlers—who were farmers and traders—were the entrepreneurial faction who took the initiative to build businesses and establish trading relationships, and put in the hard work to clear the land and develop their farms. The military, another faction, was a fledgling group of soldiers made up of volunteers and a few professionals. The volunteers were undisciplined former convicts. The professional cadre were second-class soldiers who were not needed in any of the British Empire's other "hot" locations. Generally, they were very bored, as life in the colony was quiet and, for the most part, involved nothing more than arresting drunks, stopping street fights, and keeping the Aborigines at bay. They cared little for Bligh and saw him a tragic figure given his *Bounty* fiasco. The ex-convict settlers were another faction. They were hardened men and women who had served their time in appalling conditions. They had absolute contempt for men in significant positions of authority and the British aristocrats in particular.

Each faction held a piece of the problem, and therefore a piece of the solution. It was not enough simply to go after Macarthur in order to resolve the issue. The community of New South Wales was in a state of flux. No one quite knew what the purpose of the community was. Was it simply to be a penal colony? Was it to be an independent settlement that could generate revenue for the homeland? Should more thinking and strategic planning be undertaken to make something of the colony? The uncertainty of purpose produced considerable anxiety that led people to exploit their predicament for their own self-interest.

But what Bligh did was not uncommon. Many leaders make the mistake of being preoccupied in their diagnosis with individual actors and personalities, rather than the dynamics of the system. They believe that if you can apply a technical fix, such as getting get rid of a certain person, then the problem will go away. But this is an unwise and irresponsible strategy. Individual actors might be symptoms of the problem, but rarely are they the source of the problem. In a diagnosis that focuses primarily on individual players and not the interacting, competing, and conflicting values of the larger system, leaders have a very incomplete understanding of why the problem exists. They fail to learn about the loyalties and concerns of the various factions that support and fuel the problem. They also fail to learn about the opposition they might get from disgruntled factions, as they try to make changes in the system. In being unmindful of the potential opposition, leaders put themselves and their project at risk of attack and subversion.

Detect what aspects of reality the people are avoiding

After listening to the various factions, gathering as much information as possible about the context, and testing one's assumptions for validity, the diagnostic work is to determine what aspect of reality is being avoided by the people. All factions embedded in a situation of irresolution hold a view of the problem that is limited, biased, and incomplete. That aspect of reality that the people are avoiding will be a piece of the puzzle that needs to be faced if progress is to unfold. The leadership task, therefore, is to detect what it is that the people are missing that, if surfaced and confronted, would enhance the people's capacity to solve their problems and advance. Related to that is the question, What is it that the group considers to be more important and critical to their survival than the facing of a difficult piece of reality? In other words, are there some aspects of reality that a group does not want to confront because in doing so, the group's habits, practices, priorities, and even identity might be disrupted and threatened?

For example, a community may want superior schools for their children, but the reality is that the quality of their local school is mediocre because the class sizes are too big and the school's resources are too few. Although they desire better schools, if the community is not willing to pay more in property taxes (an important source of school funding in the United States), then no progress on better schools might emerge, and teachers and principals might even be scapegoated by the community. Thus the aspiration of good schools is not supported by the practices and values needed to deliver on that aspiration.

The diagnosis of such a predicament might reveal that the community considers low property taxes more important than funding public schools. They might not want to acknowledge that reality, but the data point to that conclusion. The leadership challenge is to get the people to confront the gap between their aspiration and what they are willing to contribute or sacrifice in order to fulfill that aspiration. The group must also understand how the competing values that they hold serve to perpetuate the problem. Then, the leader must work with the community to lower its aspirations, accept an increase in property taxes, or partner with the educational system—teachers, administrators, parents, and the union—to find ways to make the system more efficient and effective by increasing the capacities of people without increasing expenditures, thus making it a development challenge.

When Lou Gerstner first took over as CEO of the troubled IBM in 1993, he spent nearly a year visiting the field and listening to the stories of the different IBM divisions to ascertain what reality the various factions were avoiding. He knew that the people were avoiding some aspect of reality, as the once highly successful company was on the verge of bankruptcy.

Everywhere that Gerstner went, analysts and employees were asking him to spell out his vision. But in that first year, Gerstner's message was always the same: "The last thing IBM needs right now is a vision."[10] IBM had real problems, and creating another vision statement was not the solution at that period in time. In Gerstner's words, "I had discovered in my first ninety days on job that IBM had file drawers full of vision statements. We had never missed predicting correctly a major technological trend in the industry." The problem, as Gerstner saw it, was that IBM was "paralyzed and unable to act on any predictions."[11]

Clearly the people in IBM were avoiding some aspect of reality and pursuing a false set of tasks that had nothing to do with creating an extraordinary company. In order to find out what reality the people were avoiding, or at least missing, Gerstner traveled the globe meeting with staff, suppliers, and customers. The value-added that he, as a new CEO, could bring to that group would be to notice something that the people had ignored or missed. It took him a while, but he finally saw the pattern of how and where the IBM managers were avoiding reality. Gerstner noticed that these very intelligent and competent professionals had ignored the details of their customers' needs while paying much attention to minor clues of "who was in and out and up and down" in the organization. They had become excessively internally focused, to the detriment of understanding customer needs, market conditions, and competitive threats. As Gerstner explained, "We may not have known much about customers, but there was one group to which we paid plenty of attention: ourselves. In the IBM culture, the organization, and how one fit into the organization, was considered a very important subject."[12]

As Gerstner analyzed the situation, he could see that the IBM managers' attention to their own organization reflected the business strategy that had made IBM highly successful during the 1960s and 1970s but that was no longer appropriate. In previous years, what drove the market was what computers could do. So it was very important to have detailed knowledge of the technology that IBM could offer the customer. Customers generally would come to IBM asking what computers could do, and then the customers would install computers in the parts of their business that could take efficient advantage of the available IBM technology, which was limited. But during the 1990s, markets had shifted, and computers were used all over the customers' organizations. So the customers had become very discriminating in expecting IBM to tailor the computer offerings to how the customers wanted to do their business.

Gerstner concluded that the reality that his organization had missed was how much the markets had changed. His job was to orchestrate a learning process that would get the various parts of his organization to face the reality of the market changes and then adapt their business strategies, management styles, and work practices to take advantage of what they had been ignoring.

Get the factions interacting with each other to develop a richer view of the problem and explore possible solutions

After the leader has identified each of the factions that make up the system and listened to their respective stories to ascertain their condition and the reality they might be avoiding, the next activity in the diagnostic process is to get the factions interacting with each other to produce a richer view of the problem and explore possible solutions. Answers to tough problems are rarely obvious, and real solutions that actually work for most or all parties are often elusive. Given that, it helps to have the various factions tangle with each other's values and perspectives to appreciate what is at stake, what shared sacrifices do the people need to make, and what the best solution might be.

Being a captain of a ship, Bligh had been used to making decisions on his own. His expertise was generally sufficient to deal with the spectrum of problems that presented themselves on the open ocean. But the rum situation was not a technical problem that could be resolved through the application of technical expertise. It was a multifaceted adaptive problem embedded in the values, habits, practices, and priorities of the people. For that reason, Bligh needed to mobilize others to participate in the diagnostic process.

Think how different Bligh's tenure might have been if he had consulted with John Macarthur and the merchants, as well as former convicts who were now free settlers, and even the militia, about how to build a new set of values and practices in the community so that rum was no longer an impediment. He might have sat down with each faction and explained, "We've got a problem. Here's my view of the problem and my idea of what needs to be done. What am I missing? What problems do you foresee with my approach? What do you see as the problem? How would you handle it? Together, let's explore what needs to be done." In other words, he might have given part of the work back to Macarthur and the other factions. Macarthur might have become an ally and worked with the merchants and key community members to diagnose the deeper nature of the problem and develop workable win-win solutions.

In his book *Leadership without Easy Answers*, Ronald Heifetz summarizes the case of a copper-smelting plant in Washington State that was the mainstay of the local economy but was so toxic that it was poisoning area communities and damaging the health of local children.[13] William Ruckelshaus, the U.S. Environmental Protection Agency (EPA) administrator at the time, knew that he had to intervene to stop the poisoning.

Unlike Bligh, Ruckelshaus did not take unilateral action without making a careful diagnosis and engaging the entire group in the process. Remedying the problem was not a case of simply closing the plant. He knew that he needed to work with residents, employees, taxpayers, and shareholders to identify what capabilities were available to address the problem and what values were most important to the affected groups. Would they pay for a sophisticated filtration and reclamation program? Could the plant operate under such a program and remain profitable? Would the resulting mitigation of the pollution be enough to allay fears about public health and long-term environmental impacts? How much sacrifice should the people and the company be willing to pay for installing poison-removing filters in the plant and surrounding area that would improve their health?

Ruckelshaus had the power to close the plant, but he chose to see his leadership challenge not simply as ending the poisoning but as getting people to take responsibility for their community. Instead of acting from a position of dominance and ordering the people to obey the law, Ruckelshaus scheduled a series of town meetings to help people understand the full extent of the problem and to orchestrate a process that could get each faction to take responsibility for making adjustments in their values and behavior to bring resolution to the problem.

The meetings were argumentative and boisterous, but in the end, rather than having insurrections and refusals to comply, Ruckelshaus managed to get the unions, shareholders, company management, taxpayers, and workers to cooperate in cleaning up the mess, develop realistic plans for changing business operations, and responsibly attend to community interests. The company eventually closed the plant, but the process had prepared the community and the employees for that outcome.

By orchestrating a learning process in which people come to discover aspects of the problem that even the leader did not fully appreciate, the leader can get the factions to take responsibility for seeking a solution even as the leader tests the validity of his or her own hunches and perceptions. Such a process not only improves the quality of diagnosis but begins the process of shifting the mind-set and values of the people who must embrace the solution and make it work. The more they feel that something is being imposed upon them without due consideration of the complexity of their reality, the more they will resist.

Frame the principal challenge

Upon ascertaining what reality the people are avoiding and exploring possible pathways to resolution of the problem, the final aspect of diagnostic work is to frame the principal challenge. Whether or not a problem area is a principal challenge is a management call based on consideration of the available data. In considering the data that have been produced, the leader should then use that data to determine (1) the condition of the people, (2) the barriers to progress, and (3) the promise or opportunity available.

In looking at the *condition of the people*, the leader seeks to understand the mood of the people and the extent and nature of the capabilities that reside in the group or enterprise. Capabilities are the skills, attitudes, and values required to resolve a complex problem or take advantage of a unique opportunity. Some capabilities may be widely recognized in the group and shared by many of its members. Others may be latent and may be discovered and developed over time. For example, when Lou Gerstner eventually declared that IBM would become the "world's leading technology company," neither he nor his people had a clear idea of how to achieve that goal. Nevertheless, he had a sense that the employees at IBM could figure out how to do it by employing their current resources and developing latent capabilities that they would discover as they went along.

In considering the *barrier*, the leader seeks to understand the nature of the danger or the piece of reality that is blocking progress. Does the barrier reside in the group, or is it external to the group? What is the relationship of the barrier to the people's current values, habits, practices, and priorities? How does the barrier connect to the reality that the people are avoiding?

In considering the available *promise*, the leader seeks to appreciate the benefit that is available if the people can muster their capabilities to attend to the adaptive challenge. In examining the promise, the leader can then ascertain whether the challenge is urgent or can be paced or even postponed. For example, the leader should ask, "Given the threat, how urgent is the problem? Should extraordinary attention and resource levels be allocated to solving this problem or taking advantage of this opportunity? What will happen if we do not provide extraordinary attention and resource levels?" To gauge the urgency of the promise, the leader must examine the consequences of denying, ignoring, or underestimating the challenge. Will there be a loss of value for the community or organization if the problem is not resolved? Will progress be thwarted if the group does not take advantage of the opportunity that has presented itself?

Some problems can be postponed if they are not so serious that they require immediate attention. If there is no danger or no sense that an opportunity must be exploited immediately, the group can take time to address the problem. For example, when Lou Gerstner became CEO of

IBM in 1993, the company faced a set of urgent problems that had to be addressed: IBM was losing money and heading toward bankruptcy. The root causes of these problems—bureaucracy, territoriality, and competition among units—had been around for decades, but they were not deemed serious because IBM was still highly profitable. The problems became serious and urgent due to a shift in the marketplace. When the market shifted, the consequences of these habits, practices, and priorities became immediately threatening.

In considering the people's condition, the barriers to progress, and the available promise, the leader thereby develops a richer view of the context in which leadership needs to be exercised. By understanding the context—the threat, the opportunity, the urgency of attention, and the resources and capabilities of the group—Gerstner knew what was required of him in the way of leadership to transform the company, and what was required of the people to do adaptive work and make authentic progress. He was then in a position to frame the challenge appropriate to the context as a transition challenge.

As we have already seen in the case of China's Cultural Revolution, a misdiagnosis and an incorrect framing can lead to dire consequences, even disaster. Mao diagnosed the condition of many of the people of China in the 1960s as ideologically corrupt and framed the problem as a crisis challenge. In his mind, it was very serious and demanded immediate attention. Had Mao diagnosed the problem as a development challenge, he might have taken a more gradual, incremental approach that allowed for midcourse corrections based on further analysis and group feedback. For example, he might have tested out his strong conviction that the eradication of "ideological corruption" leads to a better society. If this question were properly explored, more informed choices might have been made on how to proceed for the development challenge China faced.

If Bligh had taken the time to diagnose the terrain, he might have noticed that he faced a transition challenge with development tasks. In a transition challenge, the group has the resources needed to make the change, but leadership is required to plan and shepherd the process. Fundamentally, that process is one of modifying the culture by establishing new norms and shifting values, habits, and practices to the extent necessary to bring resolution to the problem and take advantage of emerging opportunities. In diagnosing the transition challenge of the Sydney settlement, Bligh would have noticed that the seriousness of the problem was moderate and therefore required immediate attention to begin the process but no urgency to complete it. Given that the group had the capacity and resources to make the transition and that the problem was not time-sensitive, he could have steadily built a coalition to support the change and then paced the reforms to ensure that they were embedded in the values of the community.

In summary, the leader needs to consider fully the data that he or she and the group have gathered about the problem, the group dynamic, the context, and other relevant information. They then might work through the following kinds of questions to determine what challenge the people face:

- Is the group, or a particular faction, refusing to face some aspect of reality? (An activist challenge)

- Is the group lacking in capacity or resources to do the job or address future demands? (A development challenge)

- Does the culture of the group need to be shifted to accommodate new realities? (A transition challenge)

- Does the group need to sustain its current values and practices because it is under threat? (A maintenance challenge)

- Does the group need to invent new practices, processes, and procedures in order to do something that has never been done before? (A creative challenge)

- Is the group facing a potentially explosive situation, and is the value it has amassed in jeopardy? (A crisis challenge)

Conclusion

Progress-generating and value-conferring leadership does not flow from dominance, confidence, or even personal conviction. Instead, the exercise of real and responsible leadership derives from the wise application of power and a diagnostic capacity that helps leaders (1) figure out the nature of the challenge the group or organization faces; (2) ascertain to what degree the problems embedded in the challenge invade the values, habits, and priorities of the people; and (3) determine who and what factions must be mobilized or engaged to address the challenge.

In Part II—the next six chapters—each of the key challenges will be explained in greater detail. I will present a set of leadership principles for each challenge that help the people face the reality of their condition, deal with the threat that impedes progress, and do the adaptive work of taking advantage of their opportunities and achieving the desired promise.

FEATURES OF DIAGNOSTIC WORK

- Set aside your convictions to see what's there.
- Diagnose factional dynamics, not personalities.
- Detect what aspects of reality the people are avoiding.
- Get the factions interacting with each other to develop a richer picture of the problem and explore possible solutions.
- Frame the principal challenge.

PART II

The Six Challenges
of Real Leadership

CHAPTER 3

The Activist Challenge

Calling Attention to a Contradiction in Values

The first challenge of leadership is to get people to wake up to the fact there is a problem—that the group is avoiding some aspect of reality, ignoring a threat, or missing a great opportunity. The leader in such a predicament faces a development challenge. Groups often avoid facing some aspect of reality, either because that piece of reality is too threatening to their current existence, or because they are so focused on what they regard as their main concerns that they cannot take the time to consider any other issues. To get the people to wake up and face the problem is an activist challenge. Often the problem is embedded in people's values and behavior. The people might espouse one view but act in ways that are not consistent with that view. The leadership task in an activist challenge is to call attention to the contradiction in values and intervene to disrupt the thinking and patterns of behavior that allow the people to persist in avoiding the reality of their condition. The following scenario illustrates a corporate activist challenge.

SCENARIO

Suppose you are a senior human resource executive in a major software company. You have spent ten years in the business and worked your way up to the ranks of senior management. In recent years, given the company's phenomenal growth, it has been difficult to get managers throughout the company to attend to the many essential activities such as coaching and developing their staff and building their own leadership capacities. It is always "go, go, go,"and, it seems, people don't have time to think about management and human resource concerns.

But this constant focus on execution and the failure to attend adequately to the nurturing of talent is now producing unintended consequences. Turnover of middle and senior managers is increasing; it is difficult to retain many of the newly recruited young and bright MBAs as they find the climate somewhat stultifying and see more enticing opportunities elsewhere; and staff, in general, are complaining more then ever about their boss's management style and the corporate culture. This is very troubling to you as management espouses one set of values about "people being our most important asset" but acts in ways that violate that belief.

You conclude it is time to give the company a wake-up call. You can't make the company change or get the managers to comply. You don't have that kind of power. But you can use what power you have to get the managers to face reality—although you will be putting yourself at risk to do so. Some people, possibly the president, will see you as a troublemaker. And troublemakers in this company don't last long.

One of your duties is to organize the annual retreat. In the past these meetings have been predominantly social events, with a brief presentation by the president. The managers would publicly salute the president, never raise any concerns or objections, or even pose questions, but complain about things among themselves on the journey home. This year it will be different.

At the off-site you make a powerful presentation with indisputable facts about turnover and bench strength. You are serious but passionate. You stir people's thinking as you challenge the prevailing management paradigm. You call attention to the "rot" that is in the culture, and you say things that have been "undiscussable" in the organization up until this moment. To ensure the message has greater credibility and potency, you invite a management guru from a leading university to join you in the presentation. Some of your colleagues look a little uncomfortable, but many have a big smile on their face. They know you are being courageous, but they also know you are speaking the truth. After the presentation, many come up and thank you, although one says, "What would you like your obituary to say?" But most of the managers are supportive.

Even the president says, "You know, this is important stuff. You've really got me thinking." You have just begun exercising leadership for an activist challenge.

The Nature of an Activist Challenge

As the leader looks to the people to see whether they are facing an activist challenge, he or she is assessing whether there is a contradiction in values in the group or whether the group is refusing to face some hard facts. The group might espouse one set of values but act in ways that are not consistent with those values. For example, since the founding of the United States, many Americans espoused the value of "all men are created equal" but acted in ways that perpetuated inequalities in the society. The activist challenge of the civil rights movement was to get Americans to see the contradiction in values, face the reality of how their laws and cultural practices were discriminatory, and make adjustments in their habits, practices, and priorities to produce a more honorable country.

In the opening case of the human resource executive, the activist challenge was to get the top one hundred managers in the company to face hard facts in regard to the reality that company progress would be jeopardized if they did not devote more time and resources to developing their people to be more significant contributors. As the HR manager looked five years into the future and examined the forces and trends that affected the company, it was obvious that the company had to change and be more responsible for the development of internal managerial capacity. Getting people to take that challenge seriously—given that the HR executive could not enforce or dictate change—provided a distinct and vital opportunity to exercise leadership. Treating the problem as an activist challenge allowed the manager to exercise leadership to get people's attention by being provocative. Had the manager complied with the working values of the corporate culture and not raised the hard facts for public discussion, the problem would have persisted and, like a ticking time bomb, put the company at great risk.

The key symptoms of an activist challenge for any group, community, or organization are as follows:

- Some enduring behaviors, values, and/or practices have become corrosive and dysfunctional—and serve to undermine the long-term integrity and survival of the group.

- An opportunity presents itself that can lead to great benefit and progress for the group, but no one is seriously considering it.

- Danger is looming due to an internal or external threat, and the group is not doing anything about it.

In diagnosing an activist challenge, the leader must examine (1) the condition of the people, (2) the barrier that impedes progress, and (3) the promise or aspiration on the other side of the barrier.

In general, the condition of the *people* facing an activist challenge is an unwillingness to change their values or thinking to accommodate some aspect of reality. The people are in denial, resistant, ignorant, or, for whatever reason, simply refuse to budge. They are comfortable where they are at.

The *barrier* to progress is the people's resistance. It might be said that a part of the individual's thinking is trapped by the prevailing system or group paradigm. Hence the leadership work is to engage that part of the individual's thinking that is not trapped by the system or group paradigm and get the people to steadily entertain the aspect of reality, or the hard facts, that they are refusing to consider.

The *promise* in an activist challenge is that if people can face the problem and seriously consider the data they have neglected or denied, then a new opportunity for progress can open up.

Generally, in an activist challenge, the person seeking to lead does not have the power or authority to make people listen and command change. Given the limitations of his or her power, the intervener must think of creative ways to get people's attention and highlight the contradiction in values. Essentially, the leader is trying to say to the people, "Some of your current values and behaviors are irreconcilable with some of your other cherished practices, beliefs, and traditions. I will show you how irreconcilable they are and stir you to learn and to change." Upon getting the people's attention, the leadership task is then to move the people to be responsible for their predicament and modify their thinking and behavior accordingly. Fundamentally, the leader wants to get the people to learn: to learn about the problem, how their behavior contributes to the problem, and what can be done to solve the problem. This kind of learning is fundamentally *deep learning*, in that the people must burrow down into their underlying assumptions and deeply held beliefs to ascertain why a problem persists and what can be done about it.[1]

But many people who try to be activists fail to exercise real leadership because they do not understand what it means to get a group engaged in deep learning and doing adaptive work. Their stirrings might make a lot of noise but do not generate any lasting focus on the real problem. The intervener in such a circumstance can easily be trivialized or ignored, as others see this person as nothing more than an irritating complainer determined to get their way at the expense of others.

If it does not teach a lesson that is fundamentally compatible with key tenets of a group's larger value system, a provocation will be both unproductive and irresponsible. The terrorists who perpetrated the horror of September 11 believed that they were teaching a provocative lesson to the United States when they attacked New York and Washington, D.C. Yet while destructive interventions such as terrorist bombings may get people's attention, they violate the fundamental values of society so much that they harden positions, reduce debate, and make change even less likely. The same can be said for demonstrators who run riot through a city wreaking havoc and destroying property. Their cause might be important, but their actions are irresponsible and abusive. Rather than getting people to focus on the problem, they end up putting the spotlight on their own destructive behavior, making engagement of the real issue even more difficult. What's more, groups assaulted by such grotesque interventions are often driven away from constructive thinking. Instead, they lash out emotionally, often generating a cycle of tit-for-tat violent reactions that never address any of the underlying problems that need attention.

As Mahatma Gandhi and Martin Luther King both realized, leadership interventions for an activist challenge need not be immoral or destructive in order to be successfully provocative. Gandhi's nonviolent and creative provocations against India's British rulers generated the space for the repugnant behavior of the British Raj to be exposed for all the world to see. He succeeded not only in mobilizing his fellow Indians to act and to learn but in garnering sympathy and support from many Britons as well. Gandhi set the modern standard for a leader facing an activist challenge who could provoke the people but also take responsibility for the stirrings that such provocations produced.

Leadership for an activist challenge is often dangerous work. It requires courage whether you are trying to get the people of a nation to take responsibility for a persistent problem or whether you are in a company and trying to get people to face hard facts and change course or adopt a new strategy. In either setting, you are putting yourself on the line and will be subject to criticism, even attack. The attack often comes from the system's authority figures. In every group are authority figures who protect the status quo and maintain their power by virtue of stability in the current order. For them, there might be much to lose if the current order is disrupted in any way. Therefore, when the system is provoked, they see their role as to neutralize the provocateur and bring the system back to a state of equilibrium.

Given that a negative reaction often occurs from some in the system, particularly the system's protectors, it is understandable that people will be reluctant to exercise real leadership and challenge the prevailing norms and beliefs of a group. In a company, for example, an executive might see something that needs to be done but not do anything about it because she does not want to upset her colleagues or the boss and be marginalized, branded a troublemaker, or possibly fired. But the reason activist leadership is needed is because things are not moving, problems are being ignored, and people are playing it too safe in the name of maintaining harmonious relations, keeping the peace, and appearing loyal. For the group or organization, if leadership is not exercised to get the people to confront reality, danger awaits.

While the risk of intervening cannot always be diminished, the purpose of this chapter is to increase one's effectiveness in the face of such risk. To begin, consider the case of Alice Paul and the women of the National Woman's Party, and their extraordinary and courageous leadership in provoking men to face reality, do the right thing, and grant women the vote.

Alice Paul: Getting Men to Do the Right Thing

Even though it prized itself in being the most democratic country in the world, the United States denied voting rights to women until 1920. Activists of the likes of Susan B. Anthony and Elizabeth Cady Stanton had done an extraordinary job in the mid- to late 1800s in organizing women to be aware of their rights, but progress was elusive. The two original activists had passed away, and the issue of the women's vote had been buried under a host of other national concerns. Alice Paul and her team embraced the challenge of getting women's suffrage back in the headlines and on the national agenda—particularly President Woodrow Wilson's agenda.

Alice Paul was born on January 11, 1885, of Quaker parents in Mount Laurel, New Jersey. She dedicated her life to the single cause of securing equal rights for all women and ensuring that women were equal partners in society. In 1911, she joined with Lucy Burns to form the Congressional Union for Women's Suffrage, which later was reorganized into the National Woman's Party (NWP).

Their first major intervention was on March 3, 1913, the day before Woodrow Wilson's inauguration as president. On that day, eight thousand women marched to the White House and demanded to meet with the president to discuss the issue of giving women the vote. They came from all ranks of society—college students, teachers, nurses, mothers, professionals, and mill workers. While many men verbally abused and belittled the marchers, saying such things as, "You ought to be home darning your husband's socks," the event was a great success in that they got the publicity that they needed. President Wilson, however, was not impressed and refused to meet with the women.

Over the next three years, Paul and her team engaged politicians, religious groups, civic leaders, and reporters. But the mood of most men in the country, as reflected by the politicians, was to do everything they could to keep women from voting. Paul was tired of the intransigence of the president and the politicians and decided it was time to turn up the heat. On January 10, 1917, the women began picketing the White House. They were known as the "Silent Sentinels." Every day, from morning to evening, the women stood in front of the White House with their banners and made speeches and passed out pamphlets. One of the banners read, "Mr. President how long must we wait for liberty?" Although each day only a small group was outside the White House, more than a thousand women took their turn on the picket line.

On April 16, 1917, the United States entered World War I. Paul and her team faced a dilemma: Do we stop the picket and support the president, or do we continue the protest? Many of the women believed that in a time of war it was not appropriate to provoke the government. Paul, however, felt otherwise. She argued that the picket must continue, particularly in a time of war, as women needed to have a voice in such issues as war and peace, given that so much was at stake. She and her team maintained the picket line more defiantly than ever. Their new banner carried Wilson's own war message: "We shall fight for things which we have always held nearest our hearts—for democracy, for the rights of those who submit to authority to have a voice in their own governments."[2]

After six months of ignoring the women outside his White House, Wilson decided it was time to move. The women would be arrested. The trigger for him was another provocative banner that they waved in front of a Russian government delegation. It read, "The women of America tell you that America is not a democracy. 20 million women are denied the right to vote. President Wilson is the chief opponent of their national enfranchisement. Help us to make this nation free. Tell our government that it must liberate its people before it can claim Russia as an ally." The police moved in, tore down the banner, broke up the picket line, and arrested many of the women.

More women took their place, and a new banner was soon displayed. It read, "Kaiser Wilson, have your forgotten your sympathy for the poor Germans because they were not self-governing? 20 million women are not self-governing. Take the beam out of your own eye."[3] On August 14, 1917, a mob of angry men tried to break up the picket and destroy the banner. It turned into a riot, and many of the women, including Alice Paul, were attacked and beaten. More women were arrested and taken to jail.

In October, Paul was arrested and sentenced to seven months in jail. She was placed in solitary confinement. She and her fellow inmates began a new protest in the jail. The protest was to get the government to recognize them as political prisoners, not petty lawbreakers. Of course, Wilson denied them that status, so Paul began a hunger strike. She was forcibly fed by putting a tube down her throat, but it did not deter her. In an attempt to discredit Paul as a "crazy woman," the authorities transferred her to an insane asylum.

Newspapers carried stories about the jail terms and forced feedings of Paul and her fellow inmates. The stories angered many Americans and created more support than ever for the suffrage amendment. After five weeks in prison, the authorities relented, and Alice Paul was set free. The attempts to stop the picketers and the "political prisoners" had backfired.

After receiving thousands of letters from women all across the country who supported Paul and her team, on January 9, 1918, Woodrow Wilson gave in and agreed to endorse women's suffrage. He could see that the tide was turning and that women in the country were becoming a force to be reckoned with. But the work was far from over. The task now was to get Congress to actually ratify the amendment that would give women the vote. As the women turned their attention toward the Congress, the Senate reacted by passing the Sabotage and Sedition Act that prescribed harsh punishment for disloyal, antigovernment citizens—such as treacherous women. With this threat, the women lay low for seven months.

In August 1918, the picket lines started up again. The women were disappointed because Wilson wasn't doing anything to advance the issue. The women lit fires in front of the White House in honor of Joan of Arc, highlighting the fact that she was burned by men for having the audacity to challenge the prevailing order. Whenever Wilson made a speech that they deemed hypocritical, they took a copy of the speech and burned it in their Joan of Arc caldron. They also burned Wilson's picture "even as the revolutionary fathers had burned a picture of King George."

These provocations were seen by many—mostly men—as going too far. The press labeled the women "Bolsheviks." In the spring of 1919, to counter the negative press, Paul organized the "Suffrage Special" and the "Prison Special," two trains that would carry former prisoners around the country to talk about their imprisonment and educate men and women on the importance of woman's suffrage. It was a tremendous success, as people met these "evil women" and saw firsthand that they were intelligent and reasonable mothers, wives, and workers.

In March 1919, Paul organized the "Opera House March." Wilson was to speak at the New York Opera House, and Paul wanted to burn his speech publicly in front of the building. The intention was to put pressure on Wilson to call a special session of Congress and have them vote on the amendment. As she and her team marched to the Opera House, they were set on by the police. Doris Stevens, one of the participants, recorded what happened as police attacked:

> Clubs were raised and lowered and the women beaten back with such cruelty as none of us had ever witnessed before. . . . Women were knocked down and trampled under foot, some of them almost unconscious, others bleeding from the hands and face; arms were bruised and twisted; pocket-books were snatched and wrist-watches were stolen.[4]

The next day the *New York Times* headline read, "200 maddened women attack police with banners and fingernails."[5] In its editorial the *Times* said the women were "maniacs who should be institutionalized."

After being inundated with phone calls and letters, and receiving relentless pressure from the American people, in early 1920 Wilson decided he needed to be more active in securing the votes needed for the Senate to pass an amendment to the constitution giving women the right to vote. He formally endorsed national women's suffrage and called for an immediate vote in Congress. On January 11, the House of Representatives passed the Susan B. Anthony Amendment 274 to 136, with the necessary two-thirds majority. On June 4, 1920, the Senate passed the amendment, and it was ratified by the states in August 1920. Alice Paul and her team had succeeded. They were successful in highlighting the issue, in getting men to face reality that women were equal and could no longer be ignored, and in asserting women's rights into the national agenda.

Intervention for an Activist Challenge

The essence of leadership for an activist challenge lies in intervening to get people's attention and engagement of an issue. In determining the strategy of intervention, you need to consider a wide spectrum of possible approaches. At one end of the spectrum lies the capacity to *evoke* or *inspire* a group to face reality and stand up for an ideal or value, and at the other end of the spectrum lies the capacity to intervene by *provoking* the group to face reality and attend to the problem, as Alice Paul and her team did.

Martin Luther King's 1963 "I Have a Dream" address delivered on the steps of the Lincoln Memorial in Washington, D.C., is an enduring example of the power to intervene by *evoking* a group's ideals and using those ideals to inspire moral action. Two years later, in Alabama, civil rights advocates illustrated the power to intervene by *provoking* a reaction in a march from Selma to Montgomery. In challenging American racism, the marchers provoked state and local police into a brutal and violent assault on defenseless men, women, and children—an event recorded in shocking detail by international television cameras. Both interventions reached the moral dimension of the problem. But the powers of *inspiring the group to face reality* and *provoking the group to face reality* addressed different dynamics in the group. Inspiring the group through an evocative intervention attempts to draw out a fragile and suppressed element in the group, such as the desire for peaceful cooperation rather than vicious competition. In contrast, provoking the group attempts to diminish some unnecessarily destructive habit of the group, such as domineering, subversive, aggressive, or prejudiced behavior.

These two approaches can be used alone or in different combinations, but they both have the same objective: to engage the people in facing hard facts and solving the problems that impede progress.

Intervening to Evoke: Inspiring the Group with the Poetry of Leadership

In Norse myth, one of the greatest powers one could have was the power to inspire, particularly through poetry. This power could be obtained only through the possession of a sacred potion known as *mead*. The mead was an intoxicating drink that gave the possessor the capacity to charm the masses through poetic verse. Given the power of the mead, the giants, dwarves, and Odin were constantly engaging in all manner of subterfuge and trickery to get the mead from the other. It could be used for good or ill—it could bring out the best in people and orient them toward a higher purpose, or it could be used for selfish and nefarious aims and to put a false set of tasks or counterfeit issues before the people, such as pursuing wasteful and destructive battles.

A leader, as with those who possessed the mead, can use the capacity to evoke and inspire for productive or destructive purposes. Wisdom is needed to use this power to activate and evoke noble ideals in people that lead to responsible action. I suggest that inside most people, even the selfish, are the higher values of altruism, compassion, and idealism. These values might be latent, but with wise leadership they can be evoked and deployed for worthwhile aims.

Many young people experience the noble ideals in their nature when they dream that they can grow up to make a difference in the world, perhaps by discovering a new medical cure, by eliminating hunger, or simply by going into a public service career, such as firefighting, teaching, or social work. But as young people get more experience in the world, many of them give up on their noble ideals as impractical idealism. Day-to-day concerns such as making a decent living take more importance, and, over time, the surrounding culture convinces people to suppress their noble ideals and express instead their self-interest. As we have all witnessed, self-interest often overrides the value of creating a better world—not only for the community in the present but for future generations.

One CEO I worked with expressed to me as we were standing outside the company headquarters his worry about the irresponsible self-interest of his employees. At the time we were working on changing the corporate culture to be more collaborative and customer focused. A group of smokers was congregated just outside the main entrance. When we were beyond where they could hear, the CEO said, "Look at those employees. They just don't seem to care. They stand there smoking and throw the butts on the pavement. Look at the image that leaves for our customers. They have a smoking room, but they want to hang outside the door. What should I do?"

Clearly, he could exert his authority and order them to stop smoking outside the main entrance. But he was not referring to his authority; he was referring to what kind of leadership would be needed to change the behavior of people who succumbed to self-interest and ignored their responsibility for the world around them—or, in this case, the organization's public image. He was referring to the challenge of shifting people's values and priorities, and what they noticed and what they ignored.

A leader can evoke the noble ideals of the group and get people to transcend self-interest by helping them to look again at what they have lost by yielding to their immediate self-interest, prejudice, or personal hungers. This is what Martin Luther King did in his "I Have a Dream" speech. King told his audience:

> When we let freedom ring . . . from every village and every ham-
> let, from every state and every city, we will be able to speed that
> day when all of God's children, black men and white men, Jews
> and Gentiles, Protestants and Catholics, will be able to join
> hands and sing in the words of the old Negro spiritual, Free at
> last! Free at last! Thank God Almighty, we are free at last.[6]

What gave the speech its power of inspiration was King's call to recognize shared noble ideals in the society that were lurking undimmed beneath oppressive layers of self-interest. When King spoke of the "dream," it was not his alone but widely held by a broad cross section of Americans. "It is a dream rooted in the American dream," he said. "I have a dream that one day this nation will rise up and live the true meaning of its creed: 'We hold these truths to be self-evident: that all men are created equal.'" King's speech inspired people because he used it to evoke values that already existed in the society but were latent.

King's speech was not a call for people to follow him. The speech's intent was to evoke moral action by calling attention to the contradiction in values that existed in society. His intervention was powerfully evocative in the way that great poetry is evocative. Great poetry generates a picture, creates an image, and explores a possible reality that draws us into it. It touches our imagination and our latent ideals, and it tells us that things can be better.

There may be a big difference between the evocative win-win solution voiced in King's "I Have a Dream" speech and the assertive "We will conquer the world" attitude that brought down Enron, but each had an inspirational essence. As Odin's mead was intoxicating, inspiration can be intoxicating. Therefore, enormous responsibility is on the leader who seeks to move people through the evocative power of poetic inspiration. The power to evoke can spring from values that are much darker than the noble ideals of altruism and compassion. Counterfeit leadership can be exercised to inspire people to do foolish things. They can be inspired to avoid facing reality by putting their faith in illusions and unattainable dreams. They may be inspired to follow a false prophet who displays the confidence of knowing where he is going when in reality he is as lost as anyone else.

For many people in post-Weimar Germany, Hitler was inspirational, and his fiery, sometimes even poetic oratory was widely regarded as compelling, potent, and deeply evocative of shared German values. Of course, those values had little to do with justice, compassion, or other enduring virtues; they led instead to war, empire, and holocaust. Sadly, he did not use his evocative power to activate the "gentle light" that was latent in the people and help them learn about their condition and attend responsibly to their *real* problems.

Psychoanalyst Margaret Rioch, who studied in detail the negative dynamics of group behavior, stated that human beings in a confused state of mind "are much like sheep in that we readily attach ourselves to a shepherd." In her classic article she quotes the French philosopher Blaise Pascal: "It is natural for the mind to believe, and for the will to love; so that, for want of true objects, they must attach themselves to false."[7]

An individual attempting to exercise real leadership for an activist challenge—or any challenge, for that matter—must be very conscious of using the power to evoke in such a way that it does not lead people to attach themselves to the false—a false promise, a false strategy, a false belief, a false god. The poetry of leadership must be about employing speech and symbols that shift people's sentiment, elevate the mood of the group, and extricate people from their mindlessness so that issues can be confronted, reality addressed, and opportunities embraced. It is the use of power to stir people to think about and engage issues beyond their immediate self-interest. The power to evoke should help people face the truth, activate learning, and take responsible action. Hence, part of the challenge is ensuring that the people who look to you for leadership stay close to their own noble ideals so that selfishness, mindlessness, and hopelessness do not prevail.

Intervening to Provoke: Challenging the Group to Face What They Do Not Want to Face

In contrast to the use of power to evoke, which knits people together in support of a shared (and preferably noble) purpose, the power to *provoke* metaphorically "slaps them in the face" with an infuriating and jarring challenge to their beliefs, their certainties, and their prevailing assumptions. It stirs people to action by forcing them to confront what they cannot see or refuse to see. It addresses the stubbornness of the group. A provocative intervention might throw the people into a temporary state of disarray, but if properly orchestrated, it also generates a tremendous opportunity for deep learning. The power to provoke can be inherently divisive, sometimes setting peaceful people against each other. Some people may support the provocative leadership intervention, but other people will decry it as uncivilized, transgressive, and sometimes even criminal, as many men felt in regard to Alice Paul and her fellow suffragettes.

Under Martin Luther King's direction, the Southern Christian Leadership Conference exerted the power to provoke by organizing a march from Selma to Montgomery, for the purpose of registering to vote. But the Alabama authorities kept putting up barriers to keep black people from voting. The white supremacists in the North, South, East, and West of the United States supported and tolerated the Alabama authorities in keeping black people from registering to vote. In a direct slap at the face of U.S. law and policing practices, the Southern Christian Leadership Conference organized a march to Montgomery, knowing that the governor, other elected officials, and most white voters felt the march was illegal. The Alabama state police, with the full force and authority of the governor, stood on the Montgomery side of the bridge just waiting for the black marchers to cross.

So certain was the white majority in Alabama that beating blacks to keep them from registering to vote was right that the Alabama state troopers on horseback did it in front of national television cameras. When the newsbreak interrupted the regular prime-time television programming across the nation, the moment was just right to slap white America right across the face with the reality of what the law, tradition, and the police were doing to the nation's citizens of color. White America was caught at a vulnerable moment—they could not turn their eyes from the live horror piped into their living rooms.

They watched Alabama state troopers on horseback chase and savagely beat unarmed and defenseless women and men, and even attack the marchers with electric cattle prods, clubs, and chains. The newsbreak happened to interrupt a nationally televised screening of *Judgment at Nuremberg*. The vivid scenes were such a wake-up call—a slap to the face—that enraged white voters who had quietly tolerated past racial bigotry and violence immediately deluged their representatives and the president with demands to stop southern whites from impeding the registration of black voters. Outrage over police conduct during the Selma march helped fuel support for the Voting Rights Act of 1965, which was a landmark initiative to address a hideous problem.

The march was thus successfully provocative. It was a slap-across-the-face intervention that was effective in several different ways. First, even to those white Americans who were prejudiced, the blacks who were beaten appeared noble. Second, the violence was graphic and live, and Americans had not yet become calloused to live violence on television. Third, the accusatory and cold-blooded part of human nature on display in the trial of Nazi judges and prosecutors in *Judgment at Nuremberg* was compellingly juxtaposed with the conduct of law enforcement and public officials in Alabama. Thus, the intervention worked in getting people to learn and respond reasonably to the real problem.

Now, I hasten to note that no one can plan all the elements of such a synchronous concatenation of events. However, a leader should practice in *noticing* when widely separated events converge to make the time right for a provocative intervention.

Similarly, in the Zen tradition, some skilled Zen masters are able to detect when two ideas lie close to each other in the student's brain, and with a sudden nudge, the Zen master can get the student for the first time to put together two and two to get four. When the student is in that ready state, the Zen master gives the student a sudden slap. The violence, suddenness, and unreasonableness of the Zen slap combine with the student's near realization, to push the student's understanding over the hump of defensiveness, enable ideas to converge, and ultimately help the student better see reality. Should the master be *wrong* in thinking the student was ready to understand, the student is merely infuriated and does not learn. And that is always a possibility when making a provocative intervention.

Provoking the system may be done in many different ways. One can make strong demands, call attention to people's irresponsible behavior, raise an issue that no one wants to discuss, or stand firm on a moral principle. This can be done through interventions that are bold, loud, and confrontational, as a way to get maximum attention. But, more often than not, in the course of everyday affairs, a provocative intervention may be a question in a meeting that asks someone to make his or her assumptions explicit or to consider a hard fact. It may be an observation that calls attention to someone or some group that has failed to live by the values that they preach. Such interventions are often like the subtle wind shifts that cause sailboats to tack quietly and smoothly onto a new course: there is little noise or struggle, but suddenly things are moving in a new direction.

Provocation should be considered a creative and artistic intervention process undertaken to catch the interest and attention of others. To be successful, it must challenge people to confront the discrepancies between their professed values and beliefs and the reality of their actions.

It must stir their hearts and their minds. Fundamentally, a well-timed provocative intervention will get people to reconsider their position and begin to deal realistically with the problems confronting the group, organization, or community.

Real Leadership for an Activist Challenge

Five key leadership principles apply for an activist challenge. In getting people to face what they do not want to face—through evocative and provocative interventions—the leader puts him- or herself in a vulnerable position, since a group can get defensive, even hostile. Therefore, the ability to read the dynamics of the setting and combine it with smart strategy is essential to success.

Know what threat you represent to the people

As a first step in exercising leadership for an activist challenge, a leader needs to know what threat he or she represents to others. This will help the leader ascertain who is going to stand in the way and who wants to see the leader fail.

Alice Paul knew at every level of American society what she was up against. She knew that many people would see her and her fellow picketers as enemies of the state, particularly in a time of war. She knew that many men, even of a more liberal nature, would resist her attempts to change the long established tradition of male dominance in the government, community, and the family. She also knew that there would be some women who would see her as being a threat to family values.

Paul realized that she needed to be careful in how she intervened. If her team was too provocative, they would alienate many people, and they would also be an easy target. But if they were too quiet, no one would notice them. She also knew she needed to be evocative—to evoke from American men in particular the cherished values of equality and common sense. Her message had to be crisp and clear: "Give women the vote! Why? Because they make up half the population of the country." She had to call attention to the contradiction in values and practices that existed in American society and work to ensure that women were not on the losing end of those contradictions.

Leaders must have the capacity for anticipating group and factional reactions and forecasting possible resistance, apathy, and danger. They cannot afford to be blind to the threat they represent. They must have their finger on the pulse of the larger group and appreciate the readiness levels of the various factions to shift their perspectives and engage new realities. They must acknowledge the difficulty for many group members to accommodate a new position and give up deeply held habits, practices, and beliefs about how the world should work. Indeed, the leader must realize that initially few people will support them in their quest, in spite of the logic of their argument and the passion with which they present it. Rather than see your opponents as enemies, it is better to view them as fellow travelers who are simply stuck in a particular mind-set or paradigm. Therefore, in the early stages in intervening, it is important not to be excessively stubborn and dogmatic with people—or they will outright reject the message, become more rigid in their position, flee from the work, or attack you.

Given that a provocative intervention will trigger defensiveness, the adaptive work should be paced to allow people time to accommodate a new reality and make adjustments in their behavior. There are times to turn up the heat by being provocative, and there are times when the heat should be turned down and the leadership work is to be evocative. Alice Paul was ultimately successful because her predecessors, Susan B. Anthony and Elizabeth Cady Stanton, had been evoking and provoking since the 1840s. In pacing the work, the people must be given time to think through what it is you are asking them to accept or change. People must be able to have the arguments and debates that can produce the needed discoveries in regard to the assumptions underlying their values and priorities, and how those values and priorities affect progress. They particularly need to discover whether there is a contradiction in values or priorities, and the consequences of allowing the contradiction to persist. The discovery process takes time for a group; therefore, the leadership interventions need to be paced as a way to ripen an issue and facilitate deep learning. Anthony and Stanton, in the latter part of the nineteenth century, spent more than four decades ripening the issue of women's voting rights with women and men, all across the United States. What was needed was the bold and provocative interventions of Alice Paul and her team to move men to action, do the right thing, and push the issue "across the finish line."

As a general principle, however, provocative interventions should be combined with evocative interventions if progress is to be made in getting people's attention and engagement of the issue. Evocative interventions appeal to the shared values, although often latent, of the people. Such interventions highlight what the people have in common by way of ideals and serve to make the provocative intervention less severe, even more palatable and effective.

Be strategic in where and how you intervene

In a hectic world where so many issues and concerns associated with day-to-day living vie for the peoples' attention, the leader should have an array of interventions that can expose the contradiction in values that exists in the system and get people to face the problem. Getting the people's attention is never easy, and this is why good strategy, creative design, and the right timing are essential to success.

Getting people's attention and moving them to action was a real concern for Alice Paul and her team. Given that the country was at war, with Americans dying every day on the front lines in Europe, how could they garner sympathy for their cause? They decided that their interventions must be seen in the context of the values of freedom and equality; after all, that was the espoused reason for U.S. involvement in the war. In their minds, it was hypocritical of President Wilson to defend the rights of others abroad and not defend the rights of women at home. Therefore, they decided to use the White House as the key focal point of their interventions. They were not simply trying to get the president's attention, but they were using the strategy of picketing in front of the White House to get the attention of the nation. The White House was supposed to symbolize the highest values and aspirations of the country; it was thus the perfect focal point to highlight the contradiction in values between what was espoused and what was practiced.

Mahatma Gandhi learned from, and was inspired by, Paul and her suffragettes. He, too, meticulously planned every aspect of an intervention to ensure that it got maximum publicity and could highlight the contradiction in values. The dates, location, duration, participants, and the possible reaction of the British were all carefully thought through to ensure that the intervention achieved the desired effect. He wanted his interventions to be controversial, provocative, evocative, and above all interventions that would move the minds and hearts of both the oppressor and the oppressed.[8] One of his most provocative and evocative interventions was the Salt March.

At 6:30 A.M. on March 12, 1930, Gandhi, with seventy-eight volunteers, commenced a historic journey to the seashore at Dandi, on India's northwest coast. Thousands more joined the march along the way. They walked 241 miles over twenty-four days, arriving at the ocean on April 6. In an act of defiance against the British imperialists, he picked up a handful of salt, an illegal act, and put it in a sack. "Today we are defying the salt law," Gandhi declared. "Tomorrow we shall have to consign other laws to the waste-paper basket. Doing so, we shall practice such severe non-cooperation that finally it will not be possible for the administration to be carried on at all."[9]

On that historic day, throughout India, more than five million people at more than five thousand sites joined Gandhi in breaking the salt law. The momentous event gained the attention of just about every Indian, certainly the British administrators, and people all over the world, just as Gandhi had intended. It provoked the authorities and stirred people to think critically about the condition of India.

In designing the intervention, Gandhi needed a strategy that could grab the attention of all Indians, as well as the British. He needed an evocative symbol, and that symbol was salt. The British had a royal monopoly on the manufacture of salt in India. No Indian could harvest salt or distribute it without a license. Even though it was a staple item and an indispensable ingredient in most foods, it was heavily taxed. Salt was a necessary commodity for every Indian, and the salt tax symbolized the absurd imposition of unjust laws by a foreign power.

The first tactic of the salt march intervention was writing to the viceroy of India, Lord Irwin, to let him know of the plan. The March 2, 1930, letter from Gandhi stated:

Dear Friend,
Before embarking on civil disobedience and taking the risk that I have dreaded to take all these years, I would fain approach you and find a way out. If India is to live as a nation, if the slow death by starvation of her people is to stop, some remedy must be found for immediate relief. I respectfully invite you to pave the way for immediate removal of those evils, and thus open a way for a real conference between equals. But if you cannot see your way to deal with these evils and my letter makes no appeal to your heart, on the 12th day of this month I shall proceed with such co-workers of the Ashram as I can take, to disregard the provisions of the salt laws.[10]

Gandhi did not want to take the British by surprise. He wanted them to be ready for the march. He was intentionally generating anxiety and concern on the part of the British, as he needed them to respond in a way that would contribute to giving greater attention to the event. In other words, if the British troops could be out in full force to try and stop the march, or at least arrest him, then this would result in greater publicity and further the objectives of his movement.

Gandhi was not just provoking the British government; he was also attempting to challenge the Indian people and shift their consciousness. He wanted the event to be a deep and profound learning experience for them. In his view, the Indians needed to be a more responsible and diligent people who were worthy of running their own affairs. He told his people, "We have come forward to win our freedom from this tyrannical and oppressive government. If we cannot put our own house in order in an organized manner, how shall we run the country's government? I ask you, therefore to learn order and organization."[11] To support the people's learning from this experience, he instructed all marchers to keep a daily diary and capture important insights about their observations and feelings along the way. The diary would serve to evoke important reflections about the purpose and meaning of this event and increase their resilience and commitment.[12]

Gandhi knew that the march would be a major act of provocation, and the potential of violence was very real. In taking responsibility for that possibility, four days before the march he had all those who were going to join him, literally thousands of men and women, make a solemn oath of nonviolent resistance. At a mass meeting at Ahmedabad the people pledged, "We the citizens of Ahmedabad, hereby resolve to follow our comrades to jail or win complete independence. We believe that India's freedom is to be won through peaceful and truthful means."

The march was designed to travel through numerous villages on the way to the ocean. At each village crowds of people thronged to greet Gandhi. He used the attention to educate and enroll the villagers in the struggle for independence. Fundamentally, this was their work, and they needed to take responsibility for it. While talking about the need to rid India of the British, Gandhi spoke also of racial tolerance and religious harmony between Hindus and Muslims. He addressed the need to embrace the untouchables—the marginalized lower caste—and highlighted the importance of having clean homes and communities. Gandhi was stirring things up, not just for the British but for his own people as well!

One month after the Salt March, Gandhi was arrested. He was to spend the next nine months in prison. He was released January 26, 1931. On March 4, the Gandhi-Irwin Pact was signed, containing decisions of the Round Table Conference in London that would eventually lead to complete independence for India. The strategic and provocative intervention of the Salt March succeeded.

When putting yourself at risk, make sure the cameras are rolling

An element of being strategic in where and how you intervene is in ensuring you get the maximum attention on the issue—particularly if you put yourself at risk. Being a provocateur puts oneself in a precarious position. As pointed out in this chapter, you might be ignored, denigrated, or even killed. It therefore requires enormous courage to persist in the face of a vehement opposition that are determined on avoiding the hard facts and examining how their behavior contributes to the problem. But it also requires shrewd strategy if you are to succeed in staying alive. Part of that strategy necessitates only putting yourself at risk when the cameras are rolling and you have an audience or witnesses. Otherwise, it is too easy for your opponents to kill you off, figuratively or literally.

When Alice Paul and her team marched, they made sure that the press was there to record the event. When they anticipated that a mob would attack and beat them, rather than walk away, they kept on going—but only if the cameras were there to capture the moment. When Louisine Havemeyer, a wealthy socialite, joined one of the marches and gave a speech, she actually hoped she would be arrested. As the widow of H. O. Havemeyer, owner of the American Sugar Refining Company, her arrest would be bound to get attention. Given who she was, the police chief hesitated and called the White House for instructions. Worried that she might not be arrested, Havemeyer said to her colleague, "I believe I will have to kick him to get him in the game."[13] Eventually she was arrested, and hundreds of cameras and journalists were there to record the event.

A number of years ago, at the waning period of the Cold War, I organized an International Human Rights Conference for the city of Boston. One of the participants was the Soviet dissident Yuri Orlov. Orlov had just been released from nine years in a Soviet gulag for his calling attention to the government's human rights record. It was a moving experience to talk with a man who only a few weeks earlier had been a prisoner of the state. His courage, audacity, and moral leadership were inspiring.

Within three years of Orlov being set free, the Soviet Union began to crumble and the Iron Curtain was pulled down. Obviously many factors contributed to the decline and eventual end of Soviet communism, but among the most important were the bold provocations of people such as Yuri Orlov, Natan Sharansky, Andre Sakharov, and Yelena Bonner. They, along with their fellow dissidents, played a critical role in getting international attention on the issues and putting pressure on the obstinate Kremlin in Moscow to make legitimate reforms. They were powerful and effective provocateurs.

As a provocateur, there is a moment when you cross the line—when you know that your act of provocation puts you in grave danger. For Orlov, it was when he gave public support to the dissident Sakharov and sent a letter to the president of the USSR, and the press, titled "Thirteen Questions to Brezhnev." The theme of his letter to the president of the Soviet Union was that "fanatic adherence to an ideology that denied the existence of freedom of choice and expression as an innate human need had resulted in a feudal relation between citizen and state as well as scientific, economic, and cultural decline."[14] Orlov proposed abolishing press censorship and instituting the free exchange of ideas.

Orlov knew that he would not receive a positive response from the president. He also knew that his letter would be considered an act of subversion. From that moment on the KGB monitored his every activity. The first thing that happened was being fired from his job at Moscow University. This act did not deter him. He immediately made another significant intervention by creating a human rights group to monitor the government's compliance of the international human rights agreement known as the Helsinki Accords. On May 14, 1978, the Voice of America announced the formation of Orlov's group, and the next day he was seized by the KGB. He was given a warning and told to stay out of trouble. He immediately went to Andre Sakharov's apartment and met with other members of his network to plan their strategy of action. They knew if any of them were to be arrested, it would be incredibly embarrassing for the Soviet Union, as all they were doing was documenting the implementation of an agreement that the government had signed. Arresting them would be a high-profile indication that the government was flouting that agreement.

Throughout 1976, Orlov's group sent press releases and reports all over the world, calling attention to Soviet violations of human rights and the contradiction in values. It was only a matter of time before the state would take action. On February 9, 1977, Orlov was arrested. He was held for nearly fifteen months in solitary confinement before even being brought to trial. He was eventually charged on May 15, 1978, with "anti-Soviet agitation and propaganda, with the purpose of subverting or weakening Soviet power." During the farcical trial, Sakharov, hundreds of supporters, and members of the international press came to the courthouse to observe, document, and protest. Orlov was found guilty of subverting the state and sentenced to seven years of hard labor and another five years of exile. He was released in 1987 and immediately went into exile in the United States.

Orlov did not simply take a moral stand. He took a moral and strategic stand. His intention was to provoke the system, realizing that he could be killed. But he made sure that the cameras were rolling to capture his provocation, so it could be broadcast around the world. It required enormous courage, but Orlov was prepared for the consequences. When I met Orlov, I asked him whether he had any regrets given his long imprisonment. "None at all," he replied. "I knew what I was doing." When I asked him why he did what he did, he responded, "I had no choice."

Courage is essential in leading for an activist challenge, but so also is the wisdom to ensure that the "work" lives on should you be attacked or marginalized. And, if you are attacked or marginalized, you should look to see to what degree your attack or marginalization triggers discoveries in society in regard to the contradiction in values you are highlighting. That is why it is important for the cameras to be rolling or someone to document your intervention. Then, you can track the effects of your intervention on the system over time. For example, if you are a Yuri Orlov living under the oppressive Soviet regime, you would want to track the effects of your interventions over time—including your imprisonment—in at least two communities: the system of your supporters and the system of your violent opponents, the government. And the mechanics of the transfer of the effect of your interventions may be entirely different in the two systems.[15] When the people begin to notice that their values are in contradiction and that some of those values are having a corrosive effect on the well-being of the society, then important work has begun—indicating that your interventions and subsequent marginalization have been effective. This was the strategy employed by Gandhi, Yuri Orlov, and Alice Paul. Each used their interventions as a heuristic tool to generate the discoveries in their respective communities concerning how certain values, practices, and priorities were not consistent with the values, practices, and priorities to produce meaningful and sustainable progress.

When the group stalls you on one front, open up another

In troubling problems where people blatantly refuse to shift their attitudes and actions, and persist in avoiding responsibility for their role in the mess, sometimes intervening from directly in the system (the group, organization, or nation) is just too dangerous. Sometimes a system is so belligerent or dysfunctional that it is virtually impossible to accomplish anything worthwhile from within, given the hostility and opposition. When such is the case, the leadership work is to open up another front, even if that means going outside the system and building forces that can collectively employ their resources and power to intervene and produce the internal shifts needed to get enough people to examine the contradiction in values and responsibly face the problem.

Alice Paul and her fellow suffragists tried many strategies to keep the issue in front of people—marches, picket lines, letter-writing campaigns, speeches, train tours, and even jail time and hunger strikes. As they were stalled on one front, they would open up another, always looking for new ways of getting and sustaining attention. But they were never persecuted to the point that they could not live and operate inside the system. The United States was a democracy and tolerated a considerable amount of dissent compared with other countries.

In the late 1970s in Afghanistan, a brave young woman known simply as Meena started RAWA, a women's movement organized for the intent of educating Afghan women about their rights and possibilities and getting men to do the right thing in supporting women.[16] The treatment of women in Afghanistan was atrocious, and it was dangerous to call attention to such values and practices. Given how dangerous her work was, particularly when the Taliban came to power, Meena had to go underground inside the country and also open up another front outside Afghanistan, in Europe and the refugee camps of Pakistan. One of her key tasks was to get the outside world to put pressure on Afghan men to stop the abuse of women and provide opportunities for their development. Meena's leadership was such a threat that the fundamentalists hunted her down in Pakistan and killed first her husband and then her. Her movement, however, lives on to this day and has made a tremendous contribution to the well-being of Afghanistan's women, although many men persist in thwarting change.[17] Meena's death is a sober reminder of the inherent dangers of leadership for an activist challenge in some parts of the world. Leadership writers Ronald Heifetz and Marty Linsky describe the exercise of leadership as "walking on the razor's edge."[18] And so it can be, particularly when the hard facts or the raw reality is so threatening to a group or some faction of the group.

Another place where it was exceptionally dangerous to intervene was East Timor. East Timor was invaded by the Indonesian military in

1975 when the Portuguese departed. The brutal occupation that followed lasted twenty-five years before the Indonesians were pressured by the international community to hand the country back to the East Timorese. During those twenty-five years, a few spirited individuals waged the battle for support on the diplomatic front and focused on the mobilization of international law and public opinion. Jose Ramos-Horta was one of those people. He fled the country on the eve of the invasion—not by choice, but because he was assigned the role of ambassador for the resistance. He lived abroad for twenty-five years, usually out of a suitcase, crisscrossing the world in search of support for the Timorese cause. I discussed with Ramos-Horta what it was like for him trying to mobilize international support. He explained:

> My task every day was to talk to diplomats. But senior ambassadors wouldn't see me. They would pretend to be busy. I would set up an appointment with junior administrators and they wouldn't show up. And then patiently and with humility you pretend that you're not upset, and make another appointment. I would try to talk to the American media, and that was quite a difficult task. Most American journalists didn't even know where East Timor was. And so often I'd talk to common American citizens, and I would say, "I'm from East Timor." And I remember someone saying, "You mean you're an Eskimo."
>
> I was very excited one day when a taxi driver asked me where I was from. I said, "From Timor." And he said, "Oh, that's where Captain Bligh landed after the mutiny on the Bounty." So, I immediately rushed and bought the book, and I went to the index to see that Timor was there. And I was so happy that I found Timor in the index. Anyway, this is only to illustrate the extraordinary difficulties to keep an issue alive, to educate people, to interest people.
>
> I even went to Tulsa, Oklahoma. Someone decided I should go there. I said, "I know a bit about the United States to know that, well, I don't think there's much interest in East Timor in Oklahoma. The gentleman insisted, so I went there. And I ended up with four or five people to talk to. So, I decided to take them for coffee.
>
> Sometimes I was really demoralized, you know, and I felt like "Why the hell did I come here?" But, these people came to listen to me. It's not their fault. So, you are nice to them because they

were really among the nicest people in the town who came to listen. . . . And at least it's one person, or at least there's five people who have heard you, who will be talking to their friends or relatives, in their school. It is a multiplying effect.[19]

In 1996, Ramos-Horta was awarded the Nobel Peace Prize for his efforts in mobilizing world attention on East Timor. The steady and persistent approach to the activist challenge, even though it included countless coffee sessions in places like Oklahoma, eventually reaped benefits. The award gave Ramos-Horta and the East Timor independence movement a much-needed platform to get attention and harness resources. Ramos-Horta commented that after receiving the prize, "I was the same person, saying the same things for the previous twenty years. But suddenly what I said carried different weight. It opened doors everywhere."[20]

By virtue of those doors being opened, Ramos-Horta and his colleagues were able to muster enough international support to generate the pressure that led the Indonesian president to declare in 1999 that he would permit a referendum for independence in East Timor—which did in fact lead to East Timor becoming a sovereign nation.

In going outside the system, the leader must be able to do four things: (1) Tell people the nature of the problem; (2) explain why they should be concerned about the problem; (3) give them some tasks to do, such as writing a letter to the government, organizing a meeting, or joining an organization; and then (4) be patient and persistent as it takes time to move from awareness to action and action to results.

Find good partners to support you and keep you alive

Given the risks inherent in leadership for an activist challenge, it is foolhardy for a person to take on an activist challenge alone. The leader must find partners to support them, give advice, provide protection, and ensure that the issues remain in the public eye. Good partners can bring a renewed sense of energy and creative expression to the work. They help carry the load and reduce the burden of having one person be alone in the spotlight. They also can bring balance and perspective, highlight blind spots, and keep the leader from doing imprudent things that jeopardize the work.[21]

In looking for partners, you should look for people who can broaden your perspective and intervention approach. You want people to tell you when you are acting in a foolhardy manner, missing an important opportunity, being excessively stubborn, or endangering the integrity of the work in some manner.

Gandhi created an extraordinary partnership with Jawaharlal Nehru. The two were very different in temperament and political outlook. Nehru was also twenty years younger than Gandhi. Nevertheless, their formidable partnership became the driving force that led to Indian independence. As one historian noted, "Despite differences of thought, temperament and style, Gandhi and Nehru stood together for more than a quarter of a century."[22]

The younger Nehru was imbued with the revolutionary spirit, socialist rhetoric, and the teachings of Karl Marx. Gandhi, however, although trained as a lawyer in South Africa, was more like an Indian ascetic with a profound spiritual view of the world. Nehru cared little for Gandhi's ashram lifestyle and considered his preoccupation with ancient Hindu ideals outdated and impractical. Gandhi taught that nonviolence must be the strategy employed to rid the British. Nehru, on the other hand, felt that armed revolution was inevitable. As one historian remarked:

> How two men, divided not only by twenty years of age but by deep intellectual and temperamental differences, could work together for so long, is an enigma to anyone who seriously studies their lives and the history of this period. . . . How could Jawaharlal Nehru with his enthusiasm for science and humanism take to a saint with prayers and fasts, inner voices and the spinning wheel?[23]

The relationship between the two was one of absolute honesty and the candid expression of their feelings. They were constantly critical of one another but at the same time extremely helpful and supportive. "Resist me always when my suggestion does not appeal to your head or heart. I shall not love you less for that resistance," Gandhi told Nehru.[24] Gandhi's reaction to young Nehru's rebellious streak was characteristic. He did not attempt to muzzle him, but he did try to educate him. He felt that Nehru was too impatient and impetuous.

In December 1927, after visiting the Soviet Union and the Brussels Congress on Oppressed Nationalities, Nehru persuaded the delegates at the Madras conference in India to pass resolutions in favor of complete independence. In his speech he denounced feudalism, capitalism, and imperialism and talked of organizing workers, peasants, and students to fight against the British. His excessively provocative speech deeply disturbed Gandhi. He wrote to Nehru, "You are going too fast; you should have taken time to think and become acclimatized. Most of the resolutions you prepared and got carried could have been delayed for one year. Your plunging into the 'republican army' was a hasty step. But I do not mind these acts of yours so much as I mind your encouraging mischief-mongers and hooligans."[25]

Nehru responded to Gandhi, "Bapu, the difference between you and me is this: You believe in gradualism; I stand for revolution." "My dear young man," Gandhi retorted, "I have made revolutions whilst others have only shouted revolutions. When your lungs are exhausted and you are really serious about it you will come to me and I shall then show you how a revolution is made."[26] Nehru, upon considering Gandhi's advice, pulled back slightly from his vitriolic attacks on the British and ceased his revolutionary call for an immediate uprising.

Another time during a very difficult period when Nehru wanted to resign as head of the Congress Party, Gandhi tried to talk him out of it. "Consider the situation calmly and not succumb to it in a moment of depression so unworthy of you," he told him.[27] Gandhi knew how temperamental and reactive Nehru could be when under stress. His advice was that of a solid and committed partner helping his dear friend get back in the game.

Nehru once said of Gandhi that he produced for India a "psychological change, almost as if some expert in psychoanalytic methods had probed deep into the patient's past, found out the origins of his complexes, exposed them to view, and thus rid him of that burden."[28] But Gandhi was the first to admit that he never did this work alone. Nehru was an integral partner. Both were joined together in the purpose of getting the British out of India. Gandhi, however, had a spiritual and philosophical mission right from the beginning. Politics was not his domain of thought. Nehru, on the other hand, was a brilliant, practical, and formidable politician. Gandhi thrust Nehru to the forefront of the political battles while he remained in the background watching him keenly and correcting where necessary. Such was the nature of their extraordinary partnership.

The Gandhi–Nehru partnership illustrates three important functions of partnership: (1) to help the leader see what he or she cannot see due to blind spots and biases; (2) to keep the leader in the game when the burden becomes too heavy or the leader feels that his or her options have been exhausted; and (3) to keep the leader from acting rashly, thereby jeopardizing the work and his or her life.

Conclusion

As we see with an activist challenge, real leadership at times can be a bold and precarious activity, as one is challenging the status quo and getting people to face difficult issues that they would prefer to avoid. Therefore, an activist challenge should not be taken on lightly, as one puts at risk not only oneself but also one's team. Nevertheless, when we see deceit, hypocrisy, and the avoidance of hard truths in whatever form, someone must find the courage to exercise leadership to get people to face reality. With sensitivity to the context and appreciation for how to evoke through the power of inspiration or provoke through the power of tough questions and symbolic interventions, steadily change can and will occur. As this chapter illustrates, it is not easy, but it can be done.

The other five leadership challenges, though distinct from the activist challenge, all require activist leadership at certain times to get people dealing realistically with issues. Often, people need to be provoked and noble ideals need to be evoked. As illustrated in the opening case of the human resource executive, even companies need activist leadership to generate the needed shifts in attitudes and behavior to mobilize people to face their most pressing concerns and do the right thing. It is not enough simply to raise a concern, as Enron's Sherron Watkins did with her boss, Kenneth Lay, in regard to deceitful accounting practices, but one must be creative and strategic in where and how to intervene to ensure that the hard facts get entertained, conflicts in values are forthrightly addressed, and the right choices are made that can truly give the team or the organization its best shot at sustainable success. If the group cannot face hard truths, then progress will remain elusive.

REAL LEADERSHIP FOR AN ACTIVIST CHALLENGE

- Know what threat you represent to the people.
- Be strategic in where and how you intervene.
- When putting yourself at risk, make sure the cameras are rolling.
- When the group stalls you on one front, open up another.
- Find good partners to support you and keep you alive.

CHAPTER 4

The Development Challenge
Cultivating the Latent Capabilities
Needed to Progress

There are times when the people's advancement is dependent on their capacity to develop their latent capabilities and take advantage of new opportunities. The development of those capabilities will allow the people, or their organization, to flourish and prosper at a higher level than they would be able to otherwise. The leadership task when faced with a development challenge is to orchestrate a learning process through designed experimentation that cultivates the group's latent capabilities. To illustrate this challenge, consider the following scenario.

SCENARIO

Imagine you are the CEO of a large financial services organization. The firm has been profitable for years, but, due to deregulation, it has many more competitors now. The rapid change in market conditions has caught the company by surprise—and without a revised strategic plan.

You determine that the new business challenge is to retain customers and leverage the entire organization to provide more services and products to the customer. Your strategy will necessitate what is called in business "cross selling." The company currently sells on average two of its products to each customer. You determine that if the divisions of the company could really work together, share sales and customer data, and give up the notion of a single division "owning" the customer, you could sell up to six products per customer and substantially increase the profitability of the business.

Many managers and sales staff resist the idea. They see cross selling as being a time-consuming exercise requiring a whole new set of processes and practices for which they are not equipped. Also, sales staff see no incentive for this "added burden" of trying to sell more products and bring more people into the selling process. The challenges of training, coordination, communication, and prioritization will be huge. Besides, the managers and staff in each division have operated successfully in their respective areas for many years and do not want to lose control of their customers and be dependent on other areas of the organization to ensure that quality service is provided to the customer. "Frankly, it will be too hard," one of your top executives tells you.

Your management team sees the importance of this concept, and some, who have experienced similar approaches in other companies, know how difficult it is to do well. But it is an idea with tremendous promise. If it is to become a reality, it will require a major refocus of the company's attention and resources. You have many questions: What kinds of resources will be needed? How hard will it be to enact? How will we measure progress? What kind of practices, processes, and systems will be needed? Because there is no road map to the desired destination, and because the capacity of the entire organization must be enhanced to deal with this new opportunity, you conclude you face a development challenge.

The Nature of a Development Challenge

A *development challenge* is when the group or organization must build new capabilities—competencies, practices, and processes—to ensure the survival and progress of the group or organization. In such a context, the routine capabilities are no longer adequate in meeting basic needs consistent with the aspirations of the enterprise and the challenges the people face. In other words, "business as usual" will not produce the levels of satisfaction, performance, or productivity that are needed to advance. Therefore, new capabilities must be developed.

The key symptoms of a development challenge are as follows:

- The group or organization faces a creeping threat, which the group's current capabilities cannot defuse, and therefore the people must develop new capabilities in order to survive and thrive.
- A new opportunity opens up for the group that requires extraordinary attention and commitment of resources if the people are to avail themselves of the opportunity.
- Problem-solving processes in the group must be significantly enhanced to ensure that the people can manage the scope and intensity of the challenges they face and make meaningful progress.

As with all the challenges, in diagnosing a development challenge, the leader must examine three essential factors: (1) the condition of the people, (2) the barrier that impedes progress, and (3) the promise or aspiration on the other side of the barrier.

The condition of the *people* in a development challenge is that they are incompetent in regard to the requirements of responding to a changing context. The people must face their incompetence and develop what latent capabilities they have and grow new competencies to respond to the new context and deliver on the promise. The "raw material" is available in the people and the enterprise but needs to be developed.

The *barrier* that thwarts progress is the lack of confidence of the people, their attachment to values and practices that have worked for them in the past, their unwillingness to take risks, and their reluctance to embrace new practices and priorities. The reality that the people are avoiding is that the world around them is changing and adherence to old skills, habits, and practices will render them mediocre performers at best and obsolete at worse.

The *promise* is that if latent capabilities and new competencies can be developed, the group or organization will enjoy a more prosperous, satisfying, or rewarding future. In other words, if the people can collectively develop, life will get better.

Leadership for a development challenge is about orchestrating processes to enhance the capacity of the entire system to make it more resilient, responsive, and relevant. The process is much like evolution in that development consists of formulating through a lot of trial and error, the capacities that allow for a higher level of functioning in changed context such as dealing with a new predator (competitors) or taking advantage of new terrain (markets). In evolution, the development process results in new capacity for the species, and for all progeny. For example, once some living forms had adopted a hemoglobin process as a result of capacity building, new innovations of viable life forms became possible, building on the innovations of the past—such as whales developing a highly specialized hemoglobin to carry enough oxygen with them in their blood into the great depths of the sea.

Unlike evolution, a development challenge is a more active, guided, and intentional process in which leadership tries to identify a new challenge early, and to intervene before the challenge becomes a threat or a crisis. A way to think about the function of leadership for a development challenge is to think of it as being a *perturbing force*. Stephen Gould, the renowned paleontologist, suggests that a species will generally remain stable until some drastic change in the environment challenges the ability of the species to cope. The drastic change exerts a perturbing force on the species, and unless it evolves a successful adaptive response, it will die off. Gould calls this pattern "punctuated equilibrium."[1] When the equilibrium of the system is punctuated by a perturbing force, a new adaptive opportunity results. Whether or not the species adapts is dependent on many factors, but the opportunity is there.

In response to the economic, social, and cultural pressures that punctuate the equilibrium in corporations, communities, and nations, responsible leaders must themselves act as a perturbing force to energize a developmental process that enhances the health and performance of the people and the enterprise. This requires wisdom and foresight, as a group or company often cannot wait until the troubles are upon them, or they will not survive. Therefore, someone must diagnose the challenge while there is still time to evolve the capacity of the group or organization to make adjustments that take advantage of the resources in the system to attend to what the future needs.

The point is that a healthy enterprise must think ahead to stock up on the resources it will need to survive, grow, and take advantage of the special opportunities that might emerge in the "desert" of hard times ahead. For a corporation, the desert of hard times might be the outcome of new competition, a change in preferences in the demand market, or the invention of new technologies.

Ideally, management would keep the corporation in a series of long-term developments of new resources so that the corporation would bring new resources to fruition just in time. For efficiency, the corporation should develop new resources (1) only if actually needed to play offense or defense in the market and (2) as the need emerges so that resources can be reality tested in the environment in which the resources are expected to give advantages. That is, there is a limit to the advantages of developing resources ahead of need, because the "solutions" must be tuned to the "challenges" that appear.

The opening scenario of the company trying to develop its cross-selling capabilities is a real case of a company that faced a development challenge. The CEO knew the organization had the latent capabilities that could be developed to make cross selling a successful strategy. He also knew that it would be a demanding task requiring dedicated time and resources to make it a reality. In regard to leadership, first and foremost he needed to become a perturbing force and perturb the complacency that existed in the culture of the company. To do that, in a public meeting of his two hundred senior managers, he highlighted the threat to the organization and explained the promise available if the organization could develop its latent capabilities. He helped the managers understand the condition of the corporate culture and provided some guidelines on what was needed by way of shared leadership at all levels of the organization to facilitate the development of the cross-selling capabilities.

The CEO explained to his team that there were a whole array of demanding and interlocking interdependent problems embedded in the cross-selling strategy that the company had to tackle. The development process would require more than a year of committed experimentation to discover what would work given the complex nature of the organization's structure, banking processes, and distribution procedures. The corporation, he explained, would be pushing outward the envelope of what was known among corporations generally and within this corporation specifically. The process, therefore, would no doubt produce friction between individuals and departments as different ideas and solutions competed to see what worked in practice. He told his managers that exercising leadership to discover what worked would require an open and experimental mind-set that encouraged risk taking; tolerated conflict; was willing to learn from errors; was patient enough not to jump to hasty conclusions; and could reach out to colleagues, build bridges, and heal the wounded egos that would occasionally result as people stepped on each other's toes in the attempt to determine what new competencies, practices, and procedures showed the greatest promise.

The company embraced the development challenge and ultimately succeeded in its efforts. We learn from such companies that a development challenge requires complete dedication from the leadership team to support and steer the process. It is a volatile activity, since it involves a willingness to experiment and considerable conflict and anxiety as people struggle to build new capacities that allow them to deal realistically with threats, accommodate new realities, and take advantage of emerging opportunities.

Singapore: Facing the Development Challenge

Singapore provides an interesting case study of leadership for the development challenge in a large complex social system. Over a three-decade period, this city-island with fewer than four million inhabitants rose from third world to first world status. Today, 95 percent of its people own their own homes, and unemployment has consistently been between 2 and 4 percent. Singapore leads the world in test scores for high school students in science and math, its port is one of the busiest in the world, it has a highly developed and successful free market economy, the business environment is corruption-free, and Singapore has the fifth highest per capita gross domestic product (GDP) in the world. Recently Singapore was named "the world's most globalized economy."[2]

How has Singapore been able to develop so fast? What has been the role of leadership in the development process? What generalizable lessons can we draw about leadership for a development challenge from analysis of this case?

Although important developmental lessons may be gleaned from the Singapore case, Singapore should by no means be considered a role model for all other communities or nations—its history and context are unique. Also, Singapore has its critics who feel the country is too autocratic, lacks creative self-expression, and needs more spontaneity. These criticisms might be valid to some degree, but some of Singapore's approach may be justified from the standpoint of dealing with the specific threats and problems it faced in the past. This is still a very young country that only sprang into existence in 1959, when the British allowed it to have self-governance as a part of Malaysia. In 1965, Singapore was unceremoniously tossed out of Malaysia and became an independent nation. Singapore's development process is still unfolding. Now its new leadership team faces a different set of challenges that will require more creativity, loosening of the reins, and even playfulness if the people are to address the next stage of development.

To appreciate the demands of leadership for a development challenge, put yourself in the role of Lee Kuan Yew, the chief authority figure for the nation, and see the challenge of those early years through his eyes. How might you exercise real and responsible leadership and orchestrate development, given the history, resources, and latent capabilities of your people?

SCENARIO

Through the Eyes of Lee Kuan Yew

The British have left. Many people now look to you for vision and leadership. Some also look to you for a fight. There is considerable discontent and divisions in the society. Singapore's factions are divided by differing languages, ethnic heritage, and religious traditions. You would like to combine the competing factions into a functioning and progressive nation, but you know how difficult, if not impossible, that task will be.

Although your party defeated the communists in the elections, you are not overjoyed by this win as you realize the work in front of you is daunting. You later write about how you felt: "It was victory, but I was not jubilant. I began to realize the weight of the problems that we were to face—unemployment, high expectations of rapid results, communist unrest, more subversion in the unions, schools and associations, . . . fewer investments, more unemployment and more trouble."[3]

As you look at the threats and possibilities, you consider the following options: Singapore could remain an undeveloped agrarian society with small traders, pig farmers, rice growers, and fishing villages. Nobody would have to change. People could continue to do what they have done since the British established the colony. Your job for that possibility would be simply to maintain what is already there. But with that scenario the people would continue to muddle along at the edge of survival. Some among the population want this option.

A second option would be, as the communists in Singapore had been advocating, to become an anticapitalist, protectionist state and align Singapore with India and China—as many other countries have done in this postcolonial period. The problem is that India and China do not seem to be doing so well. Besides, both countries have a huge population and abundant resources, and Singapore has a small population with few resources.

Another option is to get the people to take on the tough work of making themselves better, more educated, more skilled, and more industrious. If you could do that, your people might get good jobs, earn high salaries, and enjoy a better standard of living, possibly advancing to the level of first world countries, although that seems a real stretch. As you read the aspirations of the population, the prevailing sentiment seems to be a willingness to embrace the challenge of building better lives for themselves and their children through pragmatic, rather than ideological, strategies. They are ready to try new approaches and work with you—but you know it will be tough work.

Singapore is a vulnerable state: It is vulnerable internally given the ethnic divisions; it is vulnerable to the forces of the global economy, as Singapore has few resources beyond the latent capabilities yet to be developed in the people; and it is vulnerable to the aggressive instincts of other countries in the region—a region riddled with wars, assassinations, and political turmoil.

You later write:

> After pondering these problems and the limited options
> available, I concluded an island city-state in Southeast Asia
> could not be ordinary if it was to survive. We had to make
> extraordinary efforts to become a tightly knit, rugged and
> adaptable people who could do things better than our
> neighbors. . . . We had to be different. . . . We had to create
> a new kind of economy, try new methods and schemes
> never tried before anywhere else in the world, because there
> was no other country like Singapore.[4]

Given there are few role models or textbooks for leading a country, you realize that you and your team will have to experiment with the process as you go along. You might make mistakes, but with a strong team of dedicated and talented men and women—people who are willing to learn and be above reproach—there is a good chance you just might succeed.

Lee did succeed. He and his team (1) created a robust holding environment to keep people from getting distracted, (2) developed the country in stages, (3) used a combination of levers to assist people in developing new competencies and capabilities, and (4) gave people a stake in the long-term development of their capacities. What follows is a presentation of these leadership strategies and principles, along with examples from other groups. These strategies and principles are relevant to an array of different settings, be it building a country, developing a school system, or managing a corporation.

Real Leadership for a Development Challenge

Create a robust holding environment to keep people from getting distracted

In any group seeking to develop, invariably the people at times will be hesitant, distracted, or blatantly resistant. Therefore, to contain the messiness of the process and to generate the mood and climate for development to unfold, the leadership task is to create a *holding environment.*[5] This term is used by psychologists and social workers who must deal with the aberrant and irregular behavior of people under stress. Some environments are not conducive to maturing people but keep them in a state of perpetual dependence, persistent dysfunction, or constant immaturity. A robust holding environment, however, serves to "hold" people through the difficult and disorienting work of developing new capabilities and adjusting to new contexts. When the holding environment is weak or absent, invariably progress will be thwarted as people will be too anxious to learn and experiment with new practices and behaviors.

Depending on the context and the specific nature of the development challenge, the ingredients of the holding environment might vary. A leader, therefore, must give thoughtful consideration to the features of the holding environment that are absolutely essential if a group is to undertake a successful developmental journey. A holding environment might include the benevolent but firm use of authority to determine the boundaries of what the people can and cannot do. It could also include a set of nonnegotiable values or guiding principles. Some features of the holding environment might be symbols, myths, and stories, that orient people to do the adaptive work and remind them of the higher purpose. A holding environment could also be a physical presence, such as a United Nations peacekeeping force that contains the violence and aggression of a country racked with turmoil.

In determining the ingredients of the holding environment, the leader must ask, "What is it that the people need to see and be reminded of to keep them from getting distracted by self-interested pursuits such as immediate gratification or competition for scarce resources, and to ensure that they are constantly facing the reality of their predicament and pursuing their development in a conscientious manner?"

In thinking about how to get people to deal with the realities that they would prefer to avoid and to face the ongoing work of steady and progressive development, consider the behavior of adolescents. When challenged to learn and be more responsible for their world, adolescents sometimes are self-centered and exhibit scapegoating behavior to absolve themselves of the burden of responsibility. They may blame parents, teachers, peers, and even themselves inappropriately. At the same time, teenagers, caught up in a surge of hormones and a need to individuate themselves, can work themselves into win-lose competitive dynamics with peers, parents, and teachers. There may be a place for self-interested competition, but some teenagers choose to exhibit self-interested competition, not on the sports field but rather in the classroom, where it is disruptive and wasteful, or when driving a car, where it can be destructive and harmful. Cooperation, combined with focused and responsible behavior, requires a level of self-confidence, patience, and personal stability that many teenagers find difficult to muster.

I cite teenagers specifically because we have all been teenagers, so we have known intimately what this stage of life is like. We may have forgotten conveniently. As teenagers, we may have done many things and said many things we would rather forget. But I suggest that the memory of the stages of our growth through our teenage years can serve as an important resource in understanding the work avoidances that people generate when they resist paying attention to the real problems that they would rather not face. Therefore, anyone who wishes to exercise real leadership must have ways to get people to deal with reality and embrace the adaptive work of a developmental challenge, even when they are reluctant, anxious, or resistant.

Lee Kuan Yew attended to the creation of a robust holding environment that could support Singapore's intention to develop rapidly. His view was that unless Singapore accelerated the development process, it might not survive as a nation. He also knew that he could not develop people merely from the power of his own figure and personality, as the heads of many failed states had tried to do; he had to utilize the existing character of the various peoples and appeal to their values and aspirations. Some, but not all, of their cultural values could serve as important elements of the holding environment, while others would need to be discarded.

Lee looked to the values of the people and asked, "What latent values could I develop as strengths to unite them?" Common among the several cultures of Singapore were recurring sets of adages and folklore that supported the idea that "If the government is fair and just, then the people will unite for the common good."[6] Also within the diverse cultural traditions were strong individual work ethics that could be further enhanced through public support and encouragement. To activate and take advantage of these cultural assets—and as a critical component of the holding environment—Singapore's leadership team decided to establish the value that "Our government will be completely clean, and we will not tolerate corruption." This nonnegotiable value, Lee declared, would serve as a foundation for expediting the development of the latent resources of all the people of Singapore.

Lee conducted a reality check. In Singapore, as in many other Asian countries, corruption in both the public and private sectors had the effect of imposing an unofficial tax that raised the cost not only of taxed goods or services but also consumer goods. Corruption depressed the economy by decreasing cost competitiveness in the increasingly globalized marketplace and by raising the cost of capital needed to develop the nation's economic capacity. He drew the analogy with a corporation: If Singapore were a corporation, then Singapore would be less competitive to the extent that there was corruption—because corruption in a corporation amounts to waste: someone drains resources of the corporation without returning a compensating value.

The absence of corruption could also be instrumental in evoking those values in the various Singapore cultures that emphasized the benefits of fair play and rewards commensurate with hard work and initiative. Lee foresaw that Singapore's citizens would be more likely to invest in the long-term effort of becoming highly skilled if they saw a day-to-day reality in which people *did* advance in status and compensation based on an honest and accurate appraisal of merit and performance.

However, in comparing the general values of the peoples of Singapore to the reality of their lives, Lee and his leadership team recognized that an enormous gap stretched between the espoused values and the reality. With its civil institutions and civic participation stunted by its long indenture as a British colony, the country was rife with factional politics, communal strife, bribery, and deep suspicion of those not from one's clan. Racketeering infested the entire commercial sector as the Triads (the Chinese equivalent of the Mafia) extracted protection payments from most businesses and even private citizens. Corruption, in some form or another, was widespread.

The masses, generally, had little trust of politicians or groups that espoused the notion of the common good, as they had no experience of anyone delivering on their promise, certainly not under the British or the Japanese. In practice, the masses understood well a politician who was devoted to the interests of his immediate clan or community. That is, though the cultures had very powerful assertions that acting in the interest of the whole nation was the highest good, they had no direct experience of this, and many people lived as if all that mattered was furthering self-interest and the parochial interests of one's immediate family or ethnic community.

Lee and his team made a personal commitment to exercise leadership that would shift the values of the people to narrow the gap between the lofty cultural ideals of working for the common good and the common sense of self-interest. As a first step, Lee decided as a politician and prime minister that he must assume the "mantle of the ideal" and present himself and his team as totally trustworthy and above factional influence.[7] He asserted that he and his government would have to be above reproach, and failure to maintain that level of trustworthiness would be disastrous—disastrous for whoever yielded to the temptation, and disastrous for the nation as well.[8] He asked the people to hold him and his government accountable.

The mantle of the ideal, however, contains distortions of reality that a leader must manage. In other words, the leader's flaws and strengths tend to be exaggerated by the people as the people project onto the leader their fantasy of who the leader is and how he or she should behave. In wearing the "mantle of the ideal," Lee knew his fellow citizens would keep a close watch on him and his team, with some looking for any small slip as an excuse to justify their own avoidance of the hard challenges of capacity building.[9]

For example, after Lee resigned as prime minister to take an advisory position as senior minister, the Investigation Bureau received complaints from buyers of land who thought it unfair that Lee's family would receive a discount on a purchase of property from a publicly listed real estate development company who had given early buyers at a soft launch a discount to test the market. When the Investigation Bureau found that such discounts were standard business practice to establish the accounts receivable basis for further funding of a development, a rumor started that the Investigation Bureau had given Lee's family an unfair benefit of the doubt.

Though the rumor of impropriety angered Lee, he publicly revealed the details of the transactions and gave the S$1 million in the purchase discounts to the Singapore government. When the Singapore government would not take the S$1 million, saying that the discounts were normal proper business practice, Lee gave the S$1 million in the purchase discounts to charity—to avoid a "perceived unfair advantage." And when the purchase discounts did not arise as an issue in the next general election, Lee concluded that his sacrifice had succeeded in keeping the people focused on the real issues in their lives.[10]

In assuming the mantle of the ideal, the leader must also realize that perception is reality. Hence, the leader must be prepared to *manage* the perception as the reality. Wisely, Lee chose to give up the S$1 million discount as a price of managing the perception of favoritism. Lee's actions strengthened the already robust holding environment and ensured that his nation avoided the common pitfall of using the leader as a distraction from attending to their pressing development tasks.

In addition to punishments for corruption and assuming the mantle of the ideal, Lee and his leadership team revised the electoral process to minimize the role of money in currying political favor or buying electoral support. For Lee, the elections needed to serve as a time when the people held their leaders to account. Without an accountability system with integrity, the people would be subject to the artful manipulative practices of those who did not have the public interest in mind. Therefore, the government passed laws making voting compulsory. The parties could not take voters to the polls in cars, as they did in the early elections. And the spending limits were set so low that Lee referred to Singapore's electoral system as "no-money elections." The only way that parties and candidates could appeal for votes was by publicizing their policy agendas—and then delivering on their publicly-made commitments. Lee said later, "We got them to vote for us again and again by providing jobs, building schools, hospitals, community centers, and, most important of all, homes which they owned."[11]

We can learn from the Singapore case that leaders must take responsibility for the impact of their power and authority on the quality of the holding environment. In the face of considerable pressure and temptation, they must control any tendency to use their power for excessive personal gain or self-aggrandizement and be willing to embody their group's highest standards for fairness and probity. The natural self-interest of individuals and factions can easily break up a corporation, community, or nation when the authority structure does not control its display of self-interest and violates the group's fairness standards. Hence, the holding environment will be adequate only if the authority structure keeps the display of self-interest below a threshold of tolerance and does not violate the group's fairness standard. When a leader fails to honor these standards, he or she sends a signal to other self-interested parties that they no longer need to be contained by the group's holding environment or be required to work in service of its shared goals. The group then will splinter, and its progress in developing new and latent capabilities will come to a standstill.

Develop in stages: Give the people time to discover what works

Human beings and their organizations change very slowly. People have to try things out and discover, often through trial and error, what works in practice. They need time to adjust to new realities and accommodate new processes. The leadership task is to be a perturbing force to keep the people facing the work of development: to provoke them by reminding them of the threat if they do not develop, and to evoke a desire to develop by connecting the vision or purpose of development with the people's own desires for a better organization, better community, or better nation; and the leader must provide the support needed to keep people engaged in the process, particularly when it gets frustrating and difficult. Given that development is rarely a linear process involving steady progress toward a clearly defined goal, it will get difficult. The process generally includes a series of punctuated experiments, some of which fail and some of which provide new information that may warrant a change in direction (or even the occasional shortcut). It is a process rife with uncertainty, breakdowns, miscalculations, and, sometimes, quantum leaps of understanding and progress.

Those who would exercise leadership—and honor Odin's constant challenge to seek wisdom and understanding—must therefore approach the development challenge as a process of continual discovery and adjustment. With each discovery comes a platform for new experiments and further discoveries, affording the opportunity to make midcourse corrections as needed.

In the first chapter, I presented the case of David Hornbeck, the superintendent of Philadelphia's school district. Hornbeck attempted to provide leadership for a major process of systemic reform, called Children Achieving. He was a bold, visionary superintendent who truly wanted to do what was in the best interest of the children of the city— and many of the children were poor, from broken homes, and failing on statewide exams in literacy, science, and math. Hornbeck was a man who honestly cared about these kids. However, although much of the leadership Hornbeck provided was admirable, in his crusader-like zeal he overloaded the system and failed to make adjustments according to what the people discovered.

The evaluators of Hornbeck's reform initiative, in their assessment of why Children Achieving did not deliver on its promise, noted that there was a "lack of capacity and a lack of attention to building it."[12] Hornbeck and his team adopted a "one size fits all" reform strategy and did not take into consideration the "different organizational issues, professional norms, and cultures to be addressed" throughout the school district. And, in doing so, "they adhered to the dictum of the Children Achieving plan that everything had to be done simultaneously which placed enormous burdens on teachers and principals."[13]

Given the complexity of the development challenge Hornbeck was facing, he needed to orchestrate a stage-by-stage learning process to discover what actually worked in each part of the system. Pushing forward without consideration for the difficulty people had in adjusting to the new context and mastering new competencies, served to undermine the progress that was actually being made. In the absence of valid and useful data on the adaptive capacity of each distinct part of the system as it struggled to reform, it was impossible to make the necessary midcourse corrections and structural adjustments that would ensure sustainability of the reforms.

In fairness to Hornbeck and his team, in any development process it is difficult to find the best sequencing of the various initiatives that contribute to successful development, and it is also very easy to underestimate the difficulty that people face in the design and production of new capabilities. Because of this difficulty, the leadership task is to manage development as a paced experiment, with constant feedback and ongoing reflection. Only then can the people ascertain what works and what does not. However, as the evaluators of Children Achieving point out, Hornbeck and his team were not always in the frame of mind to learn from the field and ascertain where changes of strategy or midcourse corrections were needed. During the reform process, there was considerable conflict in the entire system—primarily with the union, teachers, some schools and their communities, and the state legislature—and these conflicts could have provided useful data to ascertain what was missing in the rollout strategy and what could be done differently. But the high level of conflict generated a "bunker mentality" among the leadership team, and norms developed that required "believing in the reform process in toto" and the "questioning of core beliefs was tantamount to joining the opposition."[14]

These counterproductive norms might well have developed out of people's passionate commitment to ensuring Children Achieving would succeed. A "can do" attitude can help propel people forward and overcome mental and physical barriers. But when such an attitude leads to the denigration or denial of legitimate concerns or pieces of reality, the data needed to make informed and responsible choices will not be available, and progress will be jeopardized.

Admittedly, in highly politicized environments, given the possibility that opponents might exploit one's vulnerabilities, it is understandably difficult to be open to criticism, publicly acknowledge mistakes, or make midcourse corrections. This creates a dilemma for leaders. If they do not create feedback mechanisms, even feedback mechanisms that allow harsh criticism, they will always be operating on incomplete, even distorted, information. If they do open up the process, when mistakes or miscalculations become apparent, it is always possible that such errors will reflect negatively on the leaders and they will be scapegoated by the group for not being competent enough to "get it right the first time."

Getting it right the first time is rarely possible for a development challenge. By the very nature of this type of challenge, cultivating the appropriate capabilities occurs through a series of experiments. The leadership task is to be explicit with the people and explain to them the experimental nature of the reform process. Leaders set themselves up to fail when they definitively declare that they have the magic formula for "fixing the system."

As the new prime minister of his country, Lee Kuan Yew knew that Singapore's citizens had to learn through steady experimentation about what worked, and what did not, in the context of their individual and collective efforts to build their nation's economy and civil society. He could not impose the solution on the people, even if he knew what was best for the people. He knew he needed to provide feedback mechanisms to determine (1) how hard he could push the people to develop new capabilities, (2) to what degree government development policies and strategies were contributing to the building of new capabilities, and (3) whether the right capabilities were being developed to address the nation's current and future challenges.

A significant obstacle to Singapore's future development was, given its cultural diversity, its lack of a shared national language. Lee felt that the nation's survival depended on its ability to attract international business and foreign investors by offering a skilled, reliable, and flexible workforce in a stable business environment. In Lee's view, one of the best ways to achieve this goal was to ensure that a substantial portion of the population spoke fluent English, as English had become the preeminent language of international economic activity. Given the language prejudices within the international economy, new business ventures funded by outside capital would almost certainly offer better jobs at higher pay to English speakers. If there were not enough English speakers to fill key jobs, development opportunities might bypass Singapore altogether. Hence, the Singapore leadership team felt strongly that the nation's high-skill workers—engineers, scientists, financial specialists, and managers—needed to be English speakers, and the population's English skills needed to improve rapidly.

Lee knew that he had to pursue this goal by offering incentives and gradual persuasion, because any unilateral move to impose English was likely to meet with overwhelming resistance due to the reality that Singapore was a postcolonial society. "To announce that all had to learn English when each race was intensely and passionately committed to its own mother tongue would have been disastrous," he later wrote.[15]

Under British rule, the people of Singapore were free to send their children to ethnic schools to be immersed in the language and culture of their choosing. The schools taught in English, Malay, Tamil, and Mandarin Chinese, as well as half a dozen other Chinese dialects. The people were very satisfied with this arrangement, as they valued their cultural, clan, and religious identities more than a national identity.

Initially, Lee allowed the old policy to persist and simply encouraged people to learn English. But neither Lee's admonishment nor the incentive of better jobs could get enough people to deal with this challenge. That is, many people resisted having their children learn English, even if speaking English offered significant economic advantages. As they tested the water with a few experimental English advocacy initiatives, the leaders found that people would tolerate official designation of English, Chinese dialects, Malay, and Tamil as equal languages so long as no one language was given pride of place. Furthermore, many people would tolerate learning English as a second language so long as schools that taught English also ensured that children could learn the language of their ethnic group. This scenario allowed parents to choose the English language option with minimal betrayal to their native cultures. Still, opposition persisted. Lee noted:

> We waited patiently as year by year parents in increasing numbers chose to send their children to English schools, in the face of determined opposition from the Chinese teachers' unions, and other Chinese cultural societies. Every year, around the time when parents had to register their children, these groups would mount a campaign to get parents to enroll their children in Chinese schools for the sake of their culture and identity. They berated those who chose English schools as money-minded and short-sighted.[16]

In opposing the teaching of English, the parents defended what they saw as superior moral and social values in the non-English cultures. Lee's leadership challenge was to get a new generation of students to develop their English skills while providing parents and community leaders with adequate reassurance that the values they considered more important than economic development would not suffer.

Lee thus used government policy as a heuristic tool to get people to think about the implications of their personal and public choices, and to help them find a workable approach to a shared problem that they might otherwise have ignored. By requiring that all schools offer a second-language curriculum, but allowing these schools to choose among Tamil, Malay, Chinese, or English, Singapore's leaders did not force people to favor English. Gradually, however, as graduates who learned English got better jobs, their parents began to recognize its advantages without feeling as if they had to betray their traditional cultural values in order to reap the economic benefits of English. Lee and his leadership team had created an environment of choice and experimentation that helped his people embrace the opportunities of a globalized economy while building and maintaining a distinct Singaporean identity.

We see from this case that the politically effective measure may not be the economically effective measure. The most direct route to a modernized workforce might have been to declare English as the eventual official language. And, no doubt, with a different general popular attitude, the bilingualism of Singapore would be a wasteful use of a child's limited attention span. But effective measures may require more than merely applying technical solutions, because often political opposition prevents applying obvious technical solutions. Hence, the leader must manage processes that get the people to do the sometimes tedious work of discovering for themselves which practices and priorities actually lead to increased prosperity for the community, the organization, or the nation.

Find the right combination of levers to develop new values and capabilities

Sometimes, in order to develop new capacities, the leadership work is to modify outmoded values and beliefs so that a group can transcend barriers, move to a higher level of functioning, and take advantage of new opportunities. Certainly natural evolutionary processes serve to alter people's values and beliefs as humans have proved relatively successful in adapting to changing conditions since the beginning of time. But if these normal processes are deficient, given the threat to the group, then leaders must find the right combination of levers in the organization or society that can ignite and accelerate a developmental process that gets the people dealing with the reality of their predicament and adjusting their views to accommodate a changed condition.

In the 1970s, the Australian prime minister, Malcolm Fraser, had to find the right levers to get the people to develop values of acceptance and toleration of nonwhite immigrants. When Fraser became prime minister in 1974, he felt it was time to make a change. The reality, as he saw it, was that Australia could not expand its population relying exclusively on Europeans to migrate but needed to encourage and welcome hardworking people from any cultural, racial, or religious background. Diversity, he felt, would strengthen the social fabric of Australia and make it a more creative and resilient country. The reality that the people had to confront was how to develop their capacities to operate in a more globalized context and use the resources of the region to enhance the well-being and prosperity of the nation. In facing that reality, they would also need to acknowledge that some of their values had become anachronistic.

For many years, Australians had lived by cultural values based on Anglo-Saxon roots. Since the time of colonization and the establishment of Australia as a prison colony, many Australians had thought of themselves as an English enclave, and they considered England as the "mother country." These notions persisted well into the twentieth century. Fraser explained that, "after World War II Australia was predominantly white, Anglo-Saxon, Protestant, and if you didn't come out of that mold, you probably should pretend to, to be regarded as a good Australian."[17] Until the 1960s, the government had a "white Australia policy" that excluded people of non-European countries from immigrating to Australia.

Fraser knew that the government could not impose a shift in values and beliefs from the top down. He explained to me that "if you simply had a referendum on immigration, no one would have supported the introduction of a large group of nonwhites."[18] He needed to orchestrate a process that could allow people to learn about other races through interacting with them. So to get the community to take responsibility for their development, Fraser needed to discover the right combination of levers. He found four: (1) a policy called *multiculturalism*, (2) Southeast Asian refugees, (3) a government-sponsored broadcasting network, and (4) community organizations.

Fraser and his leadership team became a perturbing force as they crafted the policy of multiculturalism—a policy that they wanted to use as a heuristic tool to get the people to learn what they needed to learn to address the realities of a more complex and diverse world. He knew Australia could not afford to have one group pitted against another, as it would wreak havoc on community relations. Race, immigration, and national identity were sensitive issues and needed to be addressed with the utmost care. The term *multiculturalism* was controversial because it touched those sensitivities. The policy, however, had few legalities but was more of a declaration of welcome and tolerance to those of different backgrounds who wanted to make Australia home. An important premise of the policy was that, first and foremost, everyone should have an overriding commitment to Australia and to its interests and future, and that the new practices and values of immigrants must exist within the structures and principles already established in Australian society: the rule of law, parliamentary democracy, freedom of speech and religion, English as the national language, and equality of the sexes.

Some people in opposition, however, raised the specter of the "Asianization" of Australia. They felt that Fraser's program reflected a deliberate strategy to fragment the nation and dilute its national identity. These changes, the critics argued, would further damage already-eroding community standards and values, and undermine economic opportunities by providing new competitors for jobs and other resources. For them, the very notion of "what it means to be an Australian" was at stake.

As a perturbing intervention into the social fabric of the country, the policy of multiculturalism generated wide debate in the pubs, schools, and homes across the land. It got people thinking about what kind of a country they wanted and what values were essential for progress. Fraser reflected on this process:

Governments clearly can do a great many things. They can lead; they can define directions; they can set the tone. But in the end . . . the essence of multiculturalism can be realized only in the attitudes and behavior of people in areas which are beyond the proper reach of democratic government. A law on the statute book punishing those who use racial or ethnic insults will not compel neighbors to respect and appreciate each other's cultural heritage. A code of conduct for the media which warns against denigrating ethnic groups will not prevent advertisers and scriptwriters using exclusively Anglo-Saxon models for their heroes and heroines. Educational institutions can introduce multicultural courses to raise awareness of social diversity, but these cannot guarantee cultural sensitivity where it is most needed, by doctors towards their patients, by teachers towards their pupils, by lawyers and social workers towards their clients. Ultimately, responsibility for multiculturalism rests on the community at large.[19]

As a second lever, Fraser capitalized on the end of the Vietnam War, a war in which Australia was directly involved. Over a six-year period, for humanitarian reasons, the government gradually allowed more than two hundred thousand refugees from the Indochina Peninsula to settle in Australia. Not only refugees, but also more and more immigrants of non-European backgrounds were quietly encouraged to make Australia their home.

As a third lever, Fraser created a new government-sponsored broadcasting network that would televise international programming and highlight local cultural issues and events. Fraser explained that "the programs are designed to enable all Australians to learn more of the history, of the culture, of the background, of the traditions of the people who make up modern Australia. In a very real sense it was a program for all Australians."[20]

As a fourth lever, the Fraser government identified—and, where necessary, created—community groups to support immigrants and to work with towns and cities in promoting racial harmony and easing historic tensions. Special community centers gave immigrants assistance in making the transition to their new country. These centers also provided language instruction, help in finding employment, and counseling for new residents. White Australians, in turn, began slowly developing new mind-sets as they experienced the food and culture of their new neighbors.

Over time, diversity was seen less as a threat and more of an enrichment of the Australian quality of life. The children of immigrants, in particular, assimilated quickly into Australian popular culture, playing football and cricket, surfing, joining the scouts, and picking up the distinctive "Aussie" accent. Today, for most Australians the experience of cultural diversity is commonplace and unremarkable, occurring at work, in the neighborhood, in community organizations, in schools, and in everyday life. Fraser noted, "In terms of the life of the nation, these changes took place with relative speed. What occurred is profound and subtle. It was not just the recognition of the needs of ethnic communities. We have not merely grafted an ethnic dimension to an otherwise unchanged view of ourselves. There is a fundamental change in the established way of seeing Australia."[21]

Malcolm Fraser's leadership efforts to develop new values and capabilities in the society illustrate important aspects of leadership for a development challenge. First, the existing culture and traditions of a group or organization likely contain positive resources as well as negative influences for getting a people to develop. The leadership task is to find the resources that can be used as levers to support development. The Australian culture had subtle forms of racial prejudice that discounted the merit and ability of people from other races. But there was also the notion of a "fair go" for all, if people were willing to get in and do their bit. Modern Australia had been built upon the labor of convicts, settlers, merchants, farmers, and a large working class. These people understood the importance of giving someone a chance. Australians would tolerate and accept new immigrants and give them a fair go, provided they tried to adapt to the new conditions and make some adjustments in their own behavior. Over time, the immigrants were seen less as a threat but more as an important resource for the growth of the nation. Fraser provided the perturbing force that set in motion this discovery process for the Australian people. His perturbing force was not blunt and abrupt, but paced and measured to allow people to make adjustments in their behavior and accommodate new realities.

Give people a stake in developing their capacity

People generally work harder to improve what they perceive is theirs. However, the ownership that matters to a person differs with the individual, the culture, and the times. For example, when the American patriot Patrick Henry said, "Give me liberty or give me death," clearly he meant, If you want hard work from me, you had better give me freedom. A leader, therefore, should be constantly searching for the right balance and distribution of stakeholding.

A very successful enterprise in the United States is the semiconductor company Xilinx, located in Silicon Valley. The company has annual revenues of over $1 billion and is the leading supplier of programmable logic in the world. It has repeatedly been chosen by *Fortune* magazine as one of the top five organizations to work for.[22] It is innovative, productive, profitable, and humane. One of the many reasons it is so successful is due to the fact that the employees have a stake in the company. By virtue of their having a stake in the company, the development processes of building new capabilities have proceeded with relative ease. At Xilinx, the employees are given a generous quantity of company stock, enjoy profit sharing, and one in five holds a patent. The CEO, Willem Roelandts, said of this strategy:

> I think it is truly a key way to reward people and make them feel connected to the company. I learned that if you want people to behave as employees then you treat them one way. If you want them to behave as owners then you treat them another way. . . . People at Xilinx care about the company and their rationale for doing their best is that they know innovation and technology and bringing things quickly to market will create breakthroughs and business opportunities that they will share in.[23]

In Singapore, people would work hard and support the government if they could be confident of enjoying the fruits of their labor. Most voters were poor and would not tolerate an unregulated economy that channeled most of the profits to a few owners and investors. On the other hand, if the government overtaxed the "high performers" to subsidize the poor, they might reduce their investment in Singapore, and the nation as a whole might be poorer—because, in Lee's words, "the high performers would cease to strive."[24] In a development challenge, wisdom is needed to strike the right balance between effort and reward for all people.

Singapore's various ethnic cultures all agreed that one definition of progress was that children should enjoy greater opportunity and prosperity than their parents.[25] These values had roots not only in the values of trust, pride, and care of children but also in the need of parents to have a source of security in their elderly years. The Singapore leaders saw the strong family ties within the Chinese, Malay, and Tamil ethnic groups as a resource. As a consequence, the leaders formulated a series of interventions to hold the wage earner "responsible for his family—his parents, wife, and children."[26]

The British had maintained a Central Provident Fund for administering a pension savings plan of matching contributions from employee and employer. After the British left, Singapore leaders reconstructed the Provident Fund to provide a mandatory savings plan to accumulate the downpayment on a home. As wages increased, the leaders increased the contribution to the Provident Fund, while ensuring that wage earners still saw "a net increase in take-home-pay." Counting the employer contribution, the savings to the Provident Fund amounted to as much as 50 percent of wages. Lee was "determined to avoid placing the burden of the present generation's welfare costs onto the next generation."[27]

As more of Singapore's workers began to have the resources to purchase their own homes, more homes were built to meet the demand, and the home-building industry created even more jobs and prosperity. Real estate prices also rose gradually, further increasing the net worth of the families who had purchased homes. In its immediate and enduring success, the Provident Fund vindicated the idea that giving citizens a stake in their society's larger success would help bind the community together and create support for shared endeavors.

Lee also wanted the people to have a stake in the process of health care. Singapore leaders saw two extremes in health care among other nations. At one extreme, the British government provided the same health care to all. At the other extreme, the U.S. government provided health care for only the elderly who had insufficient funds and destitute people. In seeking a practical approach, the Singapore leaders wanted to avoid an "all you can eat" buffet-style approach to health care because that approach would provide people with little incentive to trim waste.[28] So the leaders opted for scaled copayments by patients where the highest government subsidies went to the lowest-cost facilities. Generally, the higher-cost facilities were more comfortable but obtained less government subsidy. The Singapore government thereby gave the citizens a personal stake in trimming the costs of health care. Those less concerned about trimming costs could pay for the increased comfort from their own resources—from their own personal stake in the outcome.[29]

The Singapore strategy of giving each citizen a stake in the enterprise may have contributed to low government expenditures. For example, in Singapore, government expenditure has averaged 20 percent of GDP, compared to an average of 33 percent in the G8 economies. Furthermore, between 1960 and 2000, the Singapore government had a budget surplus for thirty-eight of those forty years. Inflation has remained low with no borrowing of foreign funds.[30]

The Singapore initiatives to give people a stake in developing their capabilities illustrate key features of real leadership for a development challenge. First, many forces work against development, steering people toward short-term gratification and profligacy. Therefore, the leader must take responsibility for the forces that support or hinder development of the entire system. For example, in Singapore's formative years, the government could not rely on free market mechanisms to provide every citizen a stake in the country's success. Realizing that an unregulated free market may waste a lot of human potential by rewarding too much stake in the outcome to the early winners in the market and encouraging short-term speculation and excessive consumption, the leadership needed to find ways to move all citizens on a developmental pathway. Hence, the Singapore leadership team developed a home ownership program and a health scheme that would appeal to the people's aspirations and long-term interest.

Second, fashioning incentives from higher-order values and assets rather than from items of consumption or immediate gratification may induce different behaviors that contribute to development. For example, in Singapore, the voters initially might have settled for government subsidy of equal health care for all instead of home ownership for all. But saving for the asset of a home induced frugal behavior and family values which government subsidy of consumption might not.

Third, the Singapore leadership team performed a regular reality check of the effect of their policies on the development process. For example, the Singapore elections every five years provided two corrective mechanisms on incentives: (1) government officials rephrased programs to accommodate the perceptions and misperceptions of the voters, and (2) voters evaluated the effectiveness of government programs. In a corporation, this regular reality check might follow from shareholder, employee, customer, and supplier feedback.

Conclusion

The cases presented in this chapter illustrate how real leadership and good policy or strategy help generate heuristic mechanisms that serve to get people engaged in the adaptive work of building new capacities to address the complexity of the problems that their institutions and communities face. The development challenge is the core challenge of all human endeavors. Without guided and context-appropriate development that allows people to take advantage of the amazing array of opportunities that are available today, groups and organizations will stagnate. Stagnation inevitably leads to decay, and decay leads to death. Leaders therefore must be vigilant in diagnosing the shifting terrain to discover emerging threats and opportunities while there is still time to evolve the latent capacity of the group or organization to make the necessary adjustments that take advantage of the system's resources to attend successfully to future needs.

In the age of globalization, leaders must think of fresh and innovative ways to approach development for the interdependent challenges that transcend cultural and geographic boundaries, such as creating economic systems that work for the benefit of the poor, dealing responsibly with environmental degradation, and attending to underlying concerns that produce ethnic wars and terrorism—all problems that traditional approaches in the past have failed to treat realistically.

REAL LEADERSHIP FOR A DEVELOPMENT CHALLENGE

- Create a robust holding environment to keep people from getting distracted.
- Develop in stages: give the people time to discover what works.
- Find the right combination of levers to develop new values and capabilities.
- Give people a stake in developing their capacity.

CHAPTER 5

The Transition Challenge

Moving from One System
of Values to Another

There are times when some of the values and mind-sets of a people are no longer useful in addressing the challenges that beset the group or organization. This could be due to a shift in the dynamics of the larger environment or the emergence of a new threat or opportunity. To ensure the group is able to adapt and thrive in a changed environment, deal with the threat, or take advantage of the opportunity, the leadership work is to transition the group to a new state of operating and refashion the values, loyalties, and mind-sets of the people. The following scenario illustrates that challenge.

SCENARIO

Suppose you are the production manager for a popular sports car manufacturer. For many years, your company has prided itself in producing handmade cars for connoisseurs. However, both the marketplace and production technology have moved on while your firm has stood still. Customers no longer view handmade as necessarily better. Precision robotics produce quality that is often indistinguishable from hand assembly at a cost that is so much lower that many customers see no point in paying extra for hand craftsmanship. In addition, your critics point out that the workers at the automated plants of your competitors make almost twice the annual wage of your workers.

You know that you must make the transition to automated manufacturing; it is only a matter of time. As part of your transition planning, you must consider the shifts in values that you are expecting of your workers, customers, and suppliers as you and they move into a more automated future. For example, your current worker motto of "Take time to take care" must change to something like "Pace, precision, performance." In addition, your marketing people must shift from the values of "Quality based on personal attention" to something like "Classic performance through cutting-edge technology."

Though your transition to automation will include some development tasks to help you refine your approach to change, you do not foresee the need for extensive experimentation or data gathering, as the way forward is all too clear. You expect the main challenge for your organization lies in making the transition to new production methods, together with the sometimes painful shift for your employees in adapting from their dedication to the beauty of handmade craftsmanship to the technical satisfaction that comes from precision automation. Given that robotics will reduce your labor requirement, some of your employees will have to find a job elsewhere—but those who remain, modify their values, and embrace the new production methods can expect significantly higher wages.

As you contemplate the leadership work ahead, you use the mental image of a group crossing a river. The crossing will be precarious, but if you handle the crossing skillfully, you can continue your forward progress in good time and order (at least until you come to the next river). If you are careless or inept, you will lose time and other resources as your group flounders in the current. If you or your people refuse to face this transition challenge, your progress will be blocked and an opportunity will be lost. Just as likely, the company could fail or be forced to sell itself to owners who then impose change with far less respect for those values that should remain enduring.

The Nature of a Transition Challenge

Transition, according to the dictionary, means the "passage from one form, state, style, or place to another."[1] In the context of real leadership, it is the process of shifting the people to a new set of norms, mind-sets, and attitudes that are more appropriate for succeeding in a changed context. It is not a process of completely replacing values but of refashioning values. The process includes sorting out what values to leave behind, what to carry forward, what values to emphasize, and what values to deemphasize.

Generally, a transition challenge emerges when those in authority have a good sense of the direction the group should take, but members of the group have various reasons for dragging their feet. Here are some of the clearer signs that a group, organization, or community is facing a transition challenge:

- Compelling evidence suggests that a new threat or opportunity has emerged, and if the people can move from one location (physical, mental, or operational) to another, their condition will be improved.

- The people have the resources to make the transition, but to do so they will have to replace one system of values for another. That is, they will have to give up, or at least modify, some of the traditions, habits, and practices that they cherish.

- Given the strong inertial influence of values, tradition, and habit, combined with the fear of the unknown, the people are reluctant to make the journey.

In diagnosing the transition challenge, the leader should consider (1) the condition of the people, (2) the barrier that impedes progress, and (3) the promise or aspiration on the other side of the barrier.

The *people* in a transition challenge might see a need to transition themselves from one system of values to another, but they are anxious and afraid, as the process of transitioning can be overwhelming and disorienting. It is not necessarily that they do not want to make a transition journey, but they are concerned about the loss that accompanies such a process.

The *barrier* includes the people's understandable reluctance to give up their routine habits, practices, and priorities and replace them with another set. This process of change can be threatening to their identity, loyalties, and sense of competence. For example, imagine that people have chains of valuable jewelry around their legs. They love their jewelry, but the chains keep them attached to the old world that they know and cherish. However, in order to move across the barrier, they will have to sacrifice the chains of jewelry. Failure to make such a sacrifice will leave them and their jewelry in the old world where their continued survival can no longer be guaranteed.

The *promise* of a transition challenge is that if the group can renegotiate their loyalties and can sift through their prevailing values and practices to determine what they can carry forward and what must be left behind, then their lives (or the organization's overall condition) might get better. The promise is not a guarantee but a hopeful possibility and a likely outcome if the people can do the requisite problem-solving and value-adjusting work along the way.

The term *change management* is sometimes used to describe this process of shifting values, habits, and attitudes, but the transition challenge is *not* about change management. That term is more properly applied to hardware, software, and technology that yields to rational, linear processes that can be planned, managed, and controlled. *In the realm of human systems, you don't manage a transition; you orchestrate a transition.* The process must allow for unpredictable events, occasional detours, and emotional explosions—which are all part of the adaptive work of adjusting to a new reality.

On the surface, a transition challenge might look very much like a development challenge, but the essential difference is a simple one. In a transition challenge, the people have the capabilities but must change their values, habits, and attitudes. In a development challenge, the capabilities—the competencies, processes, and structures—are lacking and therefore need to be built. For example, a company might need to shift its culture to respond to the demands of a changed market. This would be a transition challenge if the capacities and competencies necessary to succeed already existed in the enterprise and the leadership work was to primarily modify the people's values and mind-sets.

The Leader as Ferryman

I would liken the leadership functions in a transition challenge with the coaxing role of a ferryman trying to get people into the boat to cross the water so that they can realize a great opportunity on the other side. In Norse mythology, one of Odin's many symbolic roles was that of the ferryman. As the ferryman, he would take people to new places of prosperity. Odin is said to have led his people out of their ancient homeland in Troy to the new world in the north, known as Aegir. Troy was in a warm climate (in what is now Turkey), and Odin had to convince the people to move to the cold north (in what is now Scandinavia).

Odin was sure there was great promise in the northern lands. There was abundant hunting grounds, rich farmland, lots of water, and magnificent countryside. But people were reluctant to go there because the region's winters were so much more severe than in balmy Troy on the shores of the Aegean Sea. Those who relocated would have to give up many comforts. Moving north as far as Sweden and Iceland would mean adapting to the three months near-constant darkness and to summer weeks when the sun never sets. Daily practices, habits, and priorities would have to change radically. Furthermore, the journey might be dangerous, as the group would have to travel through regions believed to be inhabited by giants, dragons, and conniving dwarves. Although each threat might make them stronger if they prevailed, there would always be the possibility that some might not make it.

Understandably, Odin's people had good reason for their reluctance to transition. And, as you might imagine, there were great controversies whether the trip would be worth the effort, the trauma, and the sacrifice required. The actual journey from Troy to Aegir would require the fording of many rivers, but the transition first depended on Odin's ability to get his people onto the boat. Once they were committed to that first crucial step, at least they had accepted the idea that there was a possibly better world beyond the current one. Yet imagine Odin's difficulties in getting his people to make that initial commitment. He could not tell them the crossing would be easy. And he could not tell them that there were no dragons or dwarves on the other side who would cause them trouble. There probably were. Nor could he promise that they would all survive the journey. He knew better.

So suppose you are Odin. How do you get your people onto the transition boat? You could be authoritarian and order them aboard, but that approach would lead them to withhold their consent, blame you when the going gets tough, and even rebel. To the degree that they are able, you want your people to make a free and informed choice so that they can be committed to the journey. You also want them to be self-sufficient by the time they get to the new land. By making a free and informed choice, the people would be in a better position to take responsibility for the transition, and thereby use their current energy and available resources to focus on the hard work of paddling rather than the wasteful work of scapegoating the authority or fighting with one another.

Your job as leader is to talk the people through the process of giving up some of the things that they value, help them cope with their losses, and develop enough confidence to move forward at a steady pace. They will have to face some harsh realities that they would prefer to avoid. You must help them adjust their thinking, modify their expectations, be vigilant, and assume reasonable risks. As the journey progresses, given that people may feel vulnerable and lost, you will also need to help them make sense of the unfamiliar terrain and the emerging world.

Above all, you will want your people to be responsible for their actions and not excessively dependent on you to do all the work of getting them to their new home. Otherwise, they might delude themselves into thinking that they can go back, despite all rational evidence that the old ways are vanishing and cannot be recalled, no matter how much they want to cling to them. That, after all, is why the journey is necessary and why real leadership must be provided to support the people in their transition journey.

Lou Gerstner as CEO of IBM in the 1990s, as discussed in chapter 2, had to ferry his organization to a new destination. When he joined the company in 1993, he noticed that the mind-sets and attitudes of the people were not conducive to building and sustaining a productive and profitable business. The organization was cumbersome, bureaucratic, highly politicized, and internally focused. To succeed in the company's transformation, Gerstner knew that he needed to transition the values of the people so that they could respond to the realities of the changing marketplace with precision and speed. Business operations had to change, and the corporate culture had to change. He needed to take on the role of ferryman.

It took a year to figure out, in a general sense, what kind of a company IBM needed to become. But once clarity of direction emerged and the solutions became more visible on the other side of the river, the main order of business was to persuade people to board the ferry of their own free will. And, once on board, in exercising leadership, Gerstner would have to accommodate people's fears, resistance, and anxieties, and work with the people to keep them in the boat and shed their outmoded mind-sets, habits, and values.

* * *

Lou Gerstner's experience at IBM is an example of the demands and requirements of leading a difficult transition. With a group of any size—be it a team, corporation, or nation—the leadership processes for a transition challenge are similar. To illustrate the leadership work associated with a transition, consider the case of the Emperor Meiji in the latter half of the nineteenth century shepherding Japan through the modernizing of its culture, political processes, and economy. Japan's transition, as with IBM's, was unsettling for some, as it was filled with unpredictable events, uncertain terrain, periods of great danger, and moments of thrilling adventure.

Although both IBM and Meiji Japan crossed the river to a new and better state of operating with minimal loss, once they got to the new destination a whole new set of adaptive challenges began. Success in crossing the river is no guarantee that you will survive in the new place, as adaptive pressures are ongoing. For example, once the Japanese got to the new destination, they faced an array of problematic concerns related to their identity, their role in the world, and the demands of a development challenge that included building new competencies and capacities for the industrial era.

It is important to note, by way of comparison, that Meiji's transition challenge differs from Singapore's development challenge, as presented in the previous chapter. Singapore was fighting for its survival and had to develop fast. In contrast, Japan was already relatively developed, with a legal framework, an educational system, and institutions for governance. It had one of the most literate populations in the world. The problem was that Japan was insular. It had to transition the values of the people to take advantage of new opportunities in the world. The people were fairly unified and enjoyed a common tradition. They already had a significant set of capabilities. Singapore, on the other hand, had no national identity, common culture, or shared language. Singapore, therefore, had to develop new capabilities.

Transitioning Japan: Crossing the River into the Modern World

Japan's transition challenge began in 1868 when it decided to shift from an isolated feudal kingdom to an internationally connected industrial democracy. It was a difficult and painful journey—one that impressively illustrates the "dos and the don'ts" of how to lead a transition.

Japan had adopted a deliberate policy of national isolation since 1635. For more than two centuries, the people had lived in quiet seclusion from the outside world. They looked down on Westerners, regarding them as dangerous, greedy, and ignorant barbarians. They saw no value in foreign trade and little value in foreign ideas, believing that such things would fuel the destruction of their traditions and national identity. They neither knew nor cared about what was happening outside the "land of the rising sun."

All this was to change with the arrival of the American "black ships" under the command of Commodore Matthew Perry in 1853. Perry pointed his ships' cannons at Edo (now Tokyo) and told the Japanese to open up their borders for trade—or suffer the consequences. The gates to the country were forced open, and foreign influences began flooding in. By the late 1850s and early 1860s, Western ships, traders, and diplomats were plentiful in many port towns and coastal villages. However, the presence of the "barbarians" unleashed dark and injurious forces. A number of Westerners were attacked and killed by disgruntled locals. Also, many of the leading Japanese advocates of reform were assassinated. One observer noted at the time, "Any person who showed, by any will or deed, any favor towards foreigners in Japan—indeed, any person who had any interest in foreign affairs—was liable to be set upon by the unrelenting ronin (independent samurai)."[2]

One of the most troubling incidents happened on September 14, 1862. The lord of the Satsuma region, Hisamitsu, was traveling with his entourage to a meeting with the shogun when they met a group of Englishmen on the road. The English refused to move to the side of the road, bow, and make way for Lord Hisamitsu and his procession. Lord Hisamitsu's samurai took grave offense to this blatant display of disrespect and cut off the head of one of the Englishmen and wounded two others. The message was very clear to the English: "In this country we are dominant, and you are subservient. Learn that lesson, be respectful, or die."

The English refused to accept that lesson. In fact, they were infuriated. London newspapers carried articles condemning the Japanese, with some calling for immediate war. The British government made a formal complaint to the shogun, demanding that the perpetrators of the crime be executed and £100,000 be paid as compensation—or Japan would be punished. The shogun, feeling very vulnerable, had no choice but to agree. He "requested" that Lord Hisamitsu pay the indemnity and turn over the culprits. Hisamitsu refused. The British then sent warships to the coastal city of Kagoshima, in the province of Satsuma, where Lord Hisamitsu resided. The ships fired on the ancient city and partly leveled it. They burnt thousands of houses and temples, killing hundreds of people.

America, England, France, and Holland made repeated protests to the Tokugawa government (the shogunate) and lodged pleas for increased security and protection of their visiting citizens. But the shogunate had become trapped between competing factions from within and without. From within, the more progressive elements agitated in favor of rapid reform and modernization, and anti-Western clans advocated closing the borders and ridding Japan of all foreign influences. From without, the Western powers, with the constant threat of force, demanded greater influence and access. In trying to satisfy all sides, the government lost the confidence of nearly everyone.

In 1868, the progressives, sensing how weak and unstable the shogunate had become, launched a full-scale attack on the government and succeeded in toppling it. They placed on the throne a fifteen-year-old boy, who became known as the Emperor Meiji, the Mikado. They saw him as a symbol of the past who could provide continuity and stability as they transitioned into the future. Their hope in him was amply rewarded. The Meiji emperor was to become one of the most significant rulers that Japan, perhaps even the world, had ever seen. The unprecedented reforms he championed transformed his country from an isolated feudal kingdom to a powerful modern nation with global influence.

The emperor encouraged the creation of schools throughout the country (for boys *and* girls) that would teach Western arts and sciences. To placate traditionalists, he kept the teaching of Confucian philosophy and values. He also allowed hundreds of private academies to emerge, many with Western teachers and many run by Western missionaries. These schools became the agents for social, political, and cultural transformation across the country. Hundreds of young men and women were sent on study missions to the United States and Europe. By the time U.S. president Ulysses S. Grant visited the Mikado in 1879, the mood and outlook of the nation were totally different than what they had been when Perry had arrived only twenty-five years earlier. Japan was buzzing with new ideas and heated debate as people explored fascinating, novel, and sometimes threatening perspectives. The country was truly on the road to modernization, and now there was no turning back—although some dangerous, tragic, and wasteful detours would lie ahead.

What follows in this chapter is an analysis of what happened in Japan during the transition process—as well as illustrative cases from China and IBM—and a discussion about the principles and strategies that real leadership must consider if a transition is to succeed. These principles include (1) helping people understand why the journey is necessary by providing an orienting purpose, (2) getting people to own the passage, (3) determining what needs to be preserved, and (4) becoming a visible symbol of the transition ideal.

Real Leadership for a Transition Challenge

Provide an orienting purpose

As a first step in orchestrating a transition, what is needed is a compelling orienting purpose that gives the people a reason to "get on the boat" and helps them appreciate why the journey must be undertaken without delay. The orienting purpose must address the threat to the group and articulate the promise that is available if the group can succeed in making the transition. Fundamentally, it must answer the question "Is this journey really necessary?" It must be both provocative and evocative. As a provocation, it must put reality squarely in front of people, not in a way that overwhelms them, but in a way that jolts them and gets their attention. To evoke, the leader must find his or her version of Odin's mead to elevate the thinking and sentiment of the people. The mead must be potent enough to move people to persistent action, as a transition journey is usually long and frustrating with no immediate gain or benefit for the people.

To get the IBMers in the transition ferry, Lou Gerstner declared that IBM would become the world's leading technology company driven by an e-business strategy. Given the problems inside IBM, this statement of direction was a bold pronouncement. But as a first step in that direction, the people needed to understand just how broken IBM was. He told his employees:

> Clearly, what we have been doing isn't working. We lost $16 billion in three years. Since 1985, more than 175,000 employees have lost their jobs. The media and our competitors are calling us a dinosaur. Our customers are unhappy and angry. We are not growing like our competitors. Don't you agree that something is wrong and we should try something else?[3]

With that statement of reality, Gerstner got people's attention and then invited them to figure out with him what was needed for IBM to reclaim its position as the world's leader in its industry. One year later, in the spring of 1994, Gerstner called together 420 senior managers from around the world and provoked them even further. In his words, "I expressed my frustration and my bewilderment about the recurring failure to execute and the company's apparently endless tolerance of it."[4] But then Gerstner became more evocative and told the group that he "considered the people in the room to be the finest collection of talent assembled in any institution in any industry" and that IBM had virtually "unlimited potential" if management and staff could muster the resources and commitment to do the work of change.[5] Concerning this intervention, he remarked:

> It was an emotional talk for me. . . . I heard that while most of the executives were very supportive, some had simply been shocked. It wasn't so much my ideas and messages that startled

them. It was my delivery—my passion, my anger, my directness. Very un-IBM. Very un-CEO-like. . . . I wasn't surprised—or sorry. I had made the conscious decision to jolt the audience.[6]

In providing an orienting purpose, the leader must be able to connect with all members of the group. A social system of any type is not a single entity but is generally made up of many factions with different interests and competing loyalties. For example, a corporation has senior managers, middle managers, supervisors, and frontline staff. There are also employees in the regions and employees in the head office. Therefore, it is important that the orienting purpose acknowledge the values and context of each faction and holds enough aspiration to appeal to all. The leader might ask, "What image in the people's minds can help each faction overcome their reluctance and make a commitment to the journey?" The image must be powerful enough to evoke from the people the attitude that the effort they need to expend is on behalf of a noble venture and therefore worth it. Should the image be weak or inadequate, the people will feel no compelling reason to make the journey and quickly revert to habit and custom.

In appealing to the people of Japan to make the transition, the young Mikado and his leadership team crafted a letter that was published in the newspapers and sent throughout the land indicating the importance and necessity of change. To minimize resistance and maximize support, he made sure that the letter addressed the concerns of both the traditionalists and the progressives. He also tried to explain his "new" role to the people and how, as emperor, he would safeguard tradition while paving the way for changes that improved the quality of life of all citizens irrespective of their social status. Never had such a letter emanated from the most senior authority figure in the country. The letter stated:

> Ever since, quite unexpectedly, we succeeded to the throne, young and weak though we are, we have been unable to control our apprehension day and night, over how we are to remain faithful to our ancestors when dealing with foreign countries.
>
> . . . Now, at a time of renovation of rule of the country, if even one of the millions of people in this country is unable to find his place in society, this will be entirely our fault. Accordingly, we have personally exerted our physical and spiritual powers to confront the crisis.
>
> . . . At a time when every other country is progressing in all directions, only our country, being unfamiliar with the situation prevailing in the world, stubbornly maintains old customs and

does not seek the fruits of change. . . . For this reason we have sworn . . . to continue the glorious work of our ancestors. Regardless of the pain and suffering it might entail, we intend to personally rule over the entire country, to comfort you, the numberless people, and in the end open up the ten thousand leagues of ocean waves, to proclaim the glory of our country to the world and bring to the land the unshakeable security of Mount Fuji.

You, the countless numbers, have become accustomed to the evils inherited from the past and to think of the Court only as a place to be held in awe. Not knowing the acute danger threatening the Land of the Gods, you manifest extreme surprise . . . and this has given rise to doubts of every kind. The people are confused. . . . You of countless numbers, give due consideration to our aspirations and join with us. Cast away your private thoughts and choose the general good. Help us in our work and ensure the safety of the Land of the Gods. If we can comfort the spirits of our ancestors, this will be the greatest happiness of our life.[7]

The letter had an extraordinary effect. It got people's attention and got them thinking. Without the appeal of the letter and its promise of a better life, with greater personal choice and freedom for every citizen, people might have been far less willing to embrace the transition challenge.

The Mikado and his leadership team's next task was to define the guiding principles and values that would serve as the engine of the transition process. This declaration was known as the Charter Oath in Five Articles. The principles and values included the following:

- Deliberate assemblies shall be widely established and all matters decided by public discussion.
- All classes, high and low, shall unite in vigorously carrying out the administration of affairs of state.
- The common people . . . shall each be allowed to pursue his own calling so that there may be no discontent.
- Evil customs of the past shall be broken off and everything will be based on the just laws of nature.
- Knowledge shall be sought throughout the world so as to strengthen the foundations of imperial rule.[8]

The principles and values of the Charter Oath were unprecedented and revolutionary for Japan. The charter encouraged public debate of issues, something that had never happened before. It freed all citizens—even peasants—to pursue whatever vocation they chose. And it declared that the psychological, cultural, and legal walls that had isolated Japan from the rest of the world would be transcended and new knowledge would actively be sought abroad.

With his letter and the Charter Oath, the emperor successfully connected the transition purpose with the aspirations of his people by acknowledging the reality of their condition and clearly explaining what they might gain if they willingly made the journey. The leadership task was to ensure that the image of the desired future tapped into the aspirations of the people and was stronger than the values, habits, and traditions—the chains of jewelry—that perpetuated the security of the current order and an unhealthy attachment to the past.

The past, however, should not be totally discarded. Features of it can be used as a resource to evoke the group's willingness to venture forward. Paradoxically, one of the most powerful and effective ways to evoke the aspirations of the group is to couch the orienting purpose in terms of traditional values. "Remember who we are and what we have in common," says the leader. "To preserve and strengthen our shared identity, and to honor our past, we must take this journey, even if it brings change and requires great sacrifice." Indeed, this is what the emperor did in stressing that the way to honor the ancestors and to protect Japan was by embracing new knowledge and practices and embarking on the modernization process. "If we can comfort the spirit of our ancestors," he declared, "this will be the greatest happiness of our life."

As expected, many Japanese greeted the emperor's announcement with mixed emotions. They were apprehensive about change and suspicious of Western influence. The deep-dyed traditionalists, in particular, saw the new direction as a fundamental threat to the prevailing order. Small pockets of armed resistance sprung up throughout the country, and assassinations of government officials and progressive scholars became a daily occurrence. In spite of that, the majority of the people boarded the metaphorical boat.

Get people to own the passage, or they will probably deceive you

When a group or institution undertakes a transition, the natural dynamics that are a part of hierarchical relationships make it easy for some people to tell themselves, "This is what the boss wants. I'm not sure I want to go on this journey, but I have to play along in order to keep my place in the group." Consequently, the leader may find it difficult to get an accurate picture of what really is going on with the people in regard to their sentiment, concerns, and degree of progress. In order to appear loyal and committed, people might distort information, withhold data, and censor their opinions. Although they might be in the boat, the leadership challenge is to ensure that enough people own the passage and do not, when discontented, engage in distortion of information, subterfuge, or outright rebellion.[9]

A major challenge the young Mikado faced was getting the two hundred feudal lords—the *daimyo*—to be responsible for the transition journey. Would they be willing to give up their power and embrace the new order? They essentially ran their regions as independent, or at least semi-independent, kingdoms. The ordinary people were looking to their daimyo to see what they would do. The daimyo were key, because if they refused to buy into the journey, given their symbolic importance in Japanese society, then the journey would be seriously hampered. Being among the most powerful men in all Japan, the daimyo had much to lose.

The emperor invited all the daimyo to the palace to meet with him. He explained why the transition was necessary and what the work ahead would be. He also told them that their official function as daimyo was to be abolished and that civil servants would be appointed as government administrators for the regions. He told the lords that they, and all their servants and samurai, had to leave their palaces and find other jobs, although each would be given a stipend as recognition of their contribution. He also explained how the people would be looking to them for direction and that there was the potential for great turmoil if the daimyo did not do their part in displaying support for the transition.

Surprisingly, no overt opposition to this directive was expressed. Most understood and appreciated what was needed. A few, however, were bewildered and upset. They believed that the time-honored feudal system was an extension of the natural order of the universe and, when combined with the precepts of Confucianism, brought order, peace, and harmony to the society. The powerful daimyo of the Kagoshima region, in particular, believed that the reform agenda was ill conceived, dangerous, and an insult to the ancestors. He committed ritual suicide in protest.

For the most part, the daimyos anticipated the changes and gave up their power, positions, and palaces—all in the name of progress. One Western observer, who was amazed at how smoothly this aspect of the transition proceeded, wrote:

> I had full opportunity of seeing the immediate effect of this edict, when living at Fukui, in the castle under the feudal system. Three

scenes impressed me powerfully. The first was that at the local Government office, on the morning of the receipt of the Mikado's edict, July 18, 1871. Consternation, suppressed wrath, fears and forebodings mingled with emotions of loyalty. In Fukui I heard men talking of killing the Imperial representative in the city and the penman of the Charter Oath. The second scene was in the great castle hall, October 1, 1871, when Lord Ichizen, assembling his many hundreds of hereditary retainers, bade them to exchange loyalty for patriotism and in a noble address urged the transference of local to national interest. The third scene was on the morning following, when the whole population, as it seemed to me, of the city of 40,000 people, gathered in the streets to take their last look, as the lord of Ichizen left his ancestral castle and departed to Tokyo, there to live as a private gentleman without any political power.[10]

Every person—merchant, artisan, mother, father, teacher, and student—witnessed this symbolic departure in their own respective districts. It was filled with tears and mixed emotions, but it produced a profound psychological shift throughout the country. The daimyo, in supporting the emperor, thus became invaluable allies in ensuring a smooth and steady transition process. The reality was that their resistance could have led to civil war.

But there was one faction in the country who did not want to get into the boat—the samurai. The emperor and his leadership team had made radical changes in the social relationships of the people by eradicating status differentials and the privileges of the elite. The peasants appreciated this, but many samurai felt like they had been cast adrift.

In 1876, a group of samurai traditionalists known as *Shinpuren* decided that they had had enough. Their leader, Otaguro Tomo, was certain that he had been given divine authorization to stage an uprising against the Mikado and his government. This group was determined to cease the spread of Western influence and eradicate all traces of Western culture in Japan, including the wearing of Western clothes, the eating of Western food, and the adoption of the Western calendar. They even despised the use of paper money, seeing it as an imitation of a Western practice. About two hundred samurai launched their first attack on a local government military compound and killed or wounded more than three hundred conscripts, who were mostly peasants. The government troops surrounded the compound and eventually killed all the rogue samurai. By morning, after a night of bitter fighting, more than five hundred people were dead.

The Shinpuren rebellion sparked a series of uprisings by samurai in other parts of the country. Although nearly all the rebellions were easily put down by government forces, the anti-Western sentiment fueled by the samurais' audacity continued to grow. One young samurai wrote of his anger and disillusionment with the government:

What happened to their traitorous hearts?
They sold the country to the dirty foreigners and ordered us to
give up our weapons and swords, a decree never heard before or
since. . . .
We've reached a point we can take no more.
We warriors can only do our utmost to save tens of thousands of
people,
Today, our last, on the road to the other world.[11]

In 1878, the samurai of the remote area of Satsuma—the region that was bombarded by the British warships in 1862—launched a full-scale attack on the government. Under the direction of the national hero and former government minister, Saigo Takamori, thirty thousand of them, armed only with swords and bows, took on the emperor's forces with their Western tactics and weaponry. After months of bitter fighting, the Satsuma samurai were defeated, and the great Saigo committed ritual suicide. This would be the last internal rebellion against the Meiji regime.

Getting people to own the transition and become responsible players in forging the pathway forward is essential leadership work. It is not easy. On the contrary, it is exceptionally demanding. The emperor and his team did considerable work with the old feudal lords—the daimyo—but were neglectful of the needs, feelings, and aspirations of the samurai. And, sure enough, it was many samurai who put up the greatest resistance and refused to "get in the boat" to make the journey into the future.

To ensure that there were no internal rebellions at IBM, Lou Gerstner needed his "daimyo" on board. He had to create a dynamic team of internal change agents to reach every employee and enroll them in the new direction. After explaining the changes that were needed, Gerstner gave his top 420 senior managers a choice. "Those of you who are uncomfortable with it, you should think about doing something else. Those of you who are excited by it, I welcome you to the team, because I sure can't do it alone."[12] He then traveled the world to meet with regional managers and staff to explain the new strategy and build ownership. He didn't simply present the direction; he listened. Every opportunity he had, he engaged his staff in conversation, provoked them with questions, heard their fears, and incorporated their suggestions. Through this interactive process, clarity of direction was refined, and responsibility for the journey was enhanced.

The Great Leap Backward

Sometimes dogmatic and arrogant authority figures provide counterfeit leadership and take their group backward rather than forward, because they do not understand what it means to generate ownership and personal responsibility for a transition. In such a state, invariably the group, or some factions, will deceive the boss—and in doing so, jeopardize all progress. Consider the transition that Mao Tse-tung tried to make in China in 1958, before the Cultural Revolution. This transition was known as "The Great Leap Forward." In reality, it was a great leap backward. The people loved Mao and did not turn against him, but because they did not "own" the transition, they subverted the process. They wanted to please Mao, not by doing the right thing but by *appearing* to do the right thing.

Rapid industrialization, Mao asserted, would offer solutions to many of the country's problems—including the ability to produce or purchase food for a growing population. To fulfill his grand vision, Mao called for higher productivity from workers and peasants, ordering them to form "People's Communes" all across the country. These communes were expected not only to increase agricultural output but also to produce steel, which Mao declared to be the key ingredient in the industrialization process. The people were urged to build small furnaces that could melt and refine whatever scrap iron or metal goods could be found, including spoons, knives, pots, doorknobs, bed frames, tools, shovels, and small machinery. Furnaces had to be kept going night and day to meet Mao's production goals, but the problem was that sufficient coal was not widely available in the countryside. In areas already experiencing a shortage of coal or timber, the people used chairs, tables, and even coffins to heat their furnaces.

Mao's personal physician, Dr. Zhisui Li, visited the countryside with Mao and noted:

> The backyard furnaces had transformed the rural landscape. They were everywhere, and we could see peasant men in a constant frenzy of activity, transporting fuel and raw materials, keeping the fires stoked. At night, the furnaces dotted the landscape as far as the eye could see, their fires lighting the skies.

> Every commune we visited provided testimony to the abundance
> of the upcoming harvest. The statistics for both grain and steel
> production were astounding. "Good news reporting stations"
> were set up in the communal dining halls, each station compet-
> ing with nearby brigades and communes to report—red flags
> waving, gongs and drums sounding—the highest, most extrava-
> gant figures. The excitement was contagious. I was infected, too.
> Naturally, I could not help wonder how rural China could be so
> quickly transformed. But I was seeing that transformation with
> my own eyes.[13]

Dr. Li soon learned that this whole event was staged to impress
Mao. The party secretaries had ordered furnaces to be constructed all
along the route that Mao and his entourage were to travel. In one area,
the local party secretary had rice plants from distant fields uprooted and
replanted along the route to give Mao the impression of an abundant
crop. Adding to the absurdity, electric fans were used to generate enough
wind and air to reinvigorate the plants as they were beginning to die.

This drama extended into the realm of steel production as well.
Given their primitive methods, much of the steel that was produced by
the peasants was useless. It would often crack and lacked the strength
and texture to be of much use beyond making knives and spoons. This
was the irony, for each family had gathered all their household metal
goods such as knives and spoons, melted it down, and then produced
more knives and spoons. Most people thought this a bitter joke, but they
dared not raise it with the authorities. In fact, on one of their visits, Mao
and Dr. Li thought they were seeing some wonderful samples of steel
produced from backyard furnaces. The products actually had been produced by steel workers at a proper factory and brought to the peasant
commune in an attempt to impress Mao. "All of China was a stage," wrote
Dr. Li, "and the people performers in an extravaganza for Mao."[14]

The hype and euphoria of the Great Leap Forward led many people
to exaggerate their abilities, cover up their errors, and even lie about
their accomplishments. As one farmer said, "We really believed that with
the right attitude you get the corn to grow higher."[15] The "can do" attitude produced an unhealthy competition among the communes, with
each trying to outdo the other in an attempt to display their loyalty and
commitment to Mao and the Communist Party. If one commune committed to get 150 tons of grain per acre, another one would say it would
produce 180 tons. One commune's governing committee agreed to go
for 470 tons. When one of its members challenged the realism of setting

such an exaggerated target, he was accused of being an enemy of the Communist Party.

Within two years, this absurd group dynamic generated a huge shortfall in food for most of the population. Dr. Li recalled, "I did not know it then, but China was tottering on the brink of disaster. The leading cadres of the party . . . were ingratiating themselves with Mao but disregarding the welfare of hundreds of millions of peasants."[16] Due to mismanagement, deceit, and several natural disasters that further reduced agricultural production in some parts of the country, China experienced a severe famine unlike anything the nation had experienced in recent history. In the years immediately following the commencement of the Great Leap Forward, more than thirty million people needlessly died from starvation.

The Great Leap Forward may seem like a gross caricature of a transition challenge gone utterly wrong. Yet the underlying trends and patterns illustrated by this example are in fact all too common in the behavior of organizations and communities of every size and type. When a boss, attempting a transition, imposes his or her plan without testing the validity of the assumptions informing the plan, then danger awaits. The people will deceive the boss if they can, or they will resist the boss if they are able—unless the boss and the group can discover the errors of judgment, make them discussable, and then make the necessary mid-course corrections.

A transition challenge is thus made easier—and given a much greater chance of success—if management can provide a recurring mechanism for getting the people to take full possession of the vision. If people accept the reality of their situation, see a point to the journey, and understand their role in making the journey, they are much more likely to tell their boss—and each other—the truth about their concerns and the problems they see, and not get caught up in the hype and euphoria of change or succumb to the delusions or whims of the dominant authority figure. The people thereby can contribute to the transition not by following the leader deferentially but by generating a rich set of feedback processes that shape, develop, and refine the solutions to the problems they confront, and allow for corrective action as new insights take form.

Even in the middle of the river, Odin the ferryman carefully studied the currents, checked the direction of the wind, and monitored the moods of his people. His quest for new wisdom kept him alert to the need to adjust the vision as appropriate. The leadership task, therefore, must constantly be to ask, "Where are the people at emotionally? How are they coping? Are they contending with reality? Are they taking responsibility for the journey? And, does this direction still make sense?" Depending on the answers, the orienting purpose might need to be modified, even discarded. But if the people feel like they own the journey and feel like they can raise fears and concerns, they will be much more likely to be honest in their endeavors and less likely to deceive.

Determine what must be preserved, and help people deal with losses

Often in their rush to change, leaders do not give adequate attention to what must be preserved, honored, and cherished.[17] This is a vital aspect of leading a transition—to ensure that essential aspects of the culture are not discarded but kept to enrich the life of the group and to maintain continuity and well-being. There will always be something of value in the system that needs to be retained. Finding those values, practices, and traditions and protecting them will lessen the resistance because people will see some reassuring aspects of their life that can give comfort in times of uncertainty. The challenge of leadership is to work with the people to determine what it is that truly must be honored, and can actually be of value, as the transition unfolds.

Of course, all groups hold some values, habits, and practices that one would not want to carry forward. I think of the Iban and Kelabit peoples I lived with in Borneo and how, less than a century ago, they had to discard their practice of headhunting. Headhunting had a significant impact on their cultural identity as so much of their process of development as a human being was attached to this activity. It was a ritual for transitioning from boyhood to manhood. Also, the more heads that could be gathered in a village, the more protected and strengthened the people felt. Nevertheless, after being pressured by the British governor, with a significant degree of reluctance they gave up this cherished tradition (although during World War II, the British actually encouraged them to take Japanese heads).

IBM had its version of "headhunting" practices that no longer served a useful purpose and needed to be discarded. But Lou Gerstner also knew that in leading the transition, he needed to preserve many aspects of the culture. "I came to realize soon after arriving," he wrote, "that there were—and are—tremendous strengths in the company's culture—characteristics that no one would want to lose. If we could excise the bad stuff and reanimate the good, what resulted would be an unbeatable competitive advantage."[18] Gerstner worked hard to highlight those strengths and ensure that they were not lost or corrupted in the bold venture to transform the company.

The leadership task is to determine what values, symbols, and practices can be preserved and to develop a strategy for protecting them, and to dispense with the values, symbols, and practices that impede progress. The process of figuring out what is essential and what is unessential can be enormously difficult, particularly when the group or institution has overextended itself and people are in a mad rush "to get to the other side."

In the rush to transition, the Japanese during the 1880s and 1890s gave up much of their culture and traditions and hastily, even thoughtlessly, embraced Western values and practices. Basil Hall Chamberlain, a British scholar in Japan, advised his fellow Westerners:

> Whatever you do, don't expatiate in the presence of Japanese
> of the new school, on those old, quaint, and beautiful things
> Japanese which rouse our most genuine admiration. . . . Speak-
> ing generally, the educated Japanese have done with their past.
> They want to be somebody else and something else than what
> they have been and still partly are.[19]

By the end of the century, however, the loss of tradition and their mimicry of the West had generated feelings of self-doubt and confusion, among both the old and the young. One Japanese student wrote, "What is today's Japan? The old Japan has already collapsed, but the new Japan has not risen. What religion do we believe in? What moral and political principles do we favor? It is as if we were wandering in confusion through a deep fog, unable to find our way."[20] Many people were seeking something in their past that they could honor and esteem, something that need not be sacrificed in the name of progress. There was no consensus, or even debate, on what was redeemable from that heritage. As a result, this part of the transition process was poorly managed by the Meiji government.

Eventually, sensing the tiredness of the people and empathizing with the losses they were feeling, the government sought to reclaim and reemphasize many traditional values—but for questionable purposes. In the 1890s, traditional values were openly exploited to fuel a growing nationalism that was to emphasize military power and territorial expansion.

For a long time the Japanese felt like they were inferior to the West, and they now believed that the way to gain respect, even a sense of superiority, was through the expression of power, dominance, and empire building—just as Western powers had done and were continuing to do. The government, therefore, sought to place Japan alongside the great expansionist powers of the world. In doing so, the samurai Bushido spirit was revived, and the old samurai were called back to teach the young people what it meant to be a warrior. With new technology and a newfound sense of identity and pride, the Japanese embarked on the path of war. They attacked China in 1894.

Upon defeating China, the popular intellectual Tokutomi wrote, "We are no longer ashamed to stand before the world as Japanese. . . . Before we did not know ourselves, and the world did not yet know us. But now that we have tested our strength, we know ourselves and we are known by the world. Moreover, we know we are known by the world."[21]

The Japanese victories against China and then Russia served to increase national solidarity and cohesion. This renewed sense of shallow pride led the people to extricate themselves from their period of doubt and inferiority, and thereby put an end to cultural subservience to the West. They began asserting what they felt to be the distinctiveness and superiority of the Japanese way of life. These sentiments coalesced to generate a national ideology that emphasized harmony between ruler and people, loyalty, filial piety, and colonial expansion as inherent in the Japanese character.[22]

The reality was, however, that this new national pride was based on dangerous values that needed military victories and territorial acquisition to sustain. To overcome their feelings of cultural alienation and to inspire pride in their accomplishments they were, as one reformer wrote, seduced into a false sense of pride and a belief that conquest equated with greatness.[23] These values persisted through to World War II and ultimately led to devastating consequences for Japan and many other countries in the Asia Pacific region.

How was it that an open, experimental era gave way so suddenly to an era of narrow-minded, aggressive nationalism? Certainly, in little more than a generation, from 1868 to the turn of the century, Japan made an amazing transition from a predominantly agrarian society to an industrializing nation. It was an extraordinary effort by any standard. But it happened so fast. The conversation in regard to what must genuinely be cherished and preserved was never adequately addressed. The forced opening of the country in 1853 by the Americans had diminished the self-respect and dignity of the people because the opening had been "compelled by foreign intimidation rather than free choice of Japan."[24] It had been a humiliating experience. It served to propel the Japanese people forward, but at an enormous cost. They gave up so much in order to compete and prove themselves in the modern world. And when they realized the consequences of this sacrifice, they turned to the most dodgy aspects of their traditions to revive a sense of pride in being Japanese. In doing so, they ended up pursuing a set of false tasks, namely war and expansionism, to the detriment of real progress.

Become a visible symbol of the transition ideal

Consider the Old Testament story of Moses leading the Israelites from a state of bondage in Egypt to freedom in the Promised Land. According to the Book of Exodus, Moses temporarily left the group to communicate with God on top of Mount Sinai. The summit meeting went on longer than the group anticipated, and the people became quite downhearted and rebellious. In their hunger for someone to provide a visible manifestation of their values and new direction, they created a golden calf to serve as a surrogate god.[25]

I suggest that any group in the midst of a difficult transition challenge when frustrated with their predicament—and without an authority to be a visible manifestation of the transition ideal—will create their version of a golden calf and attach themselves to a set of false tasks and counterfeit issues that have little to do with maintaining the right course and generating sustainable progress. To keep the people from attaching themselves to a golden calf—a false set of tasks and counterfeit issues— the leader must use his or her authority as a means to provide a physical and symbolic presence during the transition. The leader's presence, when combined with questioning, listening, and expressions of encouragement, can be enormously beneficial in reorienting people and giving them a sense of hope.

A few years back I consulted with an executive team of a large insurance company that had embarked on a transition that included a corporate overhaul of the organizational structure through a comprehensive reengineering process. The senior management team rarely stepped out of their offices to interact with employees. For nearly six months they met regularly to analyze data provided by the consulting firm McKinsey and discuss various strategic alternatives. The midlevel managers and staff were confused and frustrated. Feeling left in the dark, they were anxious about what was happening and what they should be doing. This frustration produced a cynical mood and led many good people to leave the organization.

I raised this concern in a meeting with the senior management team. The CEO said, "We have so much planning work to do. Besides, I don't want any of my managers speaking with staff until we can all speak with one voice." I suggested that they needed to provide not just a directive voice to staff but an encouraging voice. They also needed to listen to people. The CEO and his team got the message and eventually, like Moses, left the mountain top and returned to the organizational wilderness where the people were in an anxious state. Many people had attached themselves to a "golden calf" and were engaged in counterproductive political games, not attending to quality customer service, and feeling generally disconnected from the mission of the business. And, given their general sense of alienation, many of the midlevel executives whom I spoke with admitted to distorting, even lying about, crucial performance data that would determine their budgets for the coming year. Simply stated, the people's passion for success, commitment to act with integrity, and trust in the institution had diminished significantly over the previous six months due to the benign neglect of the senior authorities during this transition period.

Leaders must wisely and responsibly use their power to be a visible symbol of the values and opportunities that change affords. As I explained in the first chapter, all groups are inclined, like chimpanzee communities, to look to their "alpha" for reassurance and direction. At times it is a burden for the chief authority figure and his or her team to be the symbolic representation of the transition promise, particularly when every aspect of the leader's behavior is scrutinized and assigned meaning by the group, but it is an essential role in a transition challenge—one from which the leader cannot and should not flee—nor is it a role that can be completely delegated.

The role should not be used to generate dependency or compliance but be used to help people deal with reality—to orient them. If no one provides the symbolic function of orienting the group, the people can all too easily regress. Certainly, the role and function of the transition ideal, in the eyes of the people, contain distortions of reality that the leader must manage. The role also exaggerates the people's sensitivity to any flaws in the leader. For example, I remember assisting a CEO in transitioning his organization from a centralized bureaucracy to empowered local districts. One day a midlevel executive told me that the CEO was not serious about the change process. Clearly she was distraught and disappointed. I asked her why she felt that way. She responded that she had recently been in the elevator with him and he never said hello to her, nor was he smiling. She concluded from this interaction that the CEO was cold, aloof, and lacking in commitment. Because I was the CEO's adviser, I knew how committed he was. He was an exceptional man with extraordinary zeal. When I confronted him about the incident, he explained that he travels up and down in the elevator a dozen times a day and generally gives a nod to whomever he meets, but at times he is deep in thought and may not notice who is there. He was surprised that the woman took it so personally.

While it is plainly impossible to meet everybody's emotional needs and expectations, those who would lead need to realize that complex psychological dynamics are at play. Trivializing this aspect of human behavior and not taking responsibility for it is like driving a car and not taking advantage of the gears. You still might get to your destination, but it will certainly take longer and might do great damage to the vehicle.

Emperor Meiji worked hard to generate and maintain the commitment of the Japanese people to the transition process, particularly in the early years before a parliamentary system of government was established and the politicians and bureaucrats took control. Through his interactions and informal behavior, the Mikado showed the people that the transition could be made. Past emperors would rarely venture out of their palace, and they certainly would not interact with commoners. Emperor Meiji broke with this tradition and made hundreds of visits to schools, businesses, villages, and government offices. The local newspaper in Nagasaki reported that after the emperor had visited their city, he had been successful in "shaking the people out of their ignorance, eradicating their narrow-mindedness, and weeding out the thorns that lay in the road to progress."[26] Given the respect the people had for the emperor, his literal presence was both inspirational and reassuring.

Those who seek to lead must ascertain how they should embody the ideal and represent the values of change to the people. It might mean smiling at everyone when in the elevator or joining staff for lunch in the corporate dining room. On the other hand, such practices might be irrelevant to the success of the transition and simply be a waste of time. Each group and each transition might need a different combination of visual and symbolic gestures. The leader must ask, "What is it that the people need to see in their authorities and leaders in order to be reminded of the spirit of the transition and reorient them in times of doubt?"

One thing is certain: To embody the transition ideal is generally not a one-time activity but an ongoing exercise. When Lou Gerstner thought about what would be required of him to provide leadership for the demanding transition challenge facing IBM, he concluded:

> I knew it would take at least five years. And I knew the leader of the revolution had to be me—I had to commit to thousands of hours of personal activity to pull off the change. I would have to

be up-front and outspoken about what I was doing. I needed to get my leadership team to join me. We had to talk openly and directly about culture, behavior, and beliefs—we could not be subtle.[27]

Gerstner realized he had to become the embodiment of the transition ideal and live and breathe new values in all his interactions with people.

To be the embodiment of the transition ideal, however, does not mean acting omniscient and omnipotent. On the contrary, the leader must display a degree of vulnerability and humility. As Odin knew, he was not smart enough to always know what direction to take his people and how to deal correctly with all the troubles they would confront along the way. He had to be the embodiment of the pursuit of wisdom and the passion for discovery. He had to show the people that he was willing to learn, thereby sending a powerful signal to the people that they too should embrace that value. We have all seen authority figures, in their commitment to a certain goal, unrelentingly pursue that goal even though the conditions change. This behavior is dangerous. The commitment should never be framed exclusively in terms of getting to a new destination, but in learning how to deal with the array of problems that ultimately allow the group to get to the new destination. Central to the notion of real leadership is not the relentless pursuit of a goal but the relentless pursuit of reality. The leader engaged in a transition challenge, above all, must be the embodiment of that pursuit. Inevitably, when engaged in a transition challenge, course corrections will need to be made as the people make new discoveries about their capacities, the environment, and the threats to the group and entertain previously unexamined assumptions and unconsidered opportunities. To the degree to which the leader shows openness to new discoveries and a willingness to adjust strategy in the face of new evidence, progress will be made on the transition journey.

REAL LEADERSHIP FOR A
TRANSITION CHALLENGE

- Provide an orienting purpose.
- Get people to own the passage, or they will probably deceive you.
- Determine what must be preserved, and help people deal with losses.
- Become a visible symbol of the transition ideal.

CHAPTER 6

The Maintenance Challenge

Protecting and Sustaining What Is
Essential during Hard Times

N ot all leadership work is about change. Sometimes the challenge is
to hold things together—to protect essential resources, maintain
core values, and keep the enterprise from falling apart. This is the objective of leadership for a maintenance challenge. To illustrate a maintenance challenge, consider the following scenario.

SCENARIO

Imagine you are CEO of one of the world's leading makers of semi-
conductors. Your company is based in San Francisco to take advantage of the abundant talent in the area and to be close to suppliers.
The company has 2,650 employees and annual revenues of more
than $1 billion. The year is 2001, and the change in the economic
conditions of the information technology industry has led to a severe downturn in the market that has jeopardized the survival of
your company. Your quarterly revenues have plunged 50 percent in
six months. The same is also happening for your competitors, and you
watch in disbelief as many of them perish under these conditions.

Through your leadership, you have developed a corporate culture that has strong core values pertaining to the respect and em-
powerment of employees, with an uncompromising focus on quality
and results. But you now face a tough and complicated challenge to
exercise leadership to keep your company from sinking.

Some members of your board are pressuring you to lay off staff—just as most other high-tech companies are doing throughout Silicon Valley. Your concern is that laying off staff will damage the level of trust that employees have in management and the company. This is a real dilemma for you. "I worry about keeping an atmosphere of trust," you ponder. "Lack of trust creeps in when there is a gap between what you say and what you do. If we say 'people are our most important asset,' and then we have layoffs as soon as a downturn comes, we'll destroy trust. Every time someone walks out the front door, it makes the company poorer. If I'm the orchestra conductor and I lose my violin player, the orchestra just won't sound as good—and eventually some people will stop coming to the orchestra."[1]

You conclude that your leadership challenge will be in keeping enough promise in the future from day to day so that the various stakeholders—employees, customers, creditors, and suppliers—do not lose hope and abandon the company. You must get people to shift their values away from the freewheeling expansiveness and boundless optimism of yesterday to hunkering down and protecting the vital resources that have made the company so successful—technical, intellectual, human, and cultural. For the immediate future, you have to get people to take satisfaction simply in surviving—yet you also must maintain their legitimate hope that eventually they will get past the current troubles and be rewarded for their patience and sacrifice. You face a maintenance challenge.

The opening scenario was the real challenge faced by Xilinx's CEO, Willem Roelandts, in 2001.[2] Xilinx did in fact weather the storm and succeeded in maintaining the core values that shaped its distinct and successful corporate culture. What made the difference?

Roelandts was not willing to mortgage the company's future for short-term actions. He insisted that the human resources department work with him to orchestrate a process to help the company protect and preserve vital resources without massive downsizing. Through a combination of actions that included taking a tiered approach to pay cuts (the CEO taking the largest cut), providing sabbaticals, offering extended vacation leave, forgoing annual bonuses, and shutting the company down for two weeks, the company was able to survive.

Of particular importance in helping employees make the necessary sacrifices were the "managing in tough times" conversations that took place throughout the company. Through forthright and open dialogue that addressed the realities of the marketplace, the financial condition of the business, and the needs of employees, the staff understood why sacrifices were needed and willingly adjusted their behavior accordingly. By virtue of the staff's participation in the process, combined with the CEO's wise and compassionate behavior, the company succeeded—in fact, it became an even better company. In 2003, Xilinx ranked fourth in *Fortune* magazine's top one hundred companies to work for in the United States.

The Nature of a Maintenance Challenge

Maintenance leadership is needed to hold a group, community, organization, or country together when it is under threat. The work for people in such a predicament is to face the reality that their survival is at stake and do what is required to preserve resources and maintain a level of energy that can allow the system to survive until the threat passes. For example, in a closed thermodynamic system, when the measure of thermal energy needed to maintain the system is unavailable, the system goes into a state of entropy—the steady and inevitable deterioration of the system. This is also true for human systems. When the system no longer has the necessary ingredients for survival, the system will deteriorate—unless leadership can be provided to revitalize the system.

The symptoms of a maintenance challenge are as follows:

- The group or enterprise is under a threat that the people cannot resolve simply by ignoring it or moving away from their current environment.
- There are significant hindrances to the group improving its lot, such as crushing debt, lack of capital resources, enslavement to a foreign power, or a severe downturn in growth.
- The mission or purpose for existing as a group has been weakened or lost, and people see no reason for staying or contributing and therefore are beginning to give up or flee.

The *people* in a maintenance challenge are generally in a state of trepidation and anxiety. The group is under threat due to dysfunctional internal practices or an external enemy, or some combination of these factors. The group's resources are eroding and they can no longer deliver on their mission. The people are at a loss in regard to what they must do to survive.

The *barrier* that impedes progress consists of the attitudes and practices of the people that lead them to further jeopardize the value and resources they have amassed. In other words, when under threat or when the group is in a state of decay, it is easy for people to become disheartened and disillusioned and fall into despair. In their depressed state, the people might simply "give up" and no longer try to survive or protect what resources they have left. Or they might lash out at the external force in a rash manner, putting themselves at even greater risk of being wiped out. The reality that the people must face is that the survival of the group is dependent on collaborative effort, persistence, a clear head, shared sacrifice, and a significant dose of inner strength.

The *promise* in a maintenance challenge is that the remaining value and resources of the people can be protected and that the people will eventually weather the storm and survive if wise and prudent leadership can be provided.

To exercise real leadership for a maintenance challenge, the leader must be able to draw on a wide range of tools and strategies to ensure continued survival and cohesion of the group or organization. Leadership interventions might include provoking the group to face the reality of the threat when they would prefer to be in denial; providing inspiration when the people are despondent and losing hope; reassuring people when they are having doubts; chastising the group when they violate their own cherished ideals and aspirations; providing a strong, symbolic presence that embodies the values critical to the group's survival; getting the various factions to distribute the pain and loss of contraction; and preparing the people for active defense.

Think of Britain in 1940, under regular attack by the Nazi bombers, struggling simply to survive until circumstances changed for the better. No one thought of bold, sweeping counterstrokes to win the war; it was a time to hang on grimly and live day to day. While Winston Churchill worked with potential allies in the United States to bring about a realignment of global forces, Britain's sole imperative was to avoid decisive defeat and endure its ordeal without collapsing. Short on food, munitions, raw materials, aircraft, productive capacity—short on *everything*—and faced by nightly bombing and the threat of invasion by a relentless enemy, Britain in 1940 was the epitome of a community facing an extreme maintenance challenge. "I have nothing to offer but blood, toil, tears, and sweat," Churchill declared, and he invited the people to join him in doing the maintenance work of protecting their families and defending the country.

In a maintenance challenge, the resources (knowledge or material) for survival may be lacking, due to neglect by group members or forces beyond the control of the group, as in wartime Britain. The shortage of resources can cascade through the group, leaving people demoralized. Keeping meaning, energy, and commitment strong when times are tough is a demanding adaptive challenge. People can easily get distracted by outside enticements, fall into a state of despair, flee to what they perceive to be a safer place, or surrender to the conquering force. They may become so tired, dispirited, and weak that they are no longer willing to do the work required to sustain themselves. When these things happen, the social fabric of the group or community might unravel, its mission can become meaningless, and the process of decay can swiftly set in.

While the plight of the British people during World War II was an extreme predicament, maintenance work should be going on all the time. To ensure that a group or organization does not simply survive but can thrive, leadership should be attending to the *maintenance tasks* of keeping the group healthy, viable, and relevant—in the same way that a person should maintain the body and mind through constant exercise and good eating habits. The sense of purpose and relevancy of the institution, if left unattended, can steadily erode over time. The people may not notice the process of erosion due to their habitual behavior. Therefore, the leader must get the people to responsibly maintain their institution and adjust it to accommodate the changing conditions.

The new prime minister of Singapore, Lee Hsien Loong, spoke to the importance of maintenance tasks to keep the system functioning well: "We can never afford to be satisfied with the status quo, even if we are still okay, even if our policies are still working. People say, 'If it ain't broke, don't fix it.' I say, if it ain't broke, better maintain it, lubricate it, inspect it, replace it, upgrade it, try something better, and make it work better than before."[3] In Singapore's case, the system was functioning well, and the country did not face a maintenance challenge requiring dedicated resources to handle the problem. But the prime minister was highlighting the importance of doing the routine maintenance work to keep the system from breaking down and operating at superior levels.

In some maintenance situations, the leader can only draw on the slender resources of the group to help it tolerate its anxiety and pain until better times arrive. Such a situation is often hard, as no one wants to admit that only a few options are left and that the best the group can hope for may be merely to endure a day at a time. Therefore, in meeting these challenges, the task of leadership often begins with helping the group face the reality of its predicament. Only then can it stave off threats and try to remain healthy enough to flourish again when times are better. This was the challenge faced by Weary Dunlop and his men in the jungles of Asia during World War II. This unusual case illustrates the demanding leadership work associated with preserving a group and their resources until better days.

The Case of Weary Dunlop

In February 1942, after spending nearly two years at war against the Germans and Italians in the Middle East, Edward "Weary" Dunlop, an Australian lieutenant colonel and doctor, was transferred to the Indonesian island of Java to lend support to the Australian, British, New Zealand, and Dutch troops who were resisting a seemingly unstoppable Japanese advance throughout Southeast Asia.

In the first few of months of 1942, Dunlop watched Malaya and then Singapore get gobbled up by the Japanese onslaught. When the Japanese arrived, Dunlop, along with his doctors, nurses, and patients, was taken into captivity. At the prison camp, where thousands of other Allied prisoners were held, the mood was one of despondency, depression, and total bewilderment. No one had expected the Japanese to defeat the Allied forces so swiftly. Troops and civilians alike had been led to believe that the mighty British army and its Allies could easily repel any enemy, particularly the Japanese. And there they were, men and women from Australia, Britain, and Holland, now rotting in the enemy's prison camps deep in the jungles of Asia.

The enlisted men harbored deep anger toward their senior officers who, they believed, had failed to plan adequately for an enemy invasion and underestimated Japanese strength and strategy. This anger surfaced in the men's unwillingness to show respect, trust, or confidence toward officers who now appeared just as lost, confused, and depressed as themselves. The situation was so bleak that senior officers were booed, heckled, and even beaten by their own men.[4]

Although the British and Australian colonels and generals tried to provide some order and discipline in the camp, clearly it was an onerous task. The men refused to follow the traditional textbook kind of military leadership that the officers bravely tried to display. Morale had hit rock-bottom. The camp's senior officers realized that they no longer had the respect and regard needed to hold the people together, and they searched for someone who could. Even though he had never commanded combat troops in battle, and even though he was not a senior officer, Dunlop was asked to take on that role.

After ten months as head of the POWs in the Java camp, Dunlop was sent to a new camp in Siam (Thailand). In his dual capacity of commanding officer and camp surgeon, he had the care and responsibility for more than one thousand troops, mostly Australian and British. This group was later called "The Dunlop Thousand." The Japanese used these men to build a continuous strategic rail line between Burma and Siam. After the war, this project achieved lasting international notoriety as the infamous Burma Railway.

For the POWs, this was to be a war within a war. Though deprived of their arms, they were nonetheless in a bitter daily fight for their sanity and dignity, and particularly their lives. Colonel Laurens van der Post, a fellow prisoner with Weary Dunlop, said it best: "We were engaged in a new war, a war for physical and moral survival, a war against disease, malnutrition and a protracted process of starvation as well as against disintegration from within by the apparent helplessness and futility of life in the prisons of an impervious, archaic and ruthless enemy."[5] This became the leadership challenge of Weary Dunlop: to help his men survive when the odds against survival were very high. He needed them to endure the daily humiliation and beatings, and preserve the belief that they would get through the experience and one day return home to their families.

The following section illustrates the principles of real leadership for a maintenance challenge, with examples from Weary Dunlop's experience and other cases.

Real Leadership for a Maintenance Challenge

Keep the fire burning: maintain hope

One vital aspect of leadership for a maintenance challenge lies in keeping the fire of hope burning. For any group to survive, its sense of purpose and hope must be strong enough to keep people from giving up or fleeing.

Under normal circumstances, people stay with an organization or group because of a shared sense of purpose or because they are paid enough to make it worth their while to stay. But when the group faces a maintenance challenge, caused by some internal or external threat, the usual reasons for people to work together are not enough to keep them focused on the tasks before them. Therefore, anyone who would exercise leadership for a maintenance challenge must focus on keeping the fire of hope burning to maintain the engagement of people—even when the threatening conditions make the organization a painful and possibly perilous place to be.

By *hope* I do not mean eternal optimism or unrealistic fantasies. The hope of leadership is grounded not in some delusional belief but in a realistic appraisal of the situation and an acknowledgment that if enough good people can be mobilized to do something about the problem, they will have a better chance to make it through the troubled times.

Hope is important. It gives people the capacity to deal with the bleakness of their predicament. When what one is doing holds little meaning, or when the effort expended does not seem worth the little return, people will be inclined to reduce their efforts, give up, or flee. While this evocative component of real leadership is needed even when a group or organization is prospering, it is even more crucial when conditions threaten the survival of the group.

In the case of Xilinx, the CEO had to get his employees to realize that they were valued and that through shared sacrifice and committed effort they could prevail against the "forces" eating away at the viability of the company. Similarly, in the jungles of Burma—a radically different setting from Silicon Valley—Weary Dunlop had to get his men to face the reality that (1) their lives did matter, (2) there were people—friends and family—who loved them and wanted to see them alive, and (3) evil must never be allowed to prevail.

Each day, Dunlop worked to convey the message of hope and persistence to his men, through his demeanor, speech, and actions. He tried to make an abnormal and barbaric situation as normal and civil as possible in order to keep the demons of despair at bay. A former POW, when asked what was it that made Weary so popular with the men, responded:

> It was his easy way. . . . He chatted away to everybody. . . . He
> went about deliberately encouraging people. Making light of
> their problems. . . . You couldn't convey what Weary conveyed,
> and that was hope—that you never knew what was around the

corner, and we're having successes. It didn't matter how few. He was able to focus on them, whereas others with the best will in the world were just overwhelmed by the losses.[6]

Dunlop could not afford to let his men succumb to despair. It was all too easy to give up and die, or make a desperate attempt to escape and be killed in the process. While he used his authority to maintain order and discipline in the camp, he did not use his authority to distance himself from his men. This was not a time for excessive displays of protocol, dominance, or privilege. They were all in this together, and through shared effort and sacrifice, they could survive. Realizing what was required to survive, Dunlop easily and freely mixed with his men. A word of encouragement, a joke, anything that brought a sense of dignity and humanity to the men in this miserable predicament could help keep the fire of hope burning. Bill Griffith, a young corporal who lost his sight and both arms just prior to joining Weary and the other prisoners in the Java camp, had this to say about him:

> With these injuries as a young man I could not envisage life at all, living like this. But Weary used to come along and he'd say, "You'll be alright, it will take time." He was a comfort then. He really was. I was only a kid, I was 21. . . . He used to instill optimism in me. He said all wasn't lost. And there was something about him that gave me hope for the future. As calm as could be was Weary, and he sort of transmitted it to me ever so quick, as soon as he'd come. I felt more secure in every way. . . . There was a certain magic when he was around, somehow.[7]

This role can be a heavy burden for a leader—to constantly be the one to shoulder the work of reviving people's spirits and encouraging them to keep going. Nevertheless, the presence of someone to anchor people in hope and shepherd them through a period of great trial is essential if the group is to survive. In that role, the leader must manage his or her own emotions, fears, and needs and cultivate a capacity to hold steady and not collapse under the load. He or she should have a strong and profound sense of purpose—so much so, that helping others is actually consistent with, and even rejuvenates, that sense of purpose.

The Jewish rabbi Maimonides, in twelfth-century Yemen, understood what was needed by way of leadership to keep the fire burning when his people faced a difficult maintenance challenge. At the time, Jews were suffering from terrible and unrelenting religious persecution. Many members of the community were killed or imprisoned. Whole villages were destroyed. This, in turn, led many members to flee, actually abandoning their beliefs and converting to other religions. The community was anxious, disillusioned, and losing hope.

Maimonides, in 1172, wrote a series of letters to the Jewish community of Yemen to inspire the people and assist them in coping with their grim predicament. He encouraged the people to remain steadfast in their commitment to the faith and hold true to their most cherished values. The epistles had an enormous impact on the Yemenite Jews and helped in maintaining the community and breathing hope into their everyday activities. Without resorting to delusion or fantasy or promoting the need for retribution, Maimonides played a crucial role in keeping the community from breaking apart, preserving its essence, and sustaining its strength.

In his letters, Maimonides did what every leader should do when confronting a difficult maintenance challenge: He displayed enormous compassion for the suffering of others and showed that he understood the threat, their fears, and their needs. Yet, according to his biographers, Maimonides "is never wholly overwhelmed by the sufferers' perspective and maintains a critical distance from his audience, enabling him to provide anchor points from which to transcend their immediate framework of experience."[8] This is an important aspect of leadership for a maintenance challenge—to provide anchor points to stabilize people's tendency to flee from the work of maintaining the value they have amassed as a community. Anchor points might include a reminder of the values, ideals, traditions, and aspirations that give purpose to life, particularly in a time of suffering. And by keeping a measure of emotional distance, Maimonides was able to speak to the community in a way that gave recognition to their plight but also provided a means for transcending the hopelessness that had gripped their souls. Steadily, he shifted their perspective from total despair to a window of hopefulness, helping the people find reasons and strategies to keep going, honor their faith, and maintain their community.

Maintain the mission and core values

All groups must maintain their sense of mission and core values if they are to survive. However, some groups are not under immediate threat, but the fire of purpose dwindles due to the people's failure in attending to the routine maintenance tasks related to the values and practices that are important in defining the group and giving purpose to their activities. When the mission becomes blurred and cracks in the core values appear due to neglectful behavior, the group is in potential danger and might suffer serious consequences. Consider what happened with the Catholic Church recently due to negligence in maintaining its mission and core practices: the Church erupted in a series of sexual abuse scandals in many different parts of the world. One of the most heated areas was Boston, which was under the direction of Archbishop Cardinal Bernard Law.

On the afternoon of June 14, 2002, Cardinal Law stood before the press looking distraught, tired, and remorseful. He had just come from a meeting with his fellow bishops where they addressed the sex scandals facing the Church.

> I said to the Bishops that never in my wildest, worst nightmare could I have imagined doing what I was then doing, and I discussed with them some of what the past six months has been like for me personally: the distrust, the anger, the sense of betrayal, the fact that for many I've become an object of contempt. I then pointed out that what added to that was the recognition that Boston, and I personally, had placed an added burden upon the Bishops, and I apologized to them for that.[9]

Six months later, the cardinal resigned.

Law had been archbishop of Boston since 1984 and was one of the most influential Catholic authorities in the United States. In January 2002, the *Boston Globe* reported details of how he had allowed Father John J. Geoghan to remain in the ministry despite knowing that Geoghan was a child molester. The story triggered a nationwide furor over the Church's handling of sexually abusive priests. As the head of the Catholic Church in Boston, Cardinal Law became the focus of the people's anger and disappointment. In essence, he had failed to do the necessary maintenance work in his diocese.

The series of scandals in the Catholic Church was a symptom of a deeper problem—the problem of parts of the Church ignoring its mission, core values, and even common sense. Many of the Church's authorities ignored the maintenance tasks and provided counterfeit leadership by sweeping the problem under the rug. The mission and vision of the Church became blurred. Hence, many priests and others in the Church had no useful standards for judging their actions and priorities. They lacked a sense of purpose that was strong enough to keep their personal hungers in check. Therefore, too many of them got seriously distracted by their personal hungers and ended up harming others, themselves, and the Catholic Church in pursuit of those hungers. In addition, many of the authorities, rather than deal with these manifestations as an indication that something was lacking in the system as a whole, tolerated the aberrant behavior and bypassed the maintenance work of sustaining the core values of justice, service, and charity.

The work of maintaining the mission and sustaining core values and essential practices is critical work for any group. There can be dire consequences when people get distracted. Even NASA, with some of the most brilliant minds in the world and being an organization charged with the noble mission of putting humans into space, became distracted by a false set of tasks and failed to protect its core values. Given that people got distracted, lives were lost. On February 1, 2003, the space shuttle *Columbia* was destroyed in a disaster that claimed the lives of all seven of its crew. A seven-month investigation into the cause of the accident revealed significant flaws in the leadership of NASA. The members of the investigative commission asked, "Why did NASA continue to fly with known foam debris problems in the years preceding the *Columbia* launch, and why did NASA managers conclude that the foam debris strike 81.9 seconds into *Columbia's* flight was not a threat to the safety of the mission, despite the concerns of their engineers?"[10]

The commission recognized that the accident was not a random event but rooted in NASA's management culture. In the wake of the 1987 *Challenger* tragedy, NASA had revamped and expanded its safety programs; a dozen years later, however, the agency's safety infrastructure had grown complacent and reactive. Independent checks and balances of safety processes had been eroded, and safety testing and monitoring had become exceedingly bureaucratized. The procedures generated massive amounts of data but failed to identify and focus on potential problems.[11] While senior management was espousing a commitment to safety, the frequent reorganizations and drive for greater efficiency sent mixed signals to employees and, according to the investigators, "created the conditions more conducive to the development of a conventional bureaucracy than to the safety-consciousness of a research and development organization."[12] Moreover, a competitive win-lose dynamic and a silo mentality had emerged between the divisions of NASA, particularly between managers and engineers. Given the bureaucratic culture and the unhealthy competitive dynamics, a pattern of ineffective communication had developed that left "risks improperly defined, problems unreported, concerns unexpressed."[13]

Had NASA's management vigilantly maintained the core values and essential practices pertaining to safety and superior quality in all of its activities, perhaps lives would not have been lost. (Certainly that is the conclusion of the *Columbia* Accident Investigation Board.) Understanding what core values and essential practices are needed for successful delivery of the mission of the organization, and then devoting time and resources to fostering and maintaining those core values and essential practices, is a critical component of real leadership.

Attend to the little big things

In maintaining the mission and core values of the organization or community, and the well-being of the group during dire times, little things can make a big difference. As Weary Dunlop knew, even a smile can make a big difference. A fellow POW remarked that

> Weary could get more from the men with a smile than an army of blooming colonels wielding big sticks. The blokes would do anything for him. He just had that quiet, assured way. "Do as I do, not do as I say," that was Weary. He gave confidence. He looked assured and he was assured and he was just brimful of confidence.[14]

The CEO of Xilinx, Willem Roelandts, also found there was enormous benefit in the little acts of leadership. He discovered that simply allowing people to come together and talk about their predicament was a useful mechanism for helping people deal with their anxiety and keep the company from falling apart. He and his senior management team joined in the "tough times" conversations, talking forthrightly about the realities of the marketplace, the threats to the organization, the financial condition of the company, and the nature of the sacrifices that needed to be made by management and staff alike. The process was a powerful "little big thing" that served to reenergize people and give them the confidence to remain focused on the work of maintaining quality in all functions of the company's operations and performance.

A group or company need not wait until things go bad to attend to the little big things. A successful company should constantly be attending to the little big things that orient the people to enact the values of the company—as a preventative measure and to inculcate good habits. Hidesaburo Kagiyama, the president of Yellow Hat, exemplified how little things could make a big difference. His company is a highly successful wholesale and retail chain that manufactures and distributes automotive parts throughout Japan.

I was invited to meet with Kagiyama at the corporate headquarters, in a suburb of outer Tokyo, at 6:00 A.M. He was not to be found inside the company but outside with a broom in hand, sweeping neighborhood streets! He invited me to participate. After cleaning the streets, we cleaned the factory grounds and were joined by many employees. Upon completing the grounds, Kagiyama, with me as his apprentice, washed and scrubbed the toilets of the employees.

We did not just clean the toilets, but we polished them as if we were preparing for a royal visitor. Kagiyama showed me how to hold the mop, fold the cloths, scrub the porcelain, fill a bucket with water, and put the materials away when the cleaning was completed. He had a "way" for every aspect of the cleaning process, a way that maximized one's energy and conserved the cleaning resources such as water, detergent, brushes, and mops. The way was exact and included scrubbing in a certain direction, cleaning different objects in a particular order, and doing these things with the right attitude—an attitude that emphasized service to others. When the cleaning was completed, the toilets were sparkling.

At Kagiyama's company, *soji* (the Japanese word for cleaning) was done every day. It was a voluntary activity that was carried out an hour and a half before formally beginning work. Every morning all the company cars were washed, all toilets cleaned, the premises swept, and the rubbish on neighboring streets was gathered. All cardboard boxes and paper collected were sent for recycling. The many drink cans that were gathered daily were taken to an old folks home so they could be sold for money.

Kagiyama explained that the purpose of soji was not just to maintain a clean working environment but to develop a soji mind—a mind that could maintain core values and be the embodiment of the spirit of service. For him, service was not a strategy purely for making money but a strategy for living life. A soji mind finds gratitude, appreciation, and satisfaction out of making others happy. It is a disciplined mind, not cluttered, able to think clearly, and committed to responsible action. It thinks not of itself but in terms of service to others. "You can talk all day long about quality, business, politics, and the environment," Kagiyama said, "but unless you are willing to act your words are empty. Action is truth. This is the core of the soji mind. Begin to take action over that environment that you have immediate control and you begin to make the world a better place. These little things make a big difference."

I asked Kagiyama how his practice of soji related to leadership. He explained that it is through leadership that you break up the self-interested behavior of others—including your own—and keep employees focused on the reality of business success, which to him was providing a quality experience for the customer. "Look at me. I'm not a charismatic man," he said. "I'm a simple man, and through simple contributions great things can be accomplished." Kagiyama then read me a Zen-like poem he had written: "When you enter the house, take off your shoes, place them neatly on the floor, and you will find that life works." For him, and certainly for his company, it was the little things that were done well and with dedication that made the difference.

Of course, not every leader needs to be like Kagiyama and scrub the employees' bathrooms, but they do need to think creatively about what they might do to maintain core values and a focus on the mission. Both Kagiyama and Weary Dunlop were able to transcend the confines of their authority role and provide leadership that was appropriate to the context, versus being constrained by hierarchical and structural relationships.

The leadership work is to ascertain what small actions, symbols, gestures, or events might serve as a way to orient the people to focus on the necessary maintenance activities that will keep them and their group or institution functioning successfully or from deteriorating any further. These little big things are generally easy to do, but they are often neglected in groups under threat or even in the best of times.

When people succumb to their hungers, give them a whack

Much of the leadership work in a maintenance challenge is evocative—you calm the group, reassure them, help them take one step at a time, and maintain a degree of hope to instill a capacity to deal with the demands of each day. However, in dire circumstances, sometimes tough actions need to be taken to keep the group alive. For example, on May 10, 1996, tragedy struck the dozens of climbers on Mount Everest as a ferocious storm enveloped the mountain. One group was stranded in the "death zone" just above twenty-six thousand feet, an area where human life cannot be sustained for long given the altitude and hazardous conditions. The group had been climbing without food for twenty hours and were exhausted and dehydrated. Their oxygen bottles were empty, and they were at serious risk of altitude sickness and cerebral or pulmonary edema. The odds of their making it through the night were slim.

Their strategy for staying alive was to huddle together and keep each other warm and awake. "Keep moving your hands and feet. Say something, shout, keep the guy next to you awake!" Danish climber Lene Gammel-gaard admonished the group. She recalled, "Neal, Tim, Klev, and I take turns shouting, moving. Klev shakes me. I shake him and kick Sandy every few minutes, 'Are you awake? You must not go to sleep. Hold out!'" Gammelgaard and her team survived. The climbers on the other side of Everest were not so lucky—eight died.[15]

Given the precarious predicament of the group in a demanding maintenance challenge, the task of leadership is to "wake people up" with a figurative kick or a whack when people get distracted in order to get them refocused on the work of survival and protection of group re-sources, just as Gammelgaard did with her team on Everest. People in an emotionally vulnerable state can easily succumb to their hungers, fan-tasies, or delusions rather than face the reality of the predicament and do what is required to maintain survival of the group. Some people might go so far as to deny that a problem even exists, while others might be to-tally overwhelmed, give up, or flee. In such a circumstance, a nudge or a whack can make a huge difference—the difference between life and death.

Such was the leadership challenge facing Colleen Rowley. Her or-ganization, the Federal Bureau of Investigation, had become distracted. Too many managers were succumbing to their hungers for power, posi-tion, and control, to the detriment of solving and preventing real crimes. The consequences were bleak. A Senate judicial hearing in 2001 indi-cated that the FBI had a bureaucratic culture riddled with arrogance, fear, and careerism. The headquarters was inclined to micromanage offi-cers and stifle initiative and responsibility. Departments refused to coop-erate with one another, and turf battles were common. A former agent testified: "Hiding behind a wall of arrogance, senior managers hold the belief that they always know what is best for the Bureau. These [man-agers] are intolerant of any suggestion that their way is wrong. They use intimidation and retaliation against anyone who would be so imperti-nent as to challenge their interests."[16]

Although these characteristics are not uncommon for a large govern-ment bureaucracy, they reveal an organization struggling to maintain focus on its mission and sustain core values, practices, and priorities. Turf battles, careerism, and the stifling of initiative are a false set of tasks—destructive forces—that have nothing to do with fighting crime and protecting the country. In fact, they detract from that purpose, as the FBI, in too many cases, belatedly discovered.[17]

After the September 11 terrorist attacks, Rowley decided it was time to intervene and give the organization a whack. Unable to sleep one night because she was troubled over the cultural behaviors that she felt may have contributed to judgment errors in events surrounding the terrorist attacks of September 11, she drove to her office and wrote a thirteen-page memo that outlined her concerns. Her intention was to send the letter to her newly appointed boss, FBI director Robert Mueller. She anguished for days about sending the letter, as she knew she would be putting her job on the line. Not only did she decide to give the letter to Mueller personally, but, given the potency and pervasiveness of the false set of tasks, she distributed copies to members of the U.S. Senate's Intelligence Committee.

Rowley made some bold assertions, one of which would get the attention of the entire nation. She accused the FBI of deliberately obstructing measures that could have prevented the terrorist attacks on that fateful September morning. She also asserted that essential information was not being disseminated to the appropriate people due to interoffice wrangling and turf wars.

Rowley stirred things up. She was eventually called before the Senate to talk about her concerns. In her testimony, Rowley presented a thoughtful and comprehensive analysis of the culture of the FBI. As chief counsel in the Minneapolis field office, she was in a position to know that culture well, having worked for the agency for twenty-one years. She painted a picture of a misaligned organization that was losing touch with its core mission and, as a result, not adequately dealing with the real problems that it had been created to address.

To highlight how many people had lost sight of what was important and were unintentionally pursuing a false set of tasks, Rowley gave a simple yet powerful illustration of a recent event in her Minneapolis office.

> One Sunday, approximately three months ago, I happened to come into our office in Minneapolis for some reason. I bumped into a supervisor who, after only about one year on the desk, told me he was reluctantly going to have to "step down." He had spent several weekends in the office completing "crime surveys," Annual Field Office Reports, pre-inspection program descriptions and other miscellaneous paperwork. The long hours were taking a toll on his family. (He's the father of four little girls.) His anguished decision to step down was, however, not solely due to the time spent away from his family but was more because of the exasperating purposelessness of the endless "reports" that were occupying his time. It's one thing to work around the clock on making a break in a kidnapping case, armored car robbery, terrorist incident, etc., but it's quite another

to have to spend hours engaged in completing the myriad of required "reports" the FBI bureaucracy has spawned in order (at
least in part), to justify its existence! This supervisor who is, in
fact, now relinquishing his management position, happened to be
one of very few who, prior to becoming a supervisor, had a long
and successful background (approximately fifteen years) as a
stellar investigator. The endless, needless paperwork and writing
exercises were actually preventing him from doing his job of su-
pervising the agents on his squad. I think this supervisor's experience is a common problem which has been echoed by many in
the FBI who say it reminds them of the old story, "The Emperor
Has No Clothes."[18]

Colleen Rowley displayed courage in highlighting the dysfunctional
dynamics in the organization in a way that people could not hide from
the problem. Hers was a bold attempt to push back the bureaucratic
forces and uncontrolled hungers for power and territory that were sabo-
taging the mission of the organization.

Keep the destructive forces at bay

Usually when a group or organization faces a maintenance challenge, a dark and destructive force threatens the survival of the group or
organization. A destructive force is an enemy of progress. It can be any
person, group, policy, pattern of behavior, or environmental condition,
from within or without, that seeks to imperil the integrity of the system.
Destructive forces might include the unbridled force of the free market
on a country ill prepared to deal with competition; it could be an invading
enemy; it could be the people's own values, habits, practices, and priorities. These forces endanger the value and worth that has been generated
by the group. The leadership task is to identify the force and protect the
group, to the degree that it is possible, from its malign assault.

For example, parents have maintenance tasks every day in protecting
their children from destructive forces. Groups, companies, and institutions inadvertently subvert parental authority by imposing new values
on children and enticing children into believing that particular items
(e.g., clothes, toys, drugs, foods, music) will make their lives better.
These destructive forces are powerful and unrelenting and will undermine family progress unless they are contended with and kept at bay.

Indeed, all groups and organizations must contend with dark, destructive forces that seek to prey on the system, exploit it, or kill it off.

Bold, moral, and strategic leadership is needed to ensure that the destructive forces do not win. Sometimes the battle is with an external enemy, but sometimes the battle is with one's own organization, one's own culture, with the very people who are supposed to be protecting the system.

Dark Forces Without

Weary Dunlop faced a destructive force from without—the prison guards.

Although he had no weapons but his own courage and moral force, Dunlop worked every day to protect his group from the destructive force that sought to make his men's lives more miserable than they already were. He discovered that a moral stand could have a powerful effect. For example, every day Dunlop and his men were required to work cutting trees and laying tracks for the railway line. It was grueling and even hazardous work, and many men were injured or killed in the process. Some simply collapsed from exhaustion. Guards beat the men to make them work harder or to punish them for alleged infractions. Some guards were excessive in their torment of the POWs. One such guard was Sergeant Okada, known to the men as "Dr. Death."

The sergeant was a ruthless and uncompromising man who repeatedly treated the prisoners in ways that violated the Geneva Convention. One morning he came to Dunlop and asked for forty men for a work detail. Dunlop found his request unacceptable because too many of his men were ill, with some on the verge of death. "You can't have forty men," he told the sergeant. "You can have ten, and that's it!" Okada got angry, finding Dunlop's insolence insulting. With his bayonet in hand, he demanded again that Dunlop give him forty men immediately. "Don't be so bloody ridiculous," Dunlop defiantly responded. "Ten men, that's all you're going to get. The rest are sick, so you're not going to get them." "Why are they sick?" the sergeant demanded to know. Dunlop didn't answer but simply pointed to the camp cemetery, which contained several hundred graves for prisoners who had died. The sergeant then relented, "Very well, today ten men will do."[19]

Clearly, Dunlop assumed the mantle of moral authority. His presence, his courage, his demeanor, and the rightness of his cause all combined to improve the mood of the situation. He repeatedly put himself in harm's way in order to protect his men but was not rash or stupid about doing so. Of course such behavior was always risky, and he was often punished himself. But his courage kept many men alive.

Moral leadership in the face of a destructive force requires an exquisite sensitivity to the mood of the enemy, a fine appreciation for what is at stake, and a sharp awareness of how one's conduct is perceived by the opposing force. The unwillingness to provide such leadership will allow the dark and destructive forces to wreak havoc on the people and resources of the group. But the exercise of leadership could also get one killed or further marginalized. To enhance the chance of success, one should find partners to support the intervention and be very strategic in where and when one intervenes. One should not push more than makes sense given the reality of the predicament. Real leadership should never be about *being right* but getting the adaptive work done. There are times to advance, times to hold steady, and times to retreat.

Dark Forces Within

Sometimes a faction within a group or organization becomes a destructive force and thwarts the advancement of the people as they seek to enact their mission. This faction persists in pursuing a false set of tasks that have nothing to do with progress. For example, I once consulted to an exceptional leader who was the superintendent of education of a large urban district in a southern state. The destructive force that was impeding progress in the school district was none other than the district school board—an elected body of ten people—who were preoccupied with trite politics, grandstanding, corrupt practices of giving school contracts to friends and family members, and trying to excessively control the superintendent for their own particular—and often selfish—purposes. This was a low-performing school district. The students were mostly poor African American and Hispanic children, many from single-parent homes. They needed all the support that they could get. The very adults who were supposed to be championing their interests were actually subverting them by engaging in all manner of political skullduggery.

The superintendent, called here by the pseudonym Betty Henderson, spent more than 80 percent of her time attending to these political distractions and keeping the board from further damaging the school system. Eventually she concluded that the powers of the board would have to be cut back. They had become too much of a dark and destructive force.

Henderson mobilized the business community, state and local legislators, and some of the key "moral" voices of the city to get the government to change the law relating to the duties and responsibilities of the school board. It was a long, painful process riddled with attack and counterattack, played out in public meetings and in the press. The law was eventually passed, and the powers of the board were significantly diminished, thus allowing the superintendent to get on with the work she was hired to do, namely, reform an ailing school district. Henderson succeeded in mobilizing a consensus in the community to reduce the potency of the destructive force, which her four predecessors had tried to do but to no avail. Her predecessors simply gave up, ignored the problem, were fired, or quit in despair. Having the courage and the commitment, combined with a wise leadership strategy, Henderson was able to ensure that the real work of schooling children was at the forefront of all those engaged politically, professionally, or administratively, in the educational system she was overseeing. Maintaining the integrity of the system was the true test of her leadership.

Conclusion

I have observed many organizations struggle with a maintenance challenge, some successfully and some poorly. Often the reason for failure is that the people are not cognizant that they are actually confronted with a maintenance challenge. In other words, they are unaware of the true nature of the threat, what needs to be preserved, and subsequently what kind of leadership is needed to address the challenge. Sometimes the people are in blatant denial and no one wants to admit that there are only a few options left. If the concern of maintenance is undistinguished then the leader and the group have no way of shaping their actions and interventions to attend to the reality that is being avoided, and the group is in danger of breaking apart and the value that it has amassed will be lost. Leaders therefore must be vigilant in looking for the threats from without or within that might damage the value and well-being of the group.

Even in good times maintenance tasks must be attended to with focus and dedication. A leader must be conscientious in maintaining the integrity of the mission, the core values of the enterprise, and essential practices that allow a group to deliver on its purpose. It is not enough to create a vision and expect people to willingly follow, but leaders must intervene, even in small ways, to remind people of what is important. In dire circumstances, when the group is under serious threat, this work is critical. Although progress can never be guaranteed, the chance of progress is greatly enhanced when real leadership is provided and the people face the reality of their condition and take personal responsibility for preserving their resources and surviving until better days.

REAL LEADERSHIP FOR A
MAINTENANCE CHALLENGE

- Keep the fire burning: maintain hope.
- Maintain the mission and core values.
- Attend to the little big things.
- When people succumb to their hungers, give them a whack.
- Keep the destructive forces at bay.

CHAPTER 7

The Creative Challenge

Doing What Has Never Been Done Before

Sometimes, a group hits a wall. It can go no further or be more productive while persisting in its current practices. To break through the wall, transcend the current paradigm, and advance to the next level of performance, the people must create. Consider the following scenario.

SCENARIO

Imagine that you are a senior manager in a large insurance company who oversees the claims-processing activity for the business. The previous four years has seen a significant slump in performance and productivity. You are getting signals from the market that your processes are not as efficient as your key competitors. "We have to change!" you tell people. "As far as I'm concerned, it is change or die." But nobody knows what to do.

You think the solution lies in inventing a completely new type of working environment that would empower people to be creative, resourceful, and accountable. "We treat people like back in the dark ages," you say. "It's disgraceful. No wonder we have these problems." You don't know exactly what kind of work environment you need to create, but you feel it must be team oriented with minimal direct supervision, even totally self-directed.

You go to the senior management committee and make a pitch to the president for funding to support a two-year experiment to

---

see whether you and your team can invent an entirely new way of managing claims offices, something that will be radically different from the prevailing paradigm. Most of the management committee thinks that this is a harebrained idea, but the president gives you the thumbs up. "You've got two years," he says. "See what you can do."

Given that you don't have the support of your colleagues, and given that you only have general ideas and no blueprint for moving forward, in the back of your mind you wonder whether you can succeed. This will be a tough leadership initiative, requiring considerable imagination and persistence. In many ways you feel like a pioneer—you are moving into unknown terrain. Your task is to do what's never been done before. You face a *creative challenge*.

The preceding scenario describes an actual organizational challenge. The manager who attempted to provide leadership for the challenge I shall call by the pseudonym Mary Jones. The company was Aetna Life and Casualty. The project was called the Experimental Office.

Jones pulled together fifty people from throughout the company who wanted to be a part of something new. They were tasked with inventing a cutting-edge claims office from scratch. They would need to design, develop, and run the office, as well as ensure that it was more dynamic, productive, and profitable than the thirty-nine traditional offices scattered across the country. They were expected to be masterful inventors and agents of change. "Just think," she told her people, "this is our version of putting a man on the moon. We are at a new frontier, and this will be, for all of us, the chance of a lifetime."

One year into her two-year creative experiment, Jones's Experimental Office was being hailed as a success; it was written about in business magazines and featured on television. The team members were truly immersed in the creative process, and it was clear that the revolution had begun. Jones was thrilled with her accomplishment. She felt her star was rising, and a huge opportunity had emerged to contribute to the transformation of the larger corporate culture. As a graduate student at Harvard University at the time, I was called in to document the success. Jones and her team wanted to capture the lessons so the concept could be rolled out to other areas of the company.

Six months later, however, to the surprise of everyone, management stepped in and quietly closed the Experimental Office down. They declared the project a failure. Mary Jones could not believe it. The distraught, onetime manager extraordinaire packed her bags and left her New England colleagues for her home state of Texas. She had been banished.

Jones had certainly faced a significant and daunting leadership challenge: how to contribute to creating a more responsible and productive work environment that would add value for the company. The analysis of her case, and others, affords an opportunity to examine the difficulties—problems and opportunities—associated with exercising leadership for a creative challenge.

The Nature of a Creative Challenge

A creative challenge necessitates doing something that has never been done before. It lies in bringing something into existence—an idea, a practice, a product—that can make a positive contribution to the group, organization, or society. It is imaginative and inventive work requiring persistence, exploratory thinking, and constant experimentation.

A creative challenge emerges when a group faces a problem or opportunity that no current strategy or practice can successfully address, and an incremental approach based on developing latent values and resources appears to hold little promise. In essence, the group must invent a solution; they must discover an answer to their predicament, or no progress will be possible. Unlike a development challenge, a creative challenge requires a significant break with the past and an unconstrained leap into the future. The group must produce a hitherto unthought-of response to the problem and then take unprecedented action.

The data indicating a group faces a creative challenge include the following:

- The group must do something for which there is no road map or blueprint—it must literally move into unexplored terrain.

- Some impediment, or threat, is blocking group progress, and no known solution is available to address the problem. The group feels ill equipped to undertake flexible, blue-sky thinking and embrace fundamental change. It is literally stuck.

- An inventory of resources and values within the group reveals that an incremental developmental strategy is inadequate to the challenge. To solve the problem or take advantage of the opportunity, the group must depart radically from its current course—and do so without delay.

In exercising leadership for a creative challenge, as with all the challenges, the leader must examine (1) the condition of the people, (2) the barrier that impedes progress, and (3) the promise or aspiration on the other side of the barrier.

The *people* facing a creative challenge are stuck. They feel like they have hit a wall and are at a loss as to what they must do or how to proceed. The group does not possess in its current repertoire of knowledge the solution to their predicament.

The *barriers* are the limitations and boundaries that contain and refrain the people's thinking—their psychological state (their arrogance, their ignorance, their imaginative capacities), the group culture (what's acceptable or unacceptable in terms of normative behavior), and the prevailing paradigm in which the problem occurs (current knowledge and the repertoire of skills). But the barriers also include those people or groups who are the gatekeepers for the current order and those who might feel threatened by creative work. Psychologist Rollo May wrote, "creativity provokes the jealousy of the gods."[1] Indeed, creative work stirs up an array of emotions in people: some get excited by the process, and some seek to squelch the process because it disrupts the world they know.

The *promise* available in a creative challenge is that if the people can accomplish something that has never done before and produce a breakthrough in their thinking and collective efforts, they can function at a higher level of productivity or profitability, or have a better shot at success. By its very nature, it can be a transformative experience. In a dire situation, creative work can make the difference between life and death.

The leadership task is to generate a mood and orchestrate a process to get the people to transcend their current thinking and discover a successful response or solution to their constraining predicament. This might include either evoking people's imagination through brainstorming or being a perturbing force that stirs the group from its comfort zone. Although this type of work is emotionally and mentally demanding, it can also be fun, since it requires a playful exploration of ideas and a willingness to be deliberately outrageous and provocative. But it can also be discomforting, because to sustain the creative state requires the willingness to challenge prevailing beliefs, tolerate conflict, and play with crazy notions. And, even then there can be no guarantee of success. In fact, the odds that you will fail are very high.

The search for the source of creative power, given how rare and valuable that power is, has been a quest conducted even by the gods. The Norse mythic tradition tells how the great Odin sought the transforming power of creativity. That power was represented in the sacred ring known as Draupner.[2] According to legend, every ninth night another ring, equally as magical, would mysteriously drop from Draupner. These rings gave enormous power to whoever possessed them. Odin's ring, in a mythological sense, symbolizes the fertility of the mind and the creative power needed to address troubling problematic realities. The dropping rings represent the way that one creative insight begets another—a veritable train, or chain, of creative thought. Folklorist R. B. Anderson has noted, "The rings fell from Draupner as drop falls from drop. Ideas do not cling to their parent but live as independent life when they are born; and the idea or thought does not slumber once awakened, but continues to grow and develop in man after man, and generation after generation, evolving constantly new ideas."[3] J. R. R. Tolkien drew from this myth in his writing of *The Lord of the Rings*.

The Odin stories influenced the medieval alchemists. Their magical quest to turn lead into gold was doomed to failure, but their novel and rigorous experimentation laid the foundation for modern chemistry. In the end, their creativity did produce something new and immensely valuable that had never existed before. As with Odin's chain of rings, one idea led to another, and magic was transformed into a new science that generated discovery after transforming discovery for succeeding generations.

Indeed, there is something magical about creative work. All of us have seen how the right mix of people, ideas, and material can generate insights and solutions that could never have been predicted—or even imagined—beforehand. The essence of exercising leadership to address a creative challenge lies in helping foster the circumstances, attitudes, and processes that make such outcomes possible (usually without having the slightest idea of what those outcomes—or the processes that will lead to them—will be).

Fundamentally, the adaptive work of a creative challenge is group work, and not to produce an individual psychological state of creativity. We have all heard the saying that "a camel is a horse designed by a committee," with its arch suggestion that only the "individual" can be truly creative. But anyone who has tried to exercise leadership in the face of a creative challenge soon learns that creativity depends on the interaction among multiple people with differing skills, perspectives, personalities, and attitudes. One individual may have a novel idea but not the ability to make it attractive or inspirational to others. Some people can get others enthusiastic but do not have the persistence or follow-through to bring a creative idea to fruition. Someone with the beginnings of a new insight may need another person with a very different viewpoint to challenge, critique, refine, and ultimately strengthen the new idea. But even when they are all working together, not everyone will share the same levels of commitment to producing an innovative solution, nor will they be able to tolerate the unwieldy process. For all these reasons, those trying to provide leadership for a creative challenge often have to deal with internal divisions—even insurrection—as group members struggle with high levels of stress, anxiety, uncertainty, and disappointment.

The creative challenge, therefore, is a confluence of high stakes, great risks, immense opportunities, profound uncertainty, exhilarating possibility, tremendous excitement, and stark fear. It may be the most difficult leadership challenge to address, but, when it is confronted with wisdom, courage, and skill, the results can be spectacular.

Taking a Mundane Assignment and Turning It into a Creative Breakthrough

The creation of the U.S. Constitution was a remarkable act of creativity, perseverance, and commitment. In 1787, fifty-five representatives from the thirteen original United States gathered in Philadelphia to transform the Articles of Confederation into a more durable and workable blueprint for a national government. Adopted by the Continental Congress in 1777, the Articles had provided a nominal and often ineffectual structure of governance that was clearly inadequate for the needs of a new and growing nation. Six years after winning independence, individual states still had their own currencies, trade rules, armed forces, and, in some cases, foreign policy. The delegates to the Constitutional Convention were "ambassadors" representing their states, sent to explore whether common ground could be found concerning what needed to be changed in the Articles of Confederation and whether it was possible to create a stronger alliance.[4]

Many of those invited to attend the convention refused to go. The prevailing belief was that the differences among the states were too great, and it would, therefore, be impossible to generate any real and lasting consensus. The hero of the Revolutionary War, George Washington, was invited to represent his state, Virginia. At first, he declined the offer, telling the Virginia legislature to choose someone else. "I have served the country long enough and it is not my business to again embark on a sea of troubles," he replied.[5] He was eventually convinced to attend.

Given the lackadaisical attitude of many of the delegates and the general sense that nothing significant would occur at the convention, a number of individuals came late, causing the opening to be delayed by eleven days. The delegate from Rhode Island actually boycotted the event. When the convention did get under way, it was immediately crippled by disagreement—disagreement over state's rights, the role of a national government, and the function of a chief executive. Each delegate brought his own agenda shaped by personal and state interests.

Still, in spite of the delegates' differences, a shared purpose emerged during the convention—to see whether the delegates could create a practical framework through which representative decision making could address their common problems and political differences. As the debates unfolded, it became abundantly clear to many of the delegates that a real opportunity was emerging that could go beyond the mere tweaking of the Articles of Confederation: the convention might yield a new constitution. Not everyone was in favor of such bold action. Luther Martin of Maryland, for example, was so vehement an opponent of the constitutional impulse that he eventually stormed out of the convention and later campaigned against ratification. Still, for four months behind closed doors and in the heat of the summer, those who stayed labored away to produce a constitution. On September 17, 1787, they completed their work, crafting what was to become one of the most remarkable documents ever produced. It was an act of extraordinary creativity.

Crucial leadership was exercised by many people, but the leadership of one delegate in particular—the eighty-one-year-old Benjamin Franklin—affords an opportunity to examine the subtle interventions that make a difference for a group in the midst of a creative challenge. From the outset, Franklin, a figure of national standing and popularity, both personified and ardently advocated a spirit of unity and goodwill that held the convention together even through the fiercest bouts of discord and conflict.[6]

Imagine, for a moment, that you are Benjamin Franklin, and consider, through his eyes, the unfolding drama of that historic event of 1787. How might you intervene to ensure that the meeting produces the best possible solution to the nation's current and future challenges?

SCENARIO

Through the Eyes of Benjamin Franklin

Now eighty-one years old, you remain in fairly good health, although you have difficulty getting around. While you were in Paris, you began to travel in a sedan chair carried by four men, and you have adopted it as your usual form of transportation. You create quite a stir wherever you go, but it beats walking.[7] You consider participation in the convention to be a unique opportunity. For you, it is not about tweaking the Articles of Confederation but seeing whether the delegates can create a constitution for the country.

Protecting the Creative Process

As the convention begins, the first task is to come up with some basic rules and procedures. One of the first procedural questions is whether to admit journalists to your sessions. You are a newspaperman yourself, so you appreciate the importance of the press in getting information to the people and engaging their participation in the debate. But you are also the veteran of many a political discussion, and you think it might be a bad idea at this fragile, exploratory stage for the convention delegates to be speaking for the applause of their factions back home. You want the delegates to work freely on the problems and come up with imaginative solutions. If the convention is reduced to political posturing and grandstanding for the home state audience, it will never succeed. You conclude it would be best to protect the creative environment from outside pressures so that the delegates will be willing to try out new ideas and explore novel perspectives.

So, to make it easier for people to speak their minds and to change their minds, you help coordinate the adoption of a secrecy rule that erects a protective boundary around the group process. You value public debate greatly, but you think that there is no reason to upset the public over the interim points of view that will be expressed within the walls of the pressure cooker that the convention will need to become if productive work is to be done. You know that you personally have a tendency to tell secrets in public, even unintentionally, so you make sure that, for your public appearances during the convention, you have another delegate with you to remind you of the secrecy rule.[8]

Getting People's "Truths" on the Table

You also know that creativity and good civics can arise from self-interest, diversity, and even discord, so long as people remain willing to engage one another openly, honestly, and with the intent to figure the problem out. In fact, you believe it is from discord that the best ideas emerge. You therefore want the delegates to feel free to express themselves openly and address their concerns and objections forthrightly *during* the meeting, so that they will not reserve their criticism for after the convention's document is made public.

After someone seconds the motion that the national executive should be one person rather than a group, there is a long, tense silence. General Washington asks whether he should put the motion to a vote. You intervene to say to the delegates, "Speak up. This is a point of great importance, and you should speak on it before you vote on it." And still no one will speak. Then one of your allies says, "We can change our minds even if we speak a strong and frank opinion." He then proceeds to say why he prefers a single person to be the national executive. Someone else says that a single executive is just the "fetus of a monarchy" and proposes that the national executive should consist of "three men." And there ensues a discussion of whether America should adopt a monarchy like Great Britain or have another form of government.

You know that this is a critical conversation and that the delegates must wrestle with their own preferences, doubts, controversies, and beliefs, even when the arguments are heated and people seem angry. So, although you have several personal views, you keep your interjections to a minimum. You deliberately provoke discussion by offering up proposals that you find intriguing but know will annoy others, such as the idea that the national executive should not be paid, as that would discourage people who are interested only in personal gain. Because you know your idea is unpopular, after you make the proposal, you say, "If it is not seconded or accepted I must be contented with the satisfaction of having delivered my opinion frankly and done my duty." You accept defeat gracefully, thereby setting an example to the rest of the delegates and winning a much greater victory for openness and candid debate.

Keeping People in the Room

After spending over a month making generous compromises on the design features of a national government, tension erupts. One delegate launches a two-day harangue defending the Articles of Confederation, in effect attacking all the progress that has been made. And in response, the delegates start attacking each other's motives. The arguments become heated, and some delegates from the smaller states attempt to reopen the question of whether each state in the new government would have the same vote in a new House of Representatives, irrespective of the size of their populations. They are afraid that the smaller states will have little power and be dominated by the larger states. The delegates become irritated as they rehash arguments presented weeks ago. They are going in circles. You know that *going in circles* is a normal occurrence in a creative process, but you also know that somebody must do something to keep people from fleeing in frustration.

When it looks like some delegates might pull up stakes and leave, given how frustrated the group is, you suggest that they could use a little divine guidance. You say, "I therefore beg leave to move—that henceforth prayers imploring the assistance of Heaven, and its blessings on our deliberations, be held in this Assembly every morning before we proceed to business."[9] Given your deist beliefs that God is the Creator but does not interfere to rescue people from the mess they make of their own world, you do not think that God will necessarily answer the prayer. However, you have some hope that prayer, or at least your mention of prayer, might have a calming effect on the passions of the delegates and remind them of the higher purpose of the work they are doing. Your motion is seconded and discussed. The delegates' anger and passion subside. And no delegates bolt the conference, even though they decide to adjourn the day's session without voting on your motion.[10] Your intervention has served to remind people of the profound importance of the work they are doing and all that is at stake.

A few days later, the struggle between the small states and the large states continues over whether each state will get one vote or several votes proportional to their population; this time the argument is over voting in the senate. It is early July and the weather is extremely hot; a despondent mood stirs among the delegates, as it does not seem likely that the group can ever break its current deadlock of opinions. Personally, you think either the small states' or the large states' solution would work for the nation's next step, as long as the delegates could emerge from the convention with a proposal that the delegates together could defend in their respective states. You intervene again, saying, "When a broad table is to be made, and the edges of planks do not fit, the artist takes a little from both, and makes a good joint. In like manner, here both sides must part with some of their demands, in order that they may join in some accommodating proposition."[11]

Sincere argument, tough debate, honest dialogue, and passionate displays of emotion continue for another two months. It is uphill all the way, but amazingly a new constitution has begun to take shape. By August, after three months of deliberation, the delegates have a complete draft of a constitution for the United States of America.

At the signing ceremony, you look at the scene and feel that something poetical should be said to capture the mood of the occasion. You declare, "I have looked toward the President's Chair these many days, and I have seen that sun painted there in the back of that chair. During these sessions, I have often wondered whether that is a rising or a setting sun. But now at length I have the happiness to know that it is a rising and not a setting sun."[12]

At the conclusion of the convention, James Madison sent a copy of the Constitution to Thomas Jefferson in Paris. "It was impossible," he wrote Jefferson, "to consider the degree of concord which ultimately prevailed, as less than a miracle."[13] As the invention of the United States Constitution shows, creative work may produce a miracle, but the process is often untidy work, riddled with friction that, in turn, generates sporadic moments of brilliance. It requires tremendous patience, persistence, and wisdom to hold steady in such a turbulent and uncertain setting and to be able to intervene at opportune times to keep the group engaging essential issues and steadily progressing. Madison remarked that when Franklin intervened, it was done "with great pertinacity and effect."[14] Indeed, when faced with a creative challenge, those who seek to lead must intervene with pertinacity and effect. They must prod people to go further in the exploration of ideas and stretch their thinking. They must keep the creative juices flowing. Drawing upon the Constitutional Convention and other cases, what follows are the principles and strategies of real leadership for a creative challenge.

Real Leadership for a Creative Challenge

Attend to the mood, energy, and focus needed to make a discovery

Creative work takes place in a particular environment or field. By *field* I mean the dynamics of the group and the contextual influences that produce a certain mood, energy, and focus that stimulate creative thinking and the exploration of ideas. The notion of a field is derived from the work of social psychologist Kurt Lewin, who argued that behavior is determined by the totality of influences on the individual in a given situation.[15] The field is the necessary sea in which discovery work occurs. It is analogous to a holding environment, as presented in the chapter on the development challenge.

The leadership task is to generate a field that is conducive to doing creative work that can produce real solutions to complex problems. Springboarding straight into creative exploration without concern for the field is never a good idea. To produce anything of value, collaborators in a creative process must be receptive, motivated, confident that they will not be penalized for playful or speculative thinking, and be reasonably respectful of one another's contributions. Therefore, a field needs to be generated that allows for genuine "outside the box" thinking.

From my experience working with groups on an array of creative challenges, I believe that three crucial features of a field directly affect the quality of creative work: mood, energy, and focus.

- *Mood* is the feeling, tone, and atmosphere of the group.
- *Energy* is the vigor and effort expended by the group.
- *Focus* pertains to the group's sense of purpose and attentiveness.

The overall mood of the group is an important variable in supporting creative exploration. If the mood is one of negativity and hopelessness—"Why bother?"—people will be reluctant to persist with the stress and anxiety of creative work. Even a slight or mild sense of hope can generate enough optimism to support creative work. So declaring and nurturing hopefulness and optimism becomes an important underlying leadership practice. If people think that their leader has lost hope and that their efforts are pointless, the creative work will die.

Creative work requires enormous energy to sustain the emotional and physical demands of generating innovative solutions that carry the group beyond incremental change and into the realm of true ingenuity. The people's minds and hearts must be quickened and stimulated to meet each succeeding challenge with confidence and a sense of competence. In many ways, the energy levels needed are like that of climbers on Mount Everest. The higher the group ascends, the more difficult it is to maintain energy levels. The closer the summit, the harder the work and the greater the threat to the climber's safety and survival.

Focus is the capacity to maintain a sense of purpose and attentiveness. It is all too easy to get distracted from the larger challenge and end up frittering away crucial energy in nonproductive ways, or to miss an important change in the environment because people are no longer paying close attention. Exhausted and depleted as they may be, mountain climbers on Everest must be alert and vigilant to attend to the shifting terrain and changing weather conditions in order to reach the summit and return safely. Similarly, groups engaged in addressing a creative challenge must stay sharply aware of signals, opportunities, and environmental shifts—especially because, unlike the mountaineers, they are defining the nature and specifics of their goal even as they approach it. One of the salient features of creative work is that those who pursue it must focus on their purpose rather than on a concrete destination. Deviations and explorations down various alleys and valleys to see "what's there" must be tolerated and even encouraged. The leadership task, however, is to be asking the group such questions as "What have we discovered?" "Are we progressing?" "Is this worthwhile?" Should the group get too distracted, someone must bring them back to the main path and get them starting afresh.

The field at the Constitutional Convention was strong due to the efforts of Benjamin Franklin, George Washington, James Madison, and others. These men intervened in a variety of ways to generate and maintain qualities of mood, energy, and focus consistent with the requirements of an unmistakably creative process. The mood needed to be positive and purposeful. Washington's mere presence as the convention chairman did wonders for the mood of the delegates. The feeling was "If

Washington thinks that it is important to be here, then perhaps I should, too." Franklin would repeatedly remind the delegates of the profound importance of the work they were doing and what was at stake—and he would often do it in a playful, provocative way that stimulated creative thought and a sense of possibility. Madison provided an enthusiasm and agility in intellectual debate that was not only instructive but infectious—and, at the same time, intensely practical.

As the convention was held in the hot summer months, an extraordinary amount of energy was needed to persist with the squabbles, arguments, and legalities of this most unpredictable process. Some delegates would speak for hours about their most pressing concerns and drive their colleagues to absolute boredom or anger. Franklin, in the evenings, would entertain delegates at his home and do what he could to maintain a spirit of good cheer in the hopes of keeping energy levels high enough to carry on the work the next day.

Now, compare the strength of the field at the Constitutional Convention to the much less sturdy field that enveloped and conditioned Mary Jones's Experimental Office. Jones wanted the experiment to be a beehive of creative activity—and for a time it was. The mood was that of excitement. Energy levels were high. The focus on creating what had never been done before was intense. However, over time, the field deteriorated because no one attended to it. People got bogged down in the technical and procedural details of "inventing" an office, without consideration for generating and maintaining a field that was sufficient to actually do the creative work. The mood became negative, even hostile. Energy levels sank. The focus became blurred.

The bleakness of the field was caused by a combination of internal and external dynamics—and lack of real leadership to know how to manage the field. Internally, the project teams could not handle the stress and pressure of creative work. Externally, senior management did not provide adequate protection for the experiment and was constantly sending mixed signals about the project's importance and efficacy.

As the members were expected to create a whole new way of working from scratch, they had to learn how to solve problems creatively and collaboratively while ensuring their decisions were sound from a business point of view. They had no idea how hard it would be to work in self-managed teams and be responsible for the resolution of demanding and complex business problems. Theoretically, the concept of creative teamwork, combined with a degree of autonomy, sounded wonderful to them, but in practice it was tough. As one person said, "This experience was more than any of us bargained for." Another team member put it like this: "We are now dealing with so many new problems. I mean, you don't get rid of any problems in this office. This is no different from any other place, except we have to be responsible for solving the problems, not the boss. You can't pass the buck." These new kinds of problems generated an incredible amount of stress for the members. In fact, most indicated that they wanted to leave the project as soon as possible because the pressure was getting to them. "Last week I was really depressed," confided one woman. "I would have walked out if I didn't stop and calm myself down. I was really upset. These people are driving me nuts. What's more, I think management wants us to fail. They don't seem interested at all in what we are doing. How do you do creative work when no one supports you?"

The leadership work is to attend to the generation and maintenance of a field conducive to achieving an outstanding result. Creative exploration and experimentation cannot flourish when the mood is bleak or the focus is blurred. Monitoring the field and managing the boundaries to ensure that stress levels, like the heat in a pressure cooker, can be released or turned up as needed is essential work. At the Experimental Office, people were overwhelmed. They were expected to be creative on many fronts on a daily basis, but they were not given sufficient support in the creative endeavors. Some people assumed that creative work would be easy, natural, and fun. The process, however, was demanding—mentally, physically, and emotionally. Given that the field was not properly attended to, the work became a heavy burden for all.

Keep the powerful from dictating "the" solution

One of the surest ways to kill off innovation and creativity is for a powerful person to try to dominate the work. It is often difficult for a boss or an "expert" to hold still and allow the group to muddle its way through the painful, unpredictable discovery work associated with a creative challenge. If you are a project manager, for example, tasked with inventing a new product, you might be tempted to "control" the creative process or shape it in a way that is consistent with your notion of what the outcome should be. However, in the realm of real leadership, one must learn when and how to get out of the way to ensure that the group can be inventive and discover solutions through their own chaotic process. And one must keep other people, particularly those with considerable power and authority, from dominating and imposing their will on the group.

Dominance dynamics are common in all groups and organizations where the stakes are high. Some people feel that they must engage in political maneuvering in order to achieve their individual aims, or their faction's interests, at the expense of a truly creative breakthrough for the system. Sometimes they genuinely believe they know better, and sometimes they simply wish to be perceived as being more knowledgeable or competent so that they can increase their status in the eyes of others. Either way, the group does not benefit from such behavior, and the creative process is thwarted. The expression of dominance stifles initiative, imaginative thinking, and creative self-expression. It generates a negative mood that makes creative work more difficult than it already is.

One reason the Constitutional Convention succeeded was because the participants had a working understanding that no one individual would be permitted to impose his will on the rest of the group. Certainly, a few demagogues did their utmost to control the floor, dominate the discussion, and bully the group into adopting a particular view, but they had no power to enforce their view. As a successful military figure with a truly national reputation for courage and leadership, George Washington was probably the most powerful person in attendance, and he was the natural choice to serve as the convention's president. In discussions about the nature of a future chief executive under a new constitution, it was natural to think of Washington in that office; he would inevitably be its first occupant. Yet Washington made no move to dominate the proceedings. He facilitated and presided over the convention with grace and finesse, never demanding that anyone abide by his precepts or using his power to get what he wanted. He was fair and evenhanded, ensuring that all had their say.

At Aetna's Experimental Office, too many powerful people started meddling with the experiment, which wreaked havoc on the creative process. Mary Jones put together an advisory board of senior managers, thinking that they would provide some protection against her projects' many critics in the company, while also contributing useful ideas and suggestions. But the very people she thought she could count on to support her began to interfere with the day-to-day running of the project and to dictate the design and function of the experiment. Unwilling to be simply advisers, they imposed their executive authority and began demanding results while the experiment was still in its formative stages. They were relentless in their criticism, recommendations, demands, and requests.

This situation led the Experimental Office team to distance themselves from the advisory board, as they saw them as a threat, even the enemy. They began presenting only positive accomplishments and with-held negative data about the real problems they were facing, for fear it would exacerbate the criticism, the control, and the demands.

The absence of clear, honest, and forthright communication about the project's real problems and dilemmas resulted in the advisory board sensing that the team was withholding data. In turn, this situation led the advisory board to redouble its efforts to take an active role in man-aging the project and assessing its performance. The project members in-creasingly felt like they did not have the freedom to make creative choices and try out innovative ideas. They resented the intrusions of the advisory board and became disillusioned and demoralized. Given the mood of the project members, a number of individuals started making serious errors in their work, which got back to the board. Rather than allow the project members to learn from their mistakes, the board saw this as a reason to close the project down. The errors were, to some of the managers on the board, confirmation that that "these young people really don't have what it takes to run a business."

Therefore, in exercising responsible leadership for a creative chal-lenge, it is essential to protect the group from those who, by the irre-sponsible use of their power, seek to stifle the creative work and impose their notion of the truth on the group. Such people might be members of the group or external to the group. Either way, the leadership task is to ensure that all the group members contend with the problem and are not confounded or distracted by those who try to impose the solution with-out due consideration for the creative process.

Allow for friction, but keep people from fleeing

Earlier in this chapter, I likened the function of leadership for the creative challenge to that of an alchemist. Irrational as they may look to us today, the medieval alchemists pushed the boundaries of the prevail-ing paradigm of their time—and the results they produced through their innovative experimentation processes laid the foundations for modern chemistry, medicine, and science. In the alchemists' den—their labora-tory—they would mix different chemicals and observe the reactions. They found that in the mixing of opposites, they could produce the needed friction to ignite the creation of a new solution. The alchemists were the first to discover that it was in dissonance and divergence that the best solutions could emerge.[16]

Likewise, in a group of any type that faces a creative challenge, people also must mix opposing and competing perspectives and generate friction to produce the sparks of creativity. Benjamin Franklin worked hard to manage the friction that was in the room by encouraging tolerant disagreement and a willingness to make concessions when appropriate. His advice to the delegates was to spend their time "not in associating with their own party and devising new arguments to fortify themselves in their old opinions but . . . mix with members of opposite sentiments, lend a patient ear to their reasonings, and candidly allow them all the weight to which they might be entitled."[17]

Still, not everyone shared Franklin's perspective, with some engaging in considerable posturing and even threatening to leave unless they got their way. From the outset, there was always the possibility that the convention might break up in furious discord. Even Washington, in a disheartened moment, wrote to Alexander Hamilton that he wished he had avoided the convention, because he found the clash of opinion so alarming.[18] Indeed, there were numerous instances of early departures and extended absences during the convention. Of the twenty-one delegates who were in place for the opening session, just over half were there to sign the Constitution. Feelings were hurt, threats were made, and, occasionally, things were said that should not have been said.

However, it is in this kind of "crucible" that creative ideas can emerge and be explored, tested, and refined, if the process is managed well. Without the heat of passionate disagreement and exuberant debate, it is often difficult to find out what people really care about and what values they hold dear to their hearts. Benjamin Franklin, reflecting on what had transpired during the convention, said it best in his final speech to the delegates on September 17, 1787:

> For when you assemble a number of men to have the advantage
> of their joint wisdom, you inevitably assemble with those men all
> their prejudices, their passions, their errors of opinion, their local
> interests, and their selfish views. From such an assembly can a per-
> fect production be expected? It therefore astonishes me to find this
> system approaching so near to perfection that it does; and I think
> it will astonish our enemies, who are waiting with confidence to
> hear that our councils are confounded like those of the Builders
> of Babel; and our States are on the point of separation, only to
> meet hereafter for the purpose of cutting one another's throats.[19]

Another reason for the failure of Mary Jones's experiment was due to the lack of leadership to manage the friction that was produced as the

Experimental Office teams engaged in problem solving for difficult organizational challenges. People were afraid of conflict. The interpersonal dynamics were riddled with tension and, at times, even rage. In their initial team training, facilitated by outside consultants, members were encouraged to be "objective" when faced with difficult issues and not let emotions cloud or distort their thinking. This proved difficult to do. While it was impossible for individuals to ignore their feelings, they often attempted to suppress them until it got to the point that they had to "explode."

In one incident, a team member named Jack attempted to get the group focused on the specifics of a tough operational problem. But in doing so, he wanted rational and nonemotional conversation, even though aspects of the problems were rooted in people's values and priorities. Mabel, a member of the group, described what happened:

> In the meeting a lot of people were angry and crying. Jack kept saying, "Mabel, tell them no feelings." I said, "I'm sorry Jack, but at this point we need these feelings because they're festering, and if we go out of this meeting without discussing it, we're never going to solve anything." But he kept saying, "No feelings!" And I was going, "People have got to talk." We ended up not dealing with the issues but fighting among ourselves. I said to the group that I know there are people in this room who feel strongly and need to speak. I think this is the time. But nobody came forth. They were scared. Jack's way of dealing with it was to go have a party afterward. No kidding—that's how we deal with problems here.

Generally, the group members assumed that friction was something negative and to be avoided. They found it difficult to express divergent opinions for fear that it could escalate into something uncontrollable. Nevertheless, the very attempt to minimize the friction by suppressing their feelings created further problems for the group as people exploded and began to vent.

One member who had mastered controlling her emotions in public explained that some of her fellow team members "took the whole experiment way too seriously." While she felt that the constant venting of emotions was not a good thing, she personally was suffering because of it. She explained: "Some of our members get too emotional over the smallest things. I mean, like you can kill an ant and they'd start crying. It takes a lot to upset me. But I guess I hold a lot of stuff in. That's why it affects me physically. I've got an ulcer."

Creative work by nature is intensely emotional, often turbulent, and riddled with conflict. But the process can be managed (not controlled) in a way that ensures this tremendous energy gets channeled into the exploration of innovative ideas and practices that help groups break through the barriers that impede real discovery and ultimately progress. Therefore, an important leadership function is to intervene to manage the tension that is inherent when a group is doing creative work. If the tension gets too great, the group might break apart. If the tension is insufficient, the energy needed to spark the emergence of novel and imaginative ideas may never emerge. A degree of tension, and even conflict, is necessary in a creative process; it should actually be encouraged, not avoided, because it can generate the sparks that allow for new ideas to develop. The challenge is to keep everyone in the room long enough to achieve a breakthrough and ensure they do not flee.

The creative process necessitates a tolerance for discord but also a willingness to inquire into the source of the discord, even if that means having people express their feelings in sloppy, hurtful ways. Harvard professor Chris Argyris's lifetime work on productive dialogue is helpful in this regard. He advocates making one's position as explicit as possible and illustrating one's views with clear, precise data to ensure that the discord allows useful and productive information to surface that can enhance the group's problem-solving endeavor and collective learning.[20] For example, someone might say, "I am really angry, and I want to leave!" In exercising real leadership, one might inquire into the source of that anger: "I understand you are angry, but what has happened that leads you to feel that way?" By presenting a position, explaining the logic of how one arrived at that position, and inquiring into the logic and reasoning of other people's positions, the work on a creative challenge can be made more productive. This advice might seem obvious, but my own research with hundreds of executives who have written personal cases on their interactions with others while addressing tough institutional problems indicates that although they subscribe to this point of view, they have great difficulty producing it real-time.

Be generous in wasting time and resources

In creative work, the solution–discovery process generally takes time for the right mixture of mood, temperature, and sparks to produce the needed breakthrough. It is important when embracing a creative challenge, therefore, to be generous in wasting time and resources and to tolerate, even encourage, a period of prolonged playfulness. I am not talking about being foolhardy, but a leader must realize that creativity in a group context is not a rational, linear, and controlled process. Groups must be allowed to meander and explore dead-end lanes that seem to produce little gain, if a solution is to eventually emerge. This was certainly true for one of the most significant creative challenges of the past century: putting a man on the moon.

On Thursday, May 25, 1961, President John F. Kennedy declared:

> I believe that this nation should commit itself to achieving the goal, before this decade is out, of landing a man on the moon and returning him safely to Earth. No single space project in this period will be more exciting, or more impressive to mankind, or more important for the long-range exploration of space; and none will be so difficult or expensive to accomplish.[21]

From the day Kennedy made his announcement, it was clear that NASA would have to learn how to do what many people thought would be impossible, including NASA. Bob Gilruth, director of the Space Task Group, the team charged with the mission, remarked to colleagues that he was fine with everything the president had said in his speech, except the part about "and returning him safely to Earth." "We don't know how to do that," Gilruth admitted. He felt that they just might be able to get a man to the moon within the decade, but only if they were willing to take the risk of killing him in the process. In 1961 they had no idea how to achieve that objective within a decade.[22]

Eight years later, on July 20, 1969, Neil Armstrong walked on the moon and then made it safely back to Earth. The Space Task Force had succeeded.

The creative process of the Space Task Force was demanding, exhausting, exhilarating, and often chaotic. It had to be approached with the cold, hard logic expected of rocket science, which it literally was, but also with the same "challenge everything" attitude of the medieval alchemists who struggled with the impossible task of trying to turn lead into gold. Caldwell Johnson, one of the lead designers of the *Apollo* spacecraft, reflected on the accounts of how the *Apollo* came to be. "The way the history books say things came about," he said, "they didn't come about that way. The official records and all, that's a long way of explaining a lot of things. It turns out that the thing was done by people, not by machines, and people have a way of coming to a very rational conclusion in a very irrational manner."[23]

By virtue of their willingness to "waste time" and allow for eccentric and even irrational thinking, the experts on the Space Task Force had the freedom to pursue their creative experiments and ultimately transcend their prevailing paradigm and achieve the needed breakthrough that produced success.

The participants in the Constitutional Convention also "wasted" a lot of time and were somewhat irrational—and the process worked. What was supposed to have been a meeting of just a few weeks, turned into a four-month-long adventure cooped up in a stifling hot room. An extraordinary amount of energy and tolerance was needed to persist with the squabbles, arguments, and legalities of this most unpredictable process. Some delegates would speak for hours about their most pressing concerns and drive their colleagues to absolute boredom or outrage. No one ever quite knew whether their efforts were paying off. Everything was riddled with so much uncertainty. Indeed, the delegates were engaged in creating a constitution for an uncertain future. As one historian noted, "The Founding Fathers were trying to legislate for a country that was certain to change but did not yet exist. They tried, with indifferent success, to look into the seeds of time."[24]

For Aetna's Experimental Office to be given a better chance at success, Mary Jones needed to explain to her colleagues in senior management that they needed to give the staff the time and space to be creative and invent a new approach to claims processing. The project was supposed to be a two-year experiment to discover whether a new form of claims processing could be invented. Management was initially tolerant of experimentation and waste, but those unfamiliar with creative work were afraid of what they saw in the formative stages and eventually demanded that the project cease. As one manager explained:

> This environment was too free. It frightened me sometimes, it really did. Because, again, being from the traditional world, I say "holy mackerel"—some of the things we allowed to go on there. It was outrageous. And sometimes it was quite discouraging, very candidly. I think the biggest thing is that we just assumed too much in terms of their ability levels. Most are just young women. Luckily we stopped it before it got out of hand.[25]

Rather than support the "young women" by being generous in expending, even wasting, time and resources during the experimental phase of figuring out what works, management backed away from their initial promise of giving the experiment two years. The creative process frightened management, so they used their power to squelch whatever excitement, imagination, and risk taking were beginning to emerge.

Get people to set aside their notions of the truth long enough for novel ideas to emerge

Sometimes, when faced with a creative challenge, the solution to the problem is right before our eyes, but we cannot see it because our prevailing assumptions—our notions of the truth—desensitize us to pieces of data that we cannot appreciate or comprehend. All of us have assumptions and beliefs that we hold dear. We use these assumptions to navigate through predictable terrain. But in uncertain terrain where we must create in order to survive, our notions of truth may be inadequate. Therefore, the leadership work in a creative challenge is to get the group to push up against prevailing wisdom, question shared assumptions, and even transcend the limitations of their cultural paradigm.

In the first chapter, I presented the case of Burke and Wills, the Australian explorers who were lost in the outback. They were trying to do something that had never been done before—by white people, at least—and that was to cross the continent. At the moment they realized they were lost, the seriousness of their creative challenge increased dramatically. Real impediments, in the environment and in their thinking, were blocking progress. Rather than persist in an attachment to their prevailing worldview, the explorers needed to suspend their assumptions, set aside their notions of the truth, and allow a solution to be discovered that could produce a breakthrough that would open up the possibility for survival. For example, as a start to the process, they could have met in the shade and said to each other, "What resources do we have that could save us? Do you think praying to God would help? Do you think cutting into the cactus would help? Do you think setting a trap for an animal would help? Might we ask the Aborigines for help? They have food somewhere." Even obvious questions need to be reexamined to discover whether faulty assumptions are constraining their options. In Burke and Wills's case, a solution to their predicament was so close yet so far away. Given they could not momentarily transcend their cultural paradigm, the explorers perished.

Similarly, at times during the Constitutional Convention, some members could not bring themselves to entertain alternative perspectives because they were so wedded to the rightness of their own position. A common way of distancing themselves from responsibility for creative exploration of alternatives was to say, "The people will never support that." That phrase occurs with considerable frequency in the transcript

of the convention. It was usually expressed as a way to stop further examination of an issue. Franklin was constantly trying to get the group
not to be stuck with their opinions of what the people would or would
not support. His view was that when the time came, the people would
make their choice but that, during the convention itself, uninhibited
exploration of ideas was absolutely essential to developing effective
solutions.[26]

Franklin made a speech during the convention that highlighted the
need not to be constrained by one's limited version of the truth.

> I confess that there are several parts of this constitution which I
> do not at present approve, but I am not sure I shall never ap-
> prove them. For having lived long, I have experienced many in-
> stances of being obliged by better information, or fuller
> consideration, to change opinions even on important subjects,
> which I once thought right, but found to be otherwise. It is there-
> fore that the older I grow, the more apt I am to doubt my judg-
> ment, and to pay more respect to the judgment of others. Most
> men indeed, as well as most sects in religion, think themselves in
> possession of all truth, and that wherever others differ from
> them it is so far error. . . . But though many private persons think
> almost as highly of their own infallibility as that of their sect,
> few express it so naturally as a certain French lady, who in a dis-
> pute with her sister, said "I don't know how it happens, Sister,
> but I meet with nobody but myself that's always in the right."[27]

In the creative challenge, the leader must be willing to subject notions of truth to critical examination to see to what degree truths and assumptions are even relevant to the immediate problem. There will be
times when leaders might even throw up their hands and say, "I am lost.
My truths don't work. I don't know what we should do." Then, in total
humility and sincerity they must put their trust in other people to become true collaborators in discovering a way out of the dire predicament
that they are in.

The former CEO of the clothing company Levi Strauss, Robert
Haas, did just that. He approached the creative work of figuring out
how to turn his company around by acknowledging he did *not* have the
answer. He said:

> When I became CEO, our business was losing altitude quickly.
> We had gone through all the usual fads and had become bureau-
> cratic and sporadic in our decision making. I was scared and didn't

even have any answers. So, I did the unthinkable for me. I reached out to my colleagues in management and said, "We're in this together. I don't have any answers. I'm not Lee Iacocca. I'm not the heroic leader. We've got to figure this out." Much of it was painful, but we got the organization back on track. I've learned a couple of lessons. It's not only okay to be vulnerable; it's important to show you are human and don't have the answers.[28]

Indeed, vulnerability and not having the answer are essential characteristics when dealing with a creative challenge. Without this orientation, the group will flounder or get attached to the dominant person's answer and think that they have "found the truth," when in fact they have bought into a false solution.

· · ·

As Rollo May warned, "Creativity provokes the jealousy of the gods." In Norse mythology, Odin and his fellow gods were in constant battles to acquire the creative power of the Mead. In all enterprises it is a real battle to produce creative, breakthrough solutions to the threats and problems that thwart progress. It is risky and dangerous work, but it also can be extremely exhilerating. The leadership challenge is to (1) turn everyone into a dissident and to get the people to question and challenge deeply held assumptions; (2) protect the creative space from marauding alphas who seek to impose their truth on the group; and (3) generate enough friction and heat by getting ideas, assumptions, and values clashing and producing sparks for birthing a creative solution. This is demanding work but absolutely critical work if the people are to progress.

REAL LEADERSHIP FOR A CREATIVE CHALLENGE

- Attend to the mood, energy, and focus needed to make a discovery.
- Keep the powerful from dictating "the" solution.
- Allow for friction, but keep people from fleeing.
- Be generous in wasting time and resources.
- Get people to set aside their notions of the truth long enough for the novel ideas to emerge.

CHAPTER 8

The Crisis Challenge

Leading in a Period of Extreme Danger

A crisis challenge is a perilous predicament in which the group is under attack from forces within or without. It is a sudden, unpredictable event that jeopardizes the accrued value and resources of the group or enterprise. In such a context, wise and responsible leadership is critical if the people are to overcome the immediate danger and return to a state of normalcy. Consider the following scenario.

SCENARIO

Imagine for a moment that you have just been appointed the CEO of one of Italy's largest state-owned companies, Eni. The company supplies much of the nation's energy resources and also does business throughout Europe. It has 135,000 employees who make up the 335 consolidated Eni companies.

The company is a national icon in Italy. It is a symbol of Italy's postwar reconstruction and modernization. Everyone knows of it, and everyone is proud of it. In your words, "Eni sends a message to the world that Italy is independent and strong, and that no country can ever control us." You are thrilled with your appointment to be at the helm, as you see a tremendous opportunity to revitalize the company and make it a more efficient and competitive operation. In its current state, it is a bureaucratic and political mess, and most observers agree it needs a major overhaul.

One of the biggest problems, as you see it, is the enormous and improper influence the government has on the company's management and strategy. Because it is a state-owned enterprise, politicians and state bureaucrats are constantly meddling in the internal affairs of the business, making it a nightmare to manage. This interference slows the decision-making process and leads to all sorts of inefficiencies. State bureaucrats regularly dictate who should be hired for, or promoted to, senior executive positions.

After four months on the job as CEO, a figurative hurricane hits. Two dozen of your top executives are arrested on charges of corruption (embezzlement, bribery, and kickbacks). You are shocked. The biggest shock of all is when your chairman, the highly respected Gabriele Cagliari, is arrested. In jail, Cagliari commits suicide. This whole experience feels like "an atomic bomb exploding on your head," you tell a journalist.

The eyes of all of Italy are on you. You have a crisis challenge and need to display some extraordinary leadership to address the danger. You and the company are in an extremely vulnerable position, and anything could happen.[1]

The Nature of a Crisis Challenge

A crisis can emerge in many forms. It may be triggered by a terrorist attack such as that experienced on September 11, 2001, in the United States. In business, it can be sparked by a terrible event such as the 1982 episode at Johnson & Johnson when someone tampered with its Tylenol product, or the 1984 disaster at Union Carbide's plant in Bhopal, India. It might be a corporate scandal of huge proportion, as faced at Eni. Or, it might be a major financial meltdown in the economy, as experienced in Asia in 1997 and 1998. Fundamentally, a crisis is a grave and urgent challenge that threatens a group, community, organization, or nation. In medical parlance, it is critical rather than acute. Danger is in the air, and the situation is volatile. The symptoms of a crisis challenge include the following:

- Hostile forces, from without or within, threaten the survival of the group.

- The situation is explosive, fueling a group's fear and anxiety while creating an urgent need to take some sort of action—to fight or flee.
- There is a widely perceived danger that the group's accumulated "value" (its resources, culture, and goods) will be lost or significantly diminished unless immediate action is taken.

The *people* in a crisis challenge are anxious and afraid. They are under threat, so naturally they worry what will become of themselves, their group, or their enterprise.

The *barrier* to progress is primarily the "forces" that have generated the crisis condition and the emotional and psychological state of the people. When people are under threat, a predictable reaction is to become defensive and fearful rather than analytical and thoughtful. The people understandably seek to blame someone or some group for their predicament and therefore may act rashly and irresponsibly. Another barrier includes the external groups who are in a position to assist in bringing resolution to the crisis but feel impotent or reluctant to get involved. Their hesitation might allow the crisis to escalate and do more damage.

The *promise* in a crisis challenge is that if the group can get beyond the "fog" of the situation, they will discover a deeper underlying issue that must addressed. If this underlying issue is attended to responsibly, the people will be in a better position to progress. If the underlying problem or challenge is not adequately understood and engaged, then the potential for the emergence of another crisis is always lurking.

The leadership work in a period of grave danger must be to restore calm; protect the people or the enterprise from further threat or attack; and assist the people in channeling their fear, anxiety, and aggression toward creative and workable solutions. In such a "hot" and "foggy" environment, wisdom and formidable intervention skills are needed to contain the fallout and refocus people's attitudes and behavior on productive actions. This necessitates managing the group's emotions, illusions, fears, and interpretations so that the people face the reality of what lies beneath the crisis and attend to the real issue that must be engaged in order for the situation of irresolution to be brought to resolution. Therefore, those who seek to exercise real leadership in such circumstances must keep their own heads clear and remain cool under pressure as they work to diagnose the reality of the predicament and figure out where and how they should intervene.

During a crisis challenge, usually two challenges must be addressed concurrently: the volatility of the situation and the unresolved issue below the surface that is actually the reason for the volatility. For example, during the 1963 Cuban Missile Crisis, when the United States and the Soviet Union came extremely close to having a nuclear confrontation due to the fact that the Soviets had placed ballistic missiles on the island of Cuba, two issues had to be addressed: (1) dissipating the immediate danger because the situation was so volatile, with trigger-happy generals and government officials on both sides ready to start shooting, and (2) undertaking the more difficult work of facing the complex development challenge of getting the two nations to be responsible for their tremendous power and deal with the real danger of the proliferation of nuclear weapons. The Cuban Missile Crisis was the symptom of deeper unresolved issues and tensions in the international community—and those unresolved issues required superior leadership.

However, from my observations, many would-be leaders in a crisis chase false solutions that may make some people feel better but avoid the real problem. Given the pressure on the leader to "do something," leaders might feel compelled to come up with a simple but palatable solution that brings temporary relief, such as finding a scapegoat for the crisis or redirecting the people's attention to some other issue and thereby bypassing the real underlying issue altogether. The work of genuine resolution is then, irresponsibly, left to others—even future generations.

Sometimes, when looking for the underlying problem, we discover nothing. In other words, there is no real problem. In such circumstances, the crisis might actually be a false crisis, manufactured for ulterior reasons or out of fear or ignorance. Mao thought that he had a crisis during the Cultural Revolution that necessitated taking radical measures to reindoctrinate the masses. Had he looked below the fog, he might have realized that there was no crisis of ideology and nothing was wrong with the people. The problem was with Mao himself and the development strategy being forced upon the people. The same thing happened during the Spanish Inquisition, when the Catholic Church, thinking that the integrity of the Church was in crisis due to heretical beliefs, embarked on a radical process of purification through intimidation, persecution, and torture. Had the authorities been wiser and exercised real leadership, they might have tested their notions of the truth, looked through the fog, and noticed that nothing threatening was there. They created a false set of tasks that had nothing to do with progress—earthly or heavenly—and wreaked havoc on the people and institutions the authorities were supposed to be supporting.

It is a heavy burden to exercise real leadership for a crisis challenge. But through thoughtful diagnosis and skilled interventions, the danger can be diminished, the people can be calmed, and the group can get back to the important work of attending to their most pressing challenges that allow them to have the best shot at success and enjoy the fruits of their labor.

It is important to note that a crisis challenge is different from a maintenance challenge, although there are overlapping qualities. In a crisis challenge, the group is under immediate threat and the air is explosive, and therefore swift action needs to be taken. In a maintenance challenge, the group is under threat, but the adaptive work of the people is to preserve themselves and their resources until better times. A maintenance challenge does not have the sense of immediacy or urgency that a crisis has.

East Timor Burning:
Where Is the Leadership?

East Timor is a small country that occupies half an island on the southern end of the Indonesian archipelago (just a few hundred miles north of Australia). In August 1999, the East Timorese voted to separate themselves from Indonesia and become an independent state. This decision was made at great cost: In a matter of weeks, 80 percent of the new nation's buildings, homes, and government offices were destroyed by gangs and militias that were actively supported by the Indonesian armed forces.

The seeds of this crisis had been sown a quarter-century before. East Timor had been a Portuguese colony for five hundred years when in 1975 it was granted independence. On December 7, 1975, the Indonesian government dispatched an army of one hundred thousand troops to occupy and annex the tiny nation.

Over the next twenty-five years, up to two hundred thousand people in East Timor were killed under Indonesia's repressive occupation. A guerilla force fought back against the Indonesian military, but death, exhaustion, and attrition wore down their strength: From an initial high of twenty thousand members, its numbers shrank to a mere three thousand by 1995. This small force of ill-equipped fighters was no match for the well-armed Indonesian military, but they did remain a constant irritant. In many ways, however, the greatest threat to the Indonesian occupation came from the extraordinary activists who worked for years to keep the issue of East Timor alive in the international media. Among them were Jose Ramos-Horta and Bishop Belo, who both received the Nobel Peace

Prize for their efforts. Xanana Gusmao, the resistance leader who languished for eight years in Indonesian jails, became the evocative symbol of the hope that one day East Timor would reclaim its independence.

The chronic crisis of East Timor became acute by the end of 1998, when Indonesia's former dictator, Suharto, was thrown out of office as his country wrestled with a severe economic depression brought on by a larger meltdown of the Asian financial system. Suharto's successor, B. J. Habibie, made an unprecedented and unexpected statement on January 27, 1999: East Timor might be granted independence if that is what its people truly desired. This statement shocked his own government, particularly the generals of the Indonesian military.

The People Vote and the People Suffer

On August 30, 1999, a referendum was conducted in East Timor with a 98 percent voter turnout. Nearly 80 percent of those casting ballots rejected any association with Indonesia and voted for independence. Within hours, however, the militias—aided and abetted by the Indonesian military—started cruising the streets of the capital, Dili, brandishing automatic weapons and machetes and intimidating anyone in their way, including United Nations observers and foreign journalists. As predicted, within days, the country plunged into total chaos. The militias, directed by the military, began a "scorched earth" campaign to burn the country to the ground. Within three weeks, more than half of the population had been displaced, with two hundred thousand people fleeing the country. Hundreds of people were killed and thousands wounded.

Containing the Violence

The world belatedly recognized how serious the crisis was and demanded that United Nations troops be sent to contain the violence. The problem was, the Indonesian government did not want any UN troops on "Indonesian" soil. In an unprecedented move, UN secretary-general Kofi Annan sent five UN ambassadors to Jakarta to meet with Habibie and the military generals. They arrived on September 8. Their mission was to stop the violence and get the Indonesians to do the right thing—immediately.

The UN team asked tough questions and demanded responsible action, but the blatant lies, denial, and obfuscation by Indonesian authorities made diplomacy a difficult task. Still, their presence was a powerful reminder that the world was now watching more closely. A journalist accompanying the ambassadors wrote:

> What has been the lowest moment for the UN Security Council ambassadors on their mission in Jakarta this past week? Was it when the puppet president, B. J. Habibie, pronounced that the reports of killings and destruction from East Timor were all "fantasies and lies"? When the rebel leader, Xanana Gusmao, fought back tears as he begged them to do something, anything, to save his people? Or when General Wiranto, the all-powerful chief of the army, spurned the offer of international troops and invited them to join him in a round of golf?[2]

The Indonesians were immovable. The international community, sensing they were being stonewalled, turned to the United States to intervene. The U.S. government, however, was hesitating. It viewed East Timor as of no strategic importance to the United States, whereas the Indonesian relationship was vital. Still, Australian prime minister John Howard and UN secretary-general Annan pled with U.S. president Bill Clinton to get involved and lend immediate support. Clinton explained that he could never get the approval from Congress to put troops in East Timor, a place that few Americans had ever heard of.

But the situation deteriorated more each day. The Australian foreign minister, Alexander Downer recalled, "The Australian public were screaming out, everybody was—I mean, it wasn't a party thing, a Left-Right thing—screaming out to do something to stop it. People were ringing up, crying over the phone; we had more phone calls on that issue than I've had in my life on anything."[3]

Australia's foreign minister continued to keep pressure on the Americans, working the issue through diplomatic channels and through the media. Howard and Downer reminded U.S. officials that Australians had supported the United States in wars in Korea, Vietnam, and the Gulf. In an interview on CNN, Downer chided the United States for not doing enough to support the East Timorese. Madeline Albright, Clinton's secretary of state, saw Downer on television in her hotel room in Hanoi. She was furious. She immediately called him and complained that he was portraying the United States in an unfavorable light, which was not particularly helpful. Downer later explained, "I believe it was actually extremely helpful, because that helped to galvanize her into action. She pushed very hard for U.S. involvement in the teeth of the Pentagon's resistance."[4]

While Australia and other countries as well as the United Nations put outside pressure on the United States, Stanley Roth of the U.S. State Department mounted a campaign of his own from within. He met with numerous members of Congress and garnered enough support that it became a relatively straightforward process to give nominal assistance to an Australian-UN peacekeeping initiative. In a matter of days, the United States started to come around. The issue had ripened to a degree that President Clinton was now ready to act. On September 9, 1999, Clinton stood on the White House lawn and made a bold declaration to the Indonesians:

> At issue is whether the democratically expressed will of the people can be overturned by violence and intimidation. . . . For these reasons, we . . . make it clear that we expect the authorities to live up to their word and responsibilities. The Indonesian government and military are responsible for the safety of the East Timorese, and of the UN mission there. If Indonesia does not end the violence, it must invite—it must invite—the international community to assist in restoring security. . . . It must move forward with the transition to independence.[5]

The speech sent a clear and unambiguous message to the Indonesians that they needed to stop the violence and repression at once or immediately allow an international peacekeeping force in to provide the security that they were unwilling to provide themselves.

The day he gave his speech from the White House, Clinton departed for New Zealand to attend the Asia-Pacific summit with the prime ministers and presidents of the region. On his journey, as Clinton took the time to learn about what was unfolding in East Timor, he became increasingly disturbed and made the decision to suspend U.S. arms sales to Indonesia immediately. Britain followed suit by suspending the delivery of nine Hawk "trainer" fighters. With Clinton's encouragement, the International Monetary Fund and World Bank joined in to lend support by suspending loans to Indonesia, further casting the country as an international pariah.[6]

On September 12, President Habibie agreed to let an international peacekeeping force into East Timor to replace the Indonesian military. Within weeks, order was restored.

a a a

Often leadership requires that people and groups are prodded and pushed to live up to their obligations, honor the values that they espouse, and do the right thing. Sadly, if a problem looks too tough to deal with, the authority figures, predictably, will be inclined to avoid it unless they can see a direct gain to being involved. Prodding people, even nations, to lend a helping hand, even at the risk of offending people, is vital, particularly when lives are at stake. Australian foreign minister Alexander Downer, even though he upset Madeline Albright (or one might say *because* he upset her), displayed effective leadership in this critical period in generating public attention on the issue that contributed, among other things, to U.S. support for East Timor. U.S. support was absolutely essential in dissipating the explosiveness of the situation and paving the way for East Timor's independence. Kofi Annan worked tirelessly to mobilize the international community to send peacekeepers to contain the mayhem. John Howard, Australia's prime minister, took the lead in negotiating with Habibie to open the door for peacekeepers and ensuring that Australia would contribute generously. Bill Clinton's voice of rebuke to Habibie was heard loud and clear in Jakarta, and it served as the tipping point that finally got the Indonesians to relent.

Clearly, the fault of the international community was in not providing leadership earlier to ensure adequate security to thwart any violence before, during, and immediately after the referendum. Xanana Gusmao and Jose Ramos-Horta had told anyone who would listen that the Indonesian military could not be trusted to provide security, and they were right. Yet because Indonesia was of such strategic importance, and its political and economic situation so precarious, few in the international community wanted to risk upsetting the Habibie government. As commentators, Greenlees and Garren state:

> There was a strong feeling that Indonesia had made the wrenching decision to hold an act of self-determination [for East Timor]. To follow this with the further concession of UN peacekeepers, at a time when the economic crisis had already left Indonesians with a sense that their sovereignty was being trampled on, would have required a degree of leadership authority and legitimacy that Habibie clearly lacked.[7]

Admittedly there was no broad appetite for a large-scale UN intervention into East Timor.[8] No foreign government was eager to send forces and have their troops possibly die on East Timor soil. Even though East Timor is in the Asia-Pacific region, nations in that area were reluctant to get directly involved because their policy had been not to interfere in the internal affairs of their neighbors. They preferred quiet diplomacy. But in this case, quiet diplomacy was inadequate. The situation called for determined, courageous leadership to get many actors to face the reality of this messy, volatile predicament. This was a crisis challenge and therefore required direct, provocative, and wise leadership.

Although many of the key players made significant mistakes in coming to grips with the East Timor crisis, its eventual resolution provides illustrations of all of the key leadership tasks that must be addressed in a crisis challenge. They are (1) dissipate the explosive gas that builds up in a crisis; (2) hold steady and remain persistent, focused, and calm; (3) keep people from striking a match, and do not allow the group's tension, anger, or fear to infect the hard work of resolving the crisis; and (4) ensure that all relevant information is surfaced and addressed so that informed choices can be made.

Real Leadership for a Crisis Challenge

Dissipate the explosive fumes, and create some time to think

In a crisis, dangerous and explosive fumes permeate the air. In other words, given people's emotional state, the predicament is explosive. Any rash or thoughtless action might trigger a response that ignites the potentially hazardous fumes and produces disastrous consequences. Those who seek to exercise leadership, as their first order of business, must remove the immediate danger of further conflagration and create some time to think through the alternatives.

In the opening case of Eni, CEO Franco Bernabe had to step forward and dissipate the explosiveness of the situation that could bring his company crashing down. The company was in dire straits due to the arrest of the twenty senior managers on corruption charges, including the chairman. Bernabe immediately went before the nation and said that he would not tolerate corruption of any sort in Eni. Eni was the people's company, he said, and needed to be managed with absolute integrity. Bernabe then demanded the resignation of the arrested managers and another two hundred senior managers of the company.

> It was a very difficult decision for me from both a psychological and managerial perspective. I could not judge the guilt or innocence of the people arrested. And replacing all the senior managers would mean putting Eni in the hands of men and women

who were untested. . . . But I did it anyway. . . . It was a big risk, but it was also a big opportunity.[9]

Bernabe wanted people to see that he was committed to cleaning house and making Eni transparent, corruption-free, and highly productive. His actions calmed the people and gave time to determine the best course of action with a brand new executive team. "The old Eni may be burning," he explained to the people of Italy, "but a new enterprise could rise from the ashes."[10]

Franklin Delano Roosevelt in the very week that he took up the job as president of the United States in 1933 faced an unparalleled and potentially explosive crisis. The economic havoc wrought by the Great Depression and a drought-plagued agricultural sector had ravaged the nation and its people. Millions were hungry and desperate. A so-called Bonus Army of World War I veterans had marched on Washington to demand promised benefits, only to be assaulted by federal troops. Internal migration of homeless farmers and laborers provoked violence and confrontation in the American West, and employers were using the hard times to break the back of organized labor. The explosive fumes of crisis were everywhere, and Roosevelt's first task as president was to vent them off and lessen the chance of societal detonation.

For the past three years, the economy had sunk deeper into depression. No relief was in sight, and the nation's banking system was teetering on the edge of total collapse. The federal deficit was a shocking $5 billion. The national income was half of what it had been four years earlier. One-quarter of the labor force was unemployed, and more industries were failing every day. In describing the leadership challenges of the era, historian Arthur Schlesinger wrote, "It was now not just a matter of staving off hunger. It was a matter of seeing whether a representative democracy could conquer economic collapse. It was a matter of staving off violence, even revolution."[11]

Into this terrible crisis came Roosevelt, with a sunny, optimistic air of patrician competence that appealed to a worn and fearful nation. Many of his supporters looked to him with incredibly high, even unrealistic, expectations that he could reverse the tides of the depression. One woman actually wrote to him saying, "People are looking to you almost as they look to God."[12] But Roosevelt's cheerful optimism concealed his deep uncertainty about how to proceed in such unprecedented and desperate circumstances. His wife Eleanor wrote at the time, "One has a feeling of going it blindly, because we're in a tremendous stream, and none of us know where we're going to land."[13]

People were in a state of panic, and many banks were collapsing due to demands by depositors to cash out their accounts. It wasn't just a run on one bank; it was a run on the entire banking system. If unchecked, it could unleash a further storm of economic destruction from which the country might never recover.

Roosevelt took office on Saturday, March 4, 1933. His first executive order was to declare Monday, March 6, as the start of a bank holiday. All banks were required to close until further notice. This important strategic action helped him buy time to make his diagnosis and to think, if only for a few crucial days, about what might be done to resolve the crisis and revive the banking system. He did not want people rushing to the banks on Monday, acting rashly, and further undermining confidence. He knew that he needed to reduce the public's anxiety and restore, to some degree at least, confidence in the banks so that the economy would not falter in his first week on the job as president. Schlesinger later wrote of this decision to declare a public holiday:

> For the country, the proclamation ushered in almost a springtime mood. The closing of the banks seemed to give the long economic descent a punctuation of a full stop, as if this were the bottom and hereafter things could only turn upward. Anything was better than nagging uncertainty. Now everyone knew where he stood. People enjoyed the sense of a common plight.[14]

In the next few days, Roosevelt pulled together a team of Treasury Department staff, government officials, economists, politicians, and bankers and gave them the task of coming up with concrete strategies for addressing the problem. This was a diverse group of people from different sectors and disciplines, as he wanted new, creative perspectives to be surfaced and engaged.

Over the next four days, the "crisis team," locked away in the U.S. Treasury Building, was stretched almost to the breaking point. But they succeeded in generating some practical solutions designed to ease the problem until more analysis could be done. One of the participants later recorded, "We had forgotten to be Republican or Democrats. We were just a bunch of men trying to save the banking system."[15] By Thursday, the group had come up with an "Emergency Banking Act." It was sent to Congress that same day. Roosevelt personally met with key members of Congress and explained to them that, with so much at stake, this was no time for party politics. (Besides, his large margin of victory and healthy Democratic majorities in both Houses of Congress gave him unstoppable momentum.) The entire legislative approval process took less than eight hours—an unprecedented accomplishment.

On Sunday, March 12, one week since taking office, Roosevelt decided to address the nation via radio and conduct a "fireside chat." He knew that the nation's banks were about to receive permission to reopen their doors—and his aim was to calm the mood of the people, reassure them that the banking system was secure, and enlist their support for an ambitious program to bring the country out of its economic decline.

In preparing for his speech, Roosevelt laid down on his couch and visualized ordinary people on the street and in their homes, and he tried to think what message they would need to hear. He imagined talking to a mason working on a building, a girl behind the counter in a store, an auto mechanic busy repairing a car, and a farmer in a field. They were all looking to him for leadership. This was to be his first major radio address as president, and the stakes were too high to contemplate.

He delivered his speech live on Sunday evening. "Let us unite in banishing fear," he said. "It is your problem no less than it is mine. Together we cannot fail." Relaxed and confident that he had done his best, he believed that the American people would understand what he was trying to say and would respond to his clear language and his call to a shared mission.

The speech was a resounding success. The humorist Will Rogers said that "the President took a complicated subject like banking, and made everybody understand it, even the bankers."[16] Within a week, the mood of the country was more upbeat. Most banks reopened, and people began returning to deposit their funds. The acute panic had come to an end.[17] One journalist wrote of Roosevelt's leadership, "In one week, the nation, which had lost confidence in everything and everybody, has regained confidence in the government and in itself."[18] Rogers also gave more kudos: "They got a man in there who is wise to Congress, wise to our so-called big men. The whole country is with him, just so he does something. If he burned down the Capitol we would cheer and say 'well, we at least got a fire started.'"[19]

Franklin Roosevelt had to dissipate the explosiveness of the situation facing the nation in 1933. By reaching out to the American people, explaining the useful role they could play, and reassuring them that he and his team were attending to the problem, he was able to diffuse the immediate danger, restore calm, and buy time to work out a course of longer-term action.

Hold steady—don't get pulled into the fracas

A leader might be outstanding in so many ways but it is often a crisis that brings them down. In a heightened state of tension, danger is ever-present, and leaders can find themselves in a highly emotional and vulnerable position. In this state of mind, and out of their own uncertainty and desire to placate a restive populace, they may lose their focus and, under these circumstances, their comments and actions may actually *deepen* the crisis and make matters worse. They can also become scapegoats for a wrathful public and get extremely defensive, going on the attack in a thoughtless and irresponsible manner. The challenge for leaders in the midst of a crisis is to hold steady, get access to their emotions, and ensure that they do not get pulled into the fracas. The sensations spawned by a crisis challenge can easily make matters even worse. Any number of the key players who sought to end the East Timor crisis could easily have given up and walked away in disgust. Instead, they kept their focus and kept up the pressure without engaging in grand gestures, wild threats, or bitter recriminations.

When Eni's CEO, Franco Bernabe, faced the perilous corruption crisis, he knew that he needed to think clearly, act rationally, and focus unswervingly on the problem at hand. "I must say I did not 'react' during the crisis. I always thought things through—I very carefully went through all the problems I had, analyzing them from every angle."[20] Bernabe kept his emotions in check, even as he, too, was accused of corruption. He knew that if he took things personally, he could easily lose control and escalate the conflict.

History is replete with episodes when even the greatest authorities, faced with a crisis challenge, took things personally and acted irresponsibly to exacerbate the crisis. One such case occurred in 1799, when Captain James Cook, who had weathered many crises with remarkable skill and flexibility, finally lost his composure, his good judgment, and his life at Hawaii's Kealakekua Bay.

In the 1770s, Cook visited, inventoried, and mapped large swathes of the Pacific and the waters around Antarctica. On his third voyage to the Pacific in 1778, he found the Hawaiian Islands, named them in honor of a patron, Lord Sandwich, and, unbeknownst to the local population, claimed them for the Crown.

As Cook's two ships, the *Discovery* and the *Resolution*, entered the beautiful Kealakekua Bay on January 17, 1779, about a thousand canoes came out to greet the tired and weary crew. Finally, when Cook came ashore, the rowdy and jubilant Hawaiians fell silent and prostrated themselves on the ground repeating the word *orono*. The Hawaiians were greeting Cook as more than just another mariner visiting their island shores. They thought he was a god. The pageantry and obsequious behavior lasted a little over a week before the Hawaiians began to suspect that Cook and his men were nothing more than mere mortals. Indeed, during that brief period, one of the crew died of a heart attack and was buried on the island, raising further doubts among the Hawaiians concerning the status of these foreign beings. They eventually concluded that they had been mistaken in their belief and suggested to Cook that he and his men best be on their way.

On February 4, 1779, Cook and his men left the island. Two days later, Cook sailed into a fierce storm. The huge waves and cyclonic winds wreaked havoc on the ships, snapping the foremast of the *Resolution*. Needing a temporary safe haven, they returned to Kealakekua Bay. This time no one paddled out to greet them.

While the men went about their repair work, one of the islanders stole a set of tongs from the ship's blacksmith. He was soon apprehended by Cook's men and given forty lashes, nearly killing the poor man. This further aggravated the Hawaiians, who demanded that the interlopers leave, once and for all. Some of the sailors who ventured ashore looking for water and food were set upon by angry, rock-throwing mobs. The situation was growing extremely tense and precarious.

When Cook and some of his men were on shore making repairs, another attempt was made to steal the blacksmith's tongs. As the thief was fleeing, Cook personally gave chase. Cook, in turn, was chased by a group of angry locals. Two of Cook's men tried to seize a canoe in the bay that they assumed to be a getaway boat of the thief. It was actually the canoe of one of the high chiefs. In the ensuing melee, the chief was beaten with an oar by the sailors. The mob gathering on the shore went berserk, hurling stones and spears at the white men. The chief intervened and brought calm to the situation, and told the sailors to return to their ship.

As Cook rested on the ship and considered his current predicament, his frustration turned to rage. To further infuriate him, he woke the next morning to find that the *Discovery*'s cutter had been stolen overnight.

To deal with the "thieving natives," Cook had men blockade the entrance to Kealakekua Bay so that no canoe could leave. Feeling very much like a great white god, the captain boldly went ashore with his armed escort and arrested the king, Tereeoboo. The intention was to take the king hostage and keep him on the *Discovery* until the cutter was returned. As the king and his captors came to the canoe for the short trip back to the ship, a hostile crowd gathered and demanded that the king not be taken away.

At the time of the king's arrest, a group of canoes tried to break the blockade at the entrance of the bay. The high chief Kalimu was shot dead in the attempt. The news of this killing arrived on shore within minutes, and, predictably, the anxious mob that had gathered around

Cook and the king became rabid. As they approached Cook, Cook fired his single-shot musket and killed a man. The crowed became hysterical, screaming and jumping. The sailors then fired randomly, killing whoever they could. A portion of the landing party was in the boat waiting for Cook and managed to flee back to the ship. Those who had gone ashore, however, met a horrible end. While Cook was walking cautiously into the water trying to reach a nearby boat, he was attacked by a warrior who clubbed him to death. Other warriors joined in and further hacked, beat, and stabbed the one-time god. Within a period of fifteen minutes, Cook and four of his crew lay lifeless in the bloody surf, along with seventeen dead Hawaiians.

Cook's behavior in Kealakekua Bay was so unlike him that it has remained a puzzle and source of controversy ever since. In a brilliant career of exploration and discovery, Cook had won the respect of his colleagues and his crews, and he was, despite his humble origins, held in high regard by the British Admiralty. He was a talented navigator, a courageous and energetic commander, and a capable diplomat. Yet a few seemingly insignificant but serious errors of judgment in a tense situation led to his death (and those of four of his crewmen) at the hands of hostile Hawaiians. Rooted in cultural differences and confrontational shows of bravado, it was a situation he handled well on other islands with other tribes. In Hawaii, he seems to have become distracted from the main issue, ignored or misjudged the dynamics of the group, and lost his composure. He made the situation worse and paid for it with his life.

Students of leadership are all too familiar with this type of uncharacteristic behavior. Momentarily, in a state of physical and psychological exhaustion, feeling unsupported and isolated, many leaders simply lose control of their emotions and their thinking capacities. Like Cook, they act rashly and make the problem worse, and the results can be devastating.

Keep people from striking a match; remind them of the higher purpose

Given the chaos and confusion that a crisis engenders, those who would exercise leadership must not only keep calm, focused, and disciplined but also be on the lookout for other individuals or factions that may, out of anger, fear, or frustration, touch off the explosive gas of crisis before it can be dissipated. One of the critical leadership tasks in a crisis challenge is to ensure that no one strikes a match—intentionally or accidentally—that destroys the opportunity to achieve successful resolution of the crisis.

In the East Timor crisis, a faction within the U.S. government was convinced that the strategic relationship with Indonesia trumped the humanitarian impulses of the international community and the cause of the East Timorese. This entrenched faction could easily have lit a match that would have enflamed the Indonesian paramilitary with a sense of invulnerability, thereby plunging the island of Timor back into decades of savage guerilla and counterinsurgent warfare. Fortunately, others in the government and in the international community saw the problem and dealt with it before it set off a new explosion of violence.

During the crisis, even the East Timorese had to manage their own internal dynamics and keep people from striking a match that would exacerbate the conflict and undermine the years of demanding activist leadership that was beginning to bear fruit. The following incident was described to me by the respective parties involved.

Immediately after the August 30, 1999, referendum for independence, the country erupted into chaos as the militias ran amok. Listening to the mayhem on the radio at his detention compound in Jakarta, Indonesia, guerrilla leader Xanana Gusmao was filled with feelings of helplessness and despair, but he kept his anger and frustration in check. Gusmao was in his seventh year of imprisonment. Before his capture, he had spent more than ten years in the mountains fighting the Indonesian military. Due to international pressure, he had recently been allowed to move from the prison to a home in Jakarta, where he was kept under house arrest. He recognized that the immediate task was to keep his fellow East Timorese guerrillas from "striking the match" that could further exacerbate the explosiveness of the intensifying crisis.

In July and August, the last of the East Timor resistance fighters had come down from the mountains to be "cantoned" by the United Nations at four special camps until after the vote. The 1,500 men were allowed to keep their weapons, although they were not allowed to carry them in the streets. When the Indonesian-backed militias went on their wild rampage, the guerrilla fighters wanted badly to engage the enemy in order to protect their families and communities. They readied their weapons and prepared for combat.

Just as they were getting ready to leave their quarters, the guerrillas' most senior field commander, Taur Matan Ruak, received a telephone call from Gusmao in Jakarta. Gusmao insisted that they should not, under any circumstance, enter the fight. He instructed Taur and his men to remain in their compounds and avoid contact with the militias. With independence so close and the eyes of the world upon them, Gusmao argued that a renewal of armed conflict would only make matters worse. The Indonesian army would devastate the guerrillas and anyone else who opposed them, the country would be thrown back into a bloody civil war, and Indonesian occupation would persist. Gusmao wanted the guerrillas to understand that, in this moment of extreme tension, their cause would be best served not by fighting but by exercising restraint. The protective work needed to be left to the few UN peacekeepers who were on the ground. It was insufficient, but this had to be the UN's battle, and not the guerrillas'. After twenty-five years of struggle and sacrifice, independence was finally within their reach, but everything they had fought and bled for could be destroyed by renewed conflict.

Reluctantly, Commander Taur obeyed Gusmao's directive, telling his men that they were not to fire a shot. The guerrillas could not believe what was being asked of them. The enemy was openly and flagrantly brutalizing and attacking the East Timorese people in front of their very eyes. This behavior could not be allowed. How could they obey such an order and stand by as their families and friends were being assaulted? Taur, who has since become the defense minister in the government of East Timor, cried with his men when he told them Gusmao did not want them to fight against the militias. In his twenty-five years as a guerrilla, this was the hardest order he had ever given. He understood the logic of what Xanana Gusmao was asking, but it pained him deeply that he and his men had to stand by watching the militia gangs destroy the country. East Timor would need the sympathy and support of the international community if, like a phoenix, it was going to rise from the ashes and become a real, viable nation. Impulsive action, however understandable and gratifying, would only serve to undermine the chances of independence and international assistance.

Nelson Mandela also had to keep his country from going up in flames. The situation was like that of a tinderbox when, on April 10, 1993, a popular antiapartheid leader named Chris Hani was shot dead near Johannesburg. Second only to Mandela, Hani had emerged as a leading symbol of resistance and was idolized by young people throughout the black townships. The killing of Hani threw the country into shock and despair.

Amazingly, a white South African woman saw the shooting of Hani and immediately reported to police the license plate of the car that the killer was driving. Within minutes the police arrested a white man who was a member of an extremist organization and charged him with the murder. Later, a white male member of parliament was also implicated.

The black population was outraged, confused, and very angry. They demanded immediate justice.

Into the fray stepped the seventy-three-year-old Nelson Mandela. The situation was heated. The people were in a heightened state of anxiety, and anything could happen. The whites were terrified, and many wanted to flee; blacks were angry and ready to fight; the police were on edge and could be excessively brutal in response to protests. The evening of the murder, Mandela made a public speech that was broadcast across the country.[21] He had a specific message for each of the factions.

The first thing he told the nation was that it was a white woman who was responsible for the capture of Hani's killer. He sought to assure the people that taking revenge on all white people was not right, as there were good, moral whites, who were committed to justice and progress. In Mandela's words: "Tonight I am reaching out to every single South African, black and white, from the depths of my being. A white man, full of prejudice and hate . . . committed a deed so foul that our whole nation now teeters on the brink of disaster. A white woman of Afrikaner origin risked her life so that we might know, and bring to justice the assassin."

Mandela then reminded his listeners that the underlying purpose of the struggle was freedom for *all* South Africans. He specifically reached out to whites, inviting them to join with him and with the black community in mourning the loss of Chris Hani, and to take a shared stand for freedom and tolerance.

Mandela then addressed the police. He knew that there would be protests and perhaps even sporadic outbursts of violence and rioting. Mandela did not want the police to exacerbate the situation by an extreme response to the rage of the black townships—and especially among young people. "Now is the time for the police to act with sensitivity and restraint," Mandela stated, "to be real community policemen and women and serve the population as a whole. There must be no further loss of life at this tragic time."

It was important for Mandela to explain to the black population just how critical it was to consider the implications of their actions when so much was at stake. He explained to them, "This is a watershed moment for all of us. Our decisions and actions will determine whether we use our pain, our grief, and our outrage to move forward to what is the only lasting solution for our country—an elected government of the people, by the people, and for the people."

In particular, Mandela directed his words to the militant factions who were demanding that "all whites be killed." Although most of the black population was not supporting the extremists, many of the youth were leaning in that direction. This was a time for incredible discipline and restraint. Mandela pled:

> We must not let the men who worship war, and those who lust for blood, precipitate actions that will plunge our country into another Angola. Chris Hani was a soldier. He believed in iron discipline. He carried out instructions to the letter. He practiced what he preached. Any lack of discipline is trampling on the values that Chris Hani stood for. . . . When we as one people, act together decisively, with discipline and determination, nothing can stop us.

Mandela's speech to the nation was a turning point in the battle against the apartheid government. The potential for the situation to burst into flames was very real. He truly understood the magnitude of the problem and did an extraordinary job in ensuring that people did not lose sight of the higher purpose.

Don't be pigheaded or naive— explore every alternative

In a time of crisis, it is important to surface all relevant information that can help bring peaceful and effective resolution to the crisis. This task is, of course, crucial in the context of any leadership challenge, but it is more time constrained in a crisis. Dealing with a crisis challenge requires a swift diagnosis and a rapacious effort to obtain feedback and seek out different perspectives. In East Timor, the danger of the Indonesian paramilitaries was obscured by the international community's sincere hope that Indonesia could be trusted to assist the East Timorese in moving toward autonomy. It took bloodshed and destruction to force the reality of the situation to the surface.

In the midst of a crisis with adrenalin flowing, it is easy for "dominance" dynamics to override the exploration of all the alternatives. The dominance dynamics could be manifest by the superior authority figure who imposes his solution prematurely on the group, or a powerful faction of the group that thinks they alone know how to resolve the crisis. The leadership work is to protect the problem-solving space and ensure that the best solution is generated.

In 1915, a "pigheaded" Winston Churchill, as Lord of the Admiralty, sent mostly Australian and New Zealand troops (ANZACs), with some British support, to battle in the ill-conceived Gallipoli campaign to take control of the Dardanelle Straits of Turkey. Although the ANZACs fought like tigers, about twelve thousand soldiers were needlessly slaughtered at Gallipoli Cove alone. More than twenty-five thousand were wounded. The British never succeeded in breaking through the Turkish lines, and after nine months, Churchill ordered the withdrawal of all troops from the Dardanelles. The British had been humiliated.

As the proverbial bull in the china shop, Churchill had imposed his Gallipoli plan on others and did not give ample space for dissident voices to challenge his assumptions, express their views, and come up with alternative strategies. The merits of his strategy seemed completely self-evident, and he was adamant on seeing that he prevailed. The primary person whom he failed to listen to was his own head of the navy, First Lord of the Sea, Admiral John Fisher. Not only did Churchill spurn Fisher's counsel, but he took steps to ensure that Fisher's perspective would never be fully considered by the prime minister and the War Cabinet. The seventy-four-year-old admiral was perhaps the most respected naval strategist in England. He certainly knew more about war than his boss, the forty-year-old Winston Churchill. Fisher, for an array of reasons, was completely against Churchill's plan for an amphibious attack on the Dardanelles, knowing his navy was ill equipped to succeed. Finding it difficult even to get a one on one meeting with Churchill, on May 11, 1915, Fisher wrote a letter to his boss:

> Although I have acquiesced in each stage of the operation up to the present, largely on account of consideration of political expediency and the political advantage which those whose business it is to judge these matters have assured me would accrue from success, or even partial success, I have clearly expressed my opinion that I did not consider the original attempt to force the Dardanelles with the fleet alone was a practical operation. . . . I therefore feel impelled to inform you definitely and formally of my conviction that such an attack by the fleet on the Dardanelles . . . is doomed to failure, and moreover is fraught with possibilities of disaster utterly incommensurate to any advantage that could be obtained there from.[22]

Fisher had a piece of the reality that Churchill needed to face in this precarious predicament and repeatedly tried to get Churchill to see it. Churchill, however, refused to entertain Fisher's argument and trivialized the old man as being too much of a traditionalist, skilled in fighting nineteenth-century battles, perhaps, but not fully appreciative of what was required for modern warfare in the twentieth century. Not knowing what else he should do, Fisher sent another letter to Churchill, this time indicating that he planned to resign. "You are bent on forcing the Dardanelles and nothing will turn you from it—nothing. I know you so well. You will remain and I shall go—it is better so."[23]

The Gallipoli campaign was a fiasco—an unnecessary crisis in the context of a larger crisis: a world war. Churchill learned from the experience; in his memoirs, he acknowledged his folly: "Looking back, with after-knowledge and increasing years, I seem to have been too ready to undertake tasks which were hazardous or even forlorn."[24]

When U.S. president John F. Kennedy faced the Cuban Missile Crisis in October 1962, it was imperative that he not get caught up in the emotion of the crisis and undertake tasks that were hazardous or forlorn. He had to take the time to ascertain what the real challenge was through the fog. His situation was the reverse of Churchill's. His generals were advocating an attack on Cuba, and Kennedy was telling them to slow down and explore all the available options. They expressed to the president that they were confident that they could succeed in destroying the weapons installations that had been placed on Cuba by the Soviet Union. Also, a piece of reality that the group did not know at the time was that more than one hundred nuclear warheads were already in Cuba. The Americans knew the installations had been constructed but were unaware that the warheads existed and were operational.

Kennedy realized that the stakes were too high for hasty action, even though he did not have knowledge of the nuclear warheads. He was wise enough to know that this was not a technical problem that could easily be fixed through the application of military expertise. On the contrary, as Kennedy looked through the fog of the crisis, it was clear to him that the underlying challenge related to the relationship between the United States and the Soviet Union. In particular, the challenge was how to ensure that both countries could take responsibility for the destructive power of their nuclear arsenals and that millions of people would never be killed. Upon seeing this challenge, Kennedy refused to accept the recommendation of the Joint Chiefs of Staff, pushing the group to consider what was at stake and to come up with a better solution.

Coming up with ways to produce a better solution was difficult work, particularly given the fact that some of the military leaders were anxious to display their fighting prowess and express their dominance. Robert McNamara, the secretary of defense and a member of Kennedy's leadership team assigned to address the crisis, told of an interaction he had with Admiral George W. Anderson, chief of naval operations and a member of the Joint Chiefs of Staff. It was about a Russian ship approaching the blockade that the United States had imposed around Cuba. McNamara had the following conversation with Admiral Anderson:

> "What are you going to do?" I said. He said, "Well, we're going to stop it." I said, "How are you going to do it?" He was beginning to get a little upset . . . and he said, "We are going to hail it." I said, "What language are you going to hail it in?" He was getting more and more exasperated. "Well, English." I said, "Do they have English speaking sailors on board the ship?" He said, "How the hell do I know?" And I said, "What are you going to do if that doesn't stop them?" "Well, we'll put a shot through the rudder." I said, "What kind of a ship is it?" "Well, it's a tanker."
>
> I said, "Look, we don't want to start a war by blowing up a tanker." And this is what he said, and these are his exact words, he said, "Mr. Secretary, the Navy has been handling blockades successfully since John Paul Jones. If you let us handle this, we will do it successfully. I said, "Admiral, you heard me. Not a shot will be fired without my permission." It was quite a controversy. . . . I had the highest respect for Admiral Anderson as a combat commander, but not as geo-politician, which was the role he was in at the time.[25]

Through constant pushing back, questioning, and examining every alternative from every angle, eventually the team came up with a diplomatic, peaceful resolution to the crisis. It was actually due to Kennedy's willingness to listen and to promote debate that the best solution emerged. Llewellyn Thompson, the former ambassador to the Soviet Union and a junior member of the problem-solving team, raised his opinion in regard to how the president should respond to a letter from the Soviet leader, Nikita Khrushchev. Kennedy and others felt it was simply a ploy to trick the Americans. Thompson, who had met with Khrushchev many times and knew his style and personality, explained to the president that he needed to take Khrushchev's letter very seriously. The conversation went as follows:

> **President Kennedy:** We're not going to get these weapons out of Cuba, probably, anyway . . . I mean by negotiation. . . . I don't think there's any doubt he's not going to retreat now that he made that public, Tommy. He's not going to take them out of Cuba.
>
> **Llewellyn Thompson:** I don't agree, Mr. President. I think there's still a chance we can get this line going.

President Kennedy: He'll back down?

Llewellyn Thompson: The important thing for Khrushchev, it seems to me, is to be able to say "I saved Cuba; I stopped an invasion," and he can get away with this, if he wants to, and he's had a go at this Turkey thing, and that we'll discuss later.

President Kennedy: All right.

McNamara said of the importance of this interaction, "Tommy proved to be exactly right. I thank God we had a president who was . . . 'fully on the job'—inquisitive, forceful, determined to find a way out short of war—and an advisor whose empathy with the Soviets allowed him to be, at that moment, virtually our in-house Russian."[26] Kennedy, in being "fully on the job" as a leader in a time of crisis, encouraged divergent views, actively inquired into people's assumptions, and always listened to discover what he might be missing—while all the time pushing the group to stretch their thinking. Indeed, he successfully (even luckily, given how volatile the situation was and the information that his team was lacking) displayed real leadership for a very real, potentially explosive crisis challenge. Had he not been open, inquisitive, and a potent perturbing force, a nuclear confrontation might have been the horrendous conclusion.

Conclusion

Politicians and presidents make errors all the time. Nevertheless, times of great danger require a particular kind of leadership that is more sensible and sensitive than what one might provide during a time of peace or relative calm. No single authority figure should be so brazen as to think that he or she alone "has the answer" and can "show the way forward" in such a foggy predicament. As the Gallipoli campaign and the Cuban Missile Crisis teach us, the complexities of the situation and unpredictable surprises can easily disorient even the most able authority—and in doing so seriously thwart progress. Therefore, taking the time to tangle with dissident perspectives, explore alternatives, and test assumptions is absolutely essential.

Taking on a crisis challenge requires the capacity to remain calm in a volatile, hot, and foggy environment that is riddled with an array of competing emotions and sensations, and to carefully intervene to reduce the heat and keep people from acting irresponsibly by exacerbating the danger. These are never easy things to do, and, with the crushing urgency of a crisis, they become even more difficult. But, as many of the cases in this chapter illustrate, leadership can be exercised in such trying circumstances, and one can succeed in seeing through the fog to identify the real work that must be attended to if the conflict is to be resolved and progress is to unfold.

REAL LEADERSHIP
FOR A CRISIS CHALLENGE

- Dissipate the explosive fumes, and create some time to think.
- Hold steady—don't get pulled into the fracas.
- Keep people from striking a match; remind them of the higher purpose.
- Don't be pigheaded or naive—explore every alternative.

PART III

Real Leadership
in Action

CHAPTER 9

Leading in Multiple Challenges
The Case of T. E. Lawrence

As the supreme god, Odin possessed multiple attributes that allowed him to play the appropriate role in many different situations. He could be a sage, an inspirational poet, a savage and vengeful warrior, or simply a mysterious pilgrim who sits for a while by the fire and offers a few words of uncanny wisdom and moves on. The demands of the situation dictated the divine aspect that he would reveal to his people, but his words and actions would always be framed by a larger purpose—to add to his store of wisdom and understanding while helping his people deal realistically and responsibly with their problems.

Few mere mortals have the transformative capacity to repeatedly exercise successful leadership in the face of multiple challenges. It is extremely difficult to modulate one's leadership style from one challenge to the next, shifting one's behavior and strategies to address a group's diverse problems or the sharply differing aspects of its single, overarching challenge. Leaders tend to get into trouble when they apply the same tactics that succeeded in one context to address another. They are inclined to believe that leadership is the consistent application of the same behaviors and strategies, irregardless of the situation. When the terrain the problem is embedded in changes, they do not know how to shift gears on the fly and modify their tactics and role to meet the new and different need.

As we have seen in this book, distinct leadership challenges require distinct leadership strategies. The capacity to alter one's approach to leadership is essential in any but the most static and simple settings. Anyone who hopes to exercise real leadership in a complex environment must learn to recognize the need for flexibility in the way that he or she intervenes and responds to the threats and opportunities confronting the group.

Real leadership is fundamentally an interactive art, in which the leader is dancing with the context, the problem, the factions, and the objective. All these factors should shape the role, style, and tactics of the leader and the leader's approach to intervention. I have attempted to categorize large and complicated phenomena under neat headings, but I also realize that real life is rarely so pristine. It is entirely reasonable to argue that some leadership challenges are really multiple challenges. That is, a challenge might not be purely an activist, development, transitional, maintenance, creative, or crisis context. One type of challenge might dominate, but elements of other challenge types are embedded in the terrain as well. This gives rise to a puzzle. Differing types of leadership challenges are best met with different types of leadership strategies, but many real-life leadership challenges are a blend of several types. How then, can someone who wishes to exercise leadership in the face of multiple challenges develop an effective and flexible approach that doesn't contradict or undo itself—or simply become a hopeless muddle?

The answer to this puzzle is to develop a hierarchy of challenges and plan one's response accordingly. The leader should give primacy to the intervention approach best suited to the *principal challenge* but have the flexibility to provide appropriate interventions for *subchallenges* and *leadership tasks* as they crop up. Therefore, in diagnosing the terrain, it is important to distinguish the overarching challenge from the many subchallenges and tasks that need to be addressed.

Take, for example, the case of the highly successful M&T Bank. Due to outstanding leadership the bank has grown from a $3 billion regional institution to a $52 billion financial services pacesetter over a twenty-year period. Recently, however, it faced a complicated development challenge of continuing to grow at a rate of 15 to 20 percent a year even though its market position had stabilized and economic conditions were less favorable than in the bank's earlier boom years. Top management did not know exactly how to meet the inflated expectations of stockholders and Wall Street in this new economic environment. After considerable deliberation, the chairman determined that the company would have to do some serious cost cutting to improve its efficiency, while simultaneously identifying inventive ways to increase revenues.

In the course of confronting the development challenge of keeping its rapid and profitable growth, the bank faced a series of important subchallenges and essential tasks that also required real leadership. These included *activist work* to get the managers and staff to face the new reality that the bank was a complex multistate operation that could no longer be managed as if it were a small regional bank; *creative work* that required the invention of new products and services to respond to the demands of increased competition and savvy consumers; *transition work* of incorporating a new acquisition into the main body of the corporation with minimal disruption to the cultures of both organizations; *maintenance work* in the areas of cutting costs, preserving current value, keeping current customers, and ensuring that talented employees did not flee to greener pastures; and *development work* to increase the capabilities of managers to become more effective leaders and problem solvers and responsibly attend to the emergence of a dynamic corporate culture.

The bank approached these challenges with notable dedication and zeal. The chairman—realizing the scope, complexity, and magnitude of the work—encouraged more aggressive and visible leadership from the two hundred members of senior management, most of whom were excellent technical specialists but were now required to be multidisciplinary managers who could lead across functional and organizational boundaries to address the complex challenges and subchallenges the bank faced, and continues to face.

Still, although it is useful (and often necessary) to engage many people in the work of leadership—especially when an organization or community faces multiple challenges—it is also vital that those who have higher authority develop the prowess to adjust their intervention strategies to meet the demands of the different and sundry challenges as they emerge. Life doesn't stay still. Contexts are shifting and changing all the time. All enterprises, therefore, need more men and women who understand the complexity of the contextual demands of leadership and authority and can provide the full array of interventions that help people face reality, address their problems, and take advantage of the opportunities before them.

What follows is the case of T. E. Lawrence—the legendary Lawrence of Arabia—a man who displayed enormous dexterity in the practice of leadership in very trying and dynamic circumstances. Although not trained as a soldier, statesman, or diplomat, Lawrence had to take on all these roles, and more, in a complex struggle over politics and nationalism in the Middle East during and after World War I. Lawrence played many parts for many audiences while trying to achieve multiple goals that had to be constantly redefined in light of changing circumstances. His story allows us to see someone who could move in and out of the different challenges, provide context appropriate leadership, and, for the most part, succeed.

Lawrence and Arabia:
The Story of the Reluctant Leader

In the introduction to the *Seven Pillars of Wisdom*, T. E. Lawrence writes:

> All men dream: but not equally. Those who dream by night in the dusty recesses of their minds wake in the day to find that it was vanity: but the dreamers of the day are dangerous men, for they may act their dreams with open eyes, to make it possible. This I did. I meant to make a new nation, to restore a lost influence, to give twenty millions of Semites the foundations on which to build an inspired dream-palace of their national thoughts.[1]

Thomas Edward Lawrence, "Ned," to his family, was born in England on August 15, 1888, the second of five boys. He attended Oxford University, where he specialized in Middle Eastern studies and developed a fluency in Arabic. He also made a number of trips to the Middle East, where he conducted research on castles constructed during the crusades. When World War I broke out in 1914, Lawrence's knowledge of the Arabic language, the culture, and the terrain led to an assignment with the British Army's Middle East intelligence section, where he was given the task of preparing maps and writing reports on Arab politics. He was perfectly content with this desk job, which seemed to him to be a logical extension of the studies he had begun at Oxford.

Given his language skills and his knowledge of the local political dynamics, he was soon asked to become a liaison officer between the British and the Arabs, and he was assigned as an adviser to Prince Feisal, the son of the sherif of Mecca, who was to become one of the key figures in the Arab resistance against the Turkish Ottoman Empire. Turkey had become an ally of Germany and therefore an enemy of Britain. Fomenting unrest in Turkey's Arab possessions was seen as an inexpensive way to tie up Turkish troops and military resources without directly engaging British forces. By 1917, the Arabs had become quite active in revolt against the Turks, who had controlled the region for five hundred years—but the Arabs were disorganized, and their actions were often ineffective and entirely unpredictable.

After a series of meetings with Feisal, Lawrence was given the daunting task of developing a crack fighting force out of Feisal's unwieldy band of part-time warriors. Lawrence was reluctant to take up this task as he did not see himself as a professional soldier, and besides, being academically inclined, he much preferred the analytical and mapping work that he was doing at headquarters. He wrote of this order:

> Clayton [Lawrence's commanding officer] . . . told me to return to Arabia and Feisal. This being against my grain I urged my complete unfitness for the job: said I hated responsibility—obviously the position of a conscientious adviser would be responsible—and that in all my life objects had been gladder to me than persons, and ideas than objects. So the duty of succeeding with men to any purpose would be doubly hard to me. They were not my medium: I was not practiced in that technique. I was unlike a soldier; I hated soldiering . . . but I had to go; leaving to others the *Arab Bulletin* I had founded, the maps I wished to draw . . . all fascinating activities . . . to take up a role for which I had no inclination.[2]

While Lawrence had no inclination to be a warrior, he reluctantly took on the task. He had a good grasp of the land, the people, and the problems they faced, but before fully committing to support the Arabs in their quest, he needed to discern the readiness of the tribal chiefs to engage in the work of fighting for independence and forging a nation. Did they really want independence? Were they ready to do what was needed, even if that meant giving their lives? Could they work together, share resources, and subjugate personal desires and self-interest for the benefit of the whole? Lawrence was not at all interested in taking on this fight purely for British purposes. This was to be for the Arabs, and they had to want this more than he.

Diagnosing the Challenge

Lawrence made a visit to Feisal's desert camp to test Feisal and a group of Arab chiefs in regard to their commitment, character, and understanding of the challenge before them. While sitting with them in their large goat-skin tent, he asked tough questions, probed their minds, and, in Lawrence's words, "threw apples of discord, inflammatory subjects of talk amongst them, to sound their mettle and beliefs without delay."[3] He was pleased with what he found. These were intelligent, passionate, and committed people.

Lawrence's next task was to discern the hearts and minds of the ordinary men who would be the actual fighters in this war. What was the nature and depth of their commitment? Did they have a passion for independence? Could they be counted on when the going got tough? He wrote:

> The next morning I was up early and out among Feisal's troops . . . trying to feel the pulse of their opinions in a moment, by such tricks as those played upon their chiefs the night before. Time was of the essence of my effort, for it was necessary to gain in ten days the impressions which would ordinarily have been the fruit of weeks of observing.[4]

Lawrence saw what he needed to see. He concluded that the Bedouin, although of disparate factions and tribes, were a noble people with noble aspirations. He detected great promise in these initial meetings and was ready to join their quest.After considering the threats and the opportunities, and condition of the people, Lawrence realized that the Arabs were facing a daunting *development challenge*. (Of course, he didn't use that term.) They had to develop their capacity to be a formidable fighting force and win the war, and ultimately to manage their own affairs and run their own country. To bring the many and varied tribes together and invent a pathway forward that would lead to independence would require enormous imagination, creativity, persistence, and resourcefulness. And, although the overall challenge was a development challenge, there would be much leadership work to be done in the other five domains as well. The work would be riddled with danger—from beginning to end.

The Development Challenge

Fundamentally, leadership for a development challenge is about increasing people's capacity to take responsibility for their problems, address their most pressing challenges, and build their future in a productive and conscientious manner. The condition of the people facing a development challenge is such that they have the latent capabilities needed for development but those latent capabilities need to be nurtured and brought to fruition if the people are to attain their aspiration, goal, or promise. Often, however, the people are hesitant and reluctant to embrace a development process because they are unsure that they will reap the benefits if they develop their latent capabilities. All this was true for the Arabs. Many joined the cause with mixed motives, aspirations, and competencies.

Facing Lawrence was a major adaptive challenge with three demanding components. First, he had to develop an alliance of Arab tribes who could work together on behalf of a larger goal. Second, he had to develop the capacity of the Bedouin to be a formidable fighting force and win the war. Finally, he had to contribute to the development of the maturity, wisdom, and leadership capacity of enough tribal chiefs, including Feisal, to be able to run their own country once that opportunity was given them.

To facilitate the development process, Lawrence had to steadily get the Arabs to "stand on their own feet."[5] He did not want to be seen as the one "leading" the Bedouin but as their trainer and coach. The relationship had to be one not of dependency but of interdependency and mutual respect. He had great respect for the chiefs, particularly Feisal, and never did anything to usurp their power or diminish their status. In 1967, John Mack interviewed several Howeitat sheiks in Jordan who fought with Lawrence. He noted:

> All of these men found dignity and personal pride in their participation in the Arab Revolt, which remained for some of them the most important period of their lives—the time when they set aside their traditional clan quarrels and worked together toward the common goal of getting rid of the Turkish oppressor and obtaining freedom for their land and people.[6]

Mack went on to note that "they took great pride in the fact that the victory was an Arab victory achieved by Arabs. Lawrence's role was deeply valued, but he was seen as a planner, the encourager and coordinator of the Revolt."[7] For the Howeitat, their leader was Feisal, and Lawrence was *serving* him.

Create a holding environment

In exercising leadership for a development challenge, part of the work is to create and sustain a holding environment to orient people in their development work. A holding environment serves to generate a set of values and practices that allows the adaptive work to persist over time. A feature of any holding environment is the role and function of authority—particularly as it pertains to being the embodiment of the desired values of the group and wearing the mantle of the ideal. The mantle of the ideal represents the group's noblest behaviors, aspirations, and features. The mantle allows the leader to set a standard or a yard-stick. Of course, the challenge thereafter is to get the people to live up to that standard. The role contains distortions of reality—for better and for worse—that the leader must manage and take responsibility for. In other words, there is a perceptual component to the mantle of the ideal that the leader must be aware of. To some degree, the mantle is a role. It is a role that allows the group to project onto the leader their hopes and even their fantasies. The challenge of the one who assumes the role is to use it productively to give the work back to the people and get them to deal with reality.

As a first step in taking up his leadership role, Lawrence decided to discard his British khakis and adopt the clothes of a Bedouin—not an or-dinary Bedouin, but a royal Bedouin. Feisal personally gave Lawrence a magnificent outfit appropriate for a prince. An observer said of him, "While in Arab dress, he outrivaled the splendor of descendants of the Prophet. This again was not merely vanity. Arabs have a respect for fine raiment, which they associate with riches and power. It made him an outstanding figure among them, excited their curiosity, and therefore in-creased his authority when dealing with them."[8] It also gave him infor-mal authority—something that he desperately needed.

While in the desert, Lawrence became, for all intents and purposes, an Arab chieftain. It was a performance, but there was authenticity in his performance. He once remarked to a friend that his experience was like being on a "foreign stage, on which one plays day and night, in fancy dress, in a strange language."[9] He adopted Bedouin habits and practices, rode camels, ate their foods, and lived with them. He told the American journalist Lowell Thomas that in order to succeed with the Arabs, one must "dress like a Shereef, if the people agree to it, and, if you use Arab costume at all, go the whole length. Leave your English friends and cus-toms on the coast, and rely entirely on Arab habits."[10] Senior British of-ficers occasionally traveled with Lawrence on exercises or met with him in a town or village. They would invariably invite him to join them in their first-rate officers' quarters, but Lawrence always declined, preferring to stay with the Bedouin on the outskirts of the town or at a remote desert dwelling.

In becoming a nominal Arab, Lawrence could see and feel what needed to be done at a more grounded level. In many ways, he became *one* with the people. The biographer John Mack noted, "My informants stated clearly that their acceptance and trust of Lawrence grew out of his willingness to live among them, speak their language, wear their clothing, and eat their food."[11] Indeed, Lawrence connected with the people at a very profound level. They did not perceive him as an Oxford-educated Englishman but as a brother, who may have looked English yet whose heart was born of the desert. Liddell Hart, a fellow soldier, said that Lawrence "got into the Arab's skin first, and then transcended it."[12]

As a second step, in assuming the mantle of the ideal, Lawrence felt that he needed to excel in all aspects of bravery and endurance to capture the imagination of the Arabs. "He represented the heart of the Arab movement for freedom," said a colleague, "and Arabs realized he vitalized their cause; that he could do everything and endure everything just a little better than the Arabs themselves."[13] W. F. Stirling, a fellow soldier with Lawrence, said:

> No one looking at Lawrence would have considered him strong physically. The fact remains that this man was to break all the records of Arabia for speed and endurance. The great sagas sung throughout the desert of phenomenal rides carried out by the dispatch riders and dating back to the days of Caliph Haroun Al-Raschid have been completely eclipsed by Lawrence's achievements. On one occasion he averaged 100 miles a day for three consecutive days. Such endurance as this is almost incredible. I myself have ridden 50 miles in a night but never do I want to do it again. The difficulty is to keep awake. After the bitter glow of the desert night when the sun begins to rise and a warm glow envelops everything, the urge to sleep becomes a veritable torture. If you sleep you are apt to fall, and it becomes a long way from the top of a camel to the ground.[14]

Lawrence endeavored to be an example to his men of the effort and courage that was needed to tolerate their circumstances and ultimately prevail. One observer noted that Lawrence "had courage and endurance beyond the ordinary: morally, he had the gift of inspiration and leadership, he had vision, determination in plenty and an absence of the personal ambition that has marred the character of many great soldiers; he knew the common man."[15] The British soldiers who joined Lawrence on various adventures also had admiration for him. "His example made it impossible for any of his force to let him down. To do well in his eyes was the ambition of every single one of us. He typified all that was best in man."[16]

Give people a stake in developing their capacities

Lawrence was constantly presenting and reiterating to the Bedouin and their chiefs that if they could put aside their tribal differences, collaborate, and learn new ways of operating, they could win the war and enjoy the benefits of having their own nation. He could see the big picture, while some of the chiefs were parochial, self-interested, and often asking, "What's in it for me?" Lawrence's answer was always "a free and independent land where people could live and pursue their dreams unencumbered by foreign powers." That evocative possibility ignited collaborative effort and concentrated action that was sufficient to transcend immediate self-interest and tribal feuds.

Although the promise of their own homeland was given to the people, not only by Lawrence but by the British authorities, Lawrence knew how hard it would be to deliver on that promise. He had to deal with three impediments: (1) the deceitfulness of the British government, (2) the powerful Turkish army that was committed to protecting a land the Turks had ruled for hundreds of years, and (3) the parochialism and fluctuating commitment of the disparate Arab tribes. But, in spite of these barriers—or perhaps because of them—Lawrence reveled in this chance to display his creativity and do what he could to deliver on the promise. He personally embodied the vision, but he also was painfully aware of what was required to deliver on it. One writer commented:

> Lawrence saw the revolt in its political wholeness and moral dynamism; not merely as it was fouled by intrigue, cupidity and narrowness of spirit, but as it might become, an ideal possibility. He possessed the vision which, historically, was the Arabs' privilege: that was cause for elation. He knew they could not sustain that vision: that was cause for despair. Balancing elation and despair Lawrence reached full knowledge of the burdens of leadership.[17]

Indeed, the responsibility of leadership for a demanding development challenge can be a heavy burden. One must hold out a tremendous sense of aspiration while simultaneously engaging the dysfunctions of the people in their current predicament. But Lawrence threw himself into the challenge with dedication, passion, and zeal. One of Lawrence's colleagues described him as having the ambition of an artist. "It was not a selfish ambition," he wrote. "Rather it was the immersed ambition of the artist sinking himself into his purpose."[18]

Maintenance Tasks

Lawrence also faced persistent maintenance subchallenges and tasks in holding his forces together. The maintenance challenge is about sustaining and preserving vital group resources that are under threat due to internal or external forces. For Lawrence, upon developing certain capabilities in the Arabs for collaborative effort, the leadership challenge was to sustain such behavior. A significant threat that served to undermine the Arabs' resources and impede progress was a combination of the people's exhaustion and their own internal cultural and political dynamics. The ongoing leadership work was in ensuring that the group did not fall apart.

Attending to the Little Big Things

Because Lawrence and his men were constantly in an exhausted state, little big things helped the people face realistically their challenge on a day-by-day basis. One can get a sense of the emotional and physical fatigue in the following words of Lawrence:

> Each day some of us passed; and the living knew themselves just sentient puppets on God's stage: indeed, our taskmaster was merciless, merciless, so long as our bruised feet could stagger forward on the road. The weak envied those tired enough to die; for success looked so remote, and failure a near and certain . . . release from toil.[19]

Given the emotional demands of surviving in the harsh desert environment during a time of war, Lawrence related to his men, not as an officer but as a colleague, an equal. S. C. Rolls (later to become chairman of Rolls-Royce), who served as a driver for a brief period in the desert with Lawrence, said of him:

> Lawrence did not wax severe and military-like, indeed he was
> the very last person one would compare with the exalted ratings
> I had served with. Orders had been snapped out like the crack of
> musketry, salutes had been expected and duly received, commands
> had been obeyed to the letter, often grudgingly and unwittingly,
> but here was a power who seemed to command one's very soul,
> of charming persuasive manner, to seduce one's rebellion and
> counteract all obstinate ideas.[20]

For Arabs accustomed to smugness and condescension from other Europeans and their Turkish overlords, Lawrence's conduct came as a welcome and winning surprise. He went out of his way to send the message that every member was valued. Moreover, he proved that belief time and again, often in quite extraordinary ways. The following story is illustrative of his commitment.

Lawrence and his men were traveling through a particularly hazardous piece of desert. They noticed a riderless camel that had the saddlebags, rifle, and food of its rider. But the man was nowhere to be found. "Gradually it dawned on us that the miserable man was lost," Lawrence wrote. The Ageyl clan members, who were one of the tribes with Lawrence, speculated that the man, whose name was Gasim, had dozed and fallen from his saddle, possibly killing himself. As no one really cared for Gasim, and given that he was of a different tribe, the fact that he was gone did not seem to bother anybody.[21] Lawrence explained what happened next:

> So, without saying anything, I turned my unwilling camel round,
> and forced her, grunting and moaning for her camel friends, back
> past the long line of men . . . into the emptiness behind. My tem-
> per was very unheroic, for I was furious with . . . my own play-
> acting as a Bedouin, and most of all with Gasim, a gap-toothed,
> grumbling fellow, scrimshank in all our marches, bad-tempered,
> suspicious, brutal, a man whose engagement I regretted, and of
> whom I had promised to rid myself as soon as we reached a
> discharging-place. It seemed absurd that I should peril my weight
> . . . for a single worthless man.[22]

After a couple of hours, Lawrence found his man. "I rode up and saw that he was nearly blinded and silly, standing there with his arms held out to me, and his black mouth gaping open."[23] Gasim got on Lawrence's camel, and together they made their way back to the main caravan. Auda, one of the chiefs, was furious with Lawrence and told him had he known Lawrence's intention, he would have stopped him from going after the man. Lawrence recalled:

> Auda pointed to the wretched hunched-up figure and denounced me, "For that thing, not worth a camel's price. . . ." I interrupted him with "Not worth a half-crown, Auda," and he, delighted in his simple mind, rode near Gasim, and struck him sharply, trying to make him repeat like a parrot his price. Gasim bared his broken teeth in a grin of rage . . . and sulked on.[24]

By going after Gasim, Lawrence communicated to the group that every person mattered and that each person, irrespective of his tribal affiliation or status, had a role to play in the liberation of their country. He bewildered the Arabs time and again but clearly earned their admiration and respect. This was no ordinary Englishman. Given what Lawrence had experienced and all the challenges he confronted, it is a testament to his wisdom and skillful leadership that he survived. Certainly leadership for a maintenance challenge is difficult in the best of times, but when one has to lead a group "through the valley of the shadow of death" and preserve their resources and morale, the difficulty is so much greater. How easy it is to give up, to walk away, and to retreat in the face of exhaustion or persistent danger. Lawrence did not do that. He stood firm and held his men together in the face of overwhelming obstacles.

Crisis Tasks

A crisis challenge is an explosive situation fraught with peril and uncertainty. The leader must seek to understand the true nature of the problem, calm the emotions of the group, restore order, and steadily lead the group through the period of volatility. In such circumstances, anything can go wrong and set the entire situation aflame. Lawrence faced many such challenges where all the goodwill, collective effort, and group resources were in danger of being lost. The following example illustrates his leadership—particularly the weight of leadership—in a very volatile moment of escalating conflict.

Dissipating the Explosive Fumes That Are Building

While lying in his tent with a terrible headache and fever trying to re-cover from dysentery, Lawrence heard a gunshot. His troops had been quarreling all day, making it difficult for him to get any rest. When he checked to see what had happened, he was shocked. A member of the Ageyl clan, a man named Salem, was dead. The other members of the Ageyl were furious and ready to start a bloodbath. The guilty culprit was Hamed, a Moroccan Moor. A court was held at once, and Hamed confessed that he had had an argument with Salem, lost his temper, and shot him. The Ageyl clan members demanded blood for blood.

Lawrence tried to calm the group and talk some reason into the Ageyl, but this approach was impossible. "My head was aching with fever and I could not think; but hardly even in health, with all eloquence, could I have begged Hamed off," Lawrence recalled.[25] The situation was particularly precarious because if the Ageyl were to kill the Moor, the other Moroccans in Lawrence's group would kill another Ageyl, starting a process of tit-for-tat reprisals that would have destroyed the unity he had worked so hard to establish. Lawrence concluded that Hamed must be executed as tribal justice required. But to ensure that a feud did not esca-late, he determined that he personally must do the killing. "Perhaps they would count me not qualified for feud," he reasoned. "At least no re-venge could lie against my followers; for I was a stranger and kinless."[26]

Lawrence was successful in restoring order and ensuring that no more revenge killings in his band took place. It was a heavy burden for him to bear, but given his role in the group, and given what was at stake, he had no other choice.

Leadership during a crisis challenge is never an easy thing to exer-cise. There are so many unpredictable elements. One must take stock of the situation and examine the group dynamics (the factions, the compet-ing values, and the mood of the group) and consider what actions might trigger other negative reactions and produce an explosion. Lawrence was able to note that the potential for a clan feud would be inevitable if the two families were left to their own devices to "resolve" the conflict. He realized that if the dispute were to remain unresolved it would be very damaging to the morale of his men. To bring resolution would require a drastic measure: for Lawrence to kill Hamed. As disturbing as this ac-tion was, in the context that he was in, the action that he took was criti-cal to ensuring that a bloodbath did not erupt. Certainly, few of us today can appreciate what it would be like to be in such a predicament and have to make such a choice.

The Activist Challenge

In an activist challenge, the leadership work is to provoke and evoke the group to face certain realities they would prefer to avoid. The process includes both inspiring people with a uniting purpose and calling attention to the contradiction between what the group espouses and what they actually do. It is demanding and risky work, as one must become a thorn in the side, an irritant, to the group or some faction of the group, if one is to succeed in getting the attention of key people who are in a position to make the necessary changes or adjustments.

After the war, the reality that the British were avoiding was the fact that they had promised the Arabs independence and were now reneging on that promise. To Lawrence, and of course to the Arabs, it was sheer hypocrisy and deceit. Both Britain and France wished to carve up the region to meet their own particular interests, irrespective of what promises had been made. Lawrence was depressed to think that the real reason thousands of Arabs had been allowed to sacrifice their lives was "not to win the war but that the corn and rice and oil of Mesopotamia might be ours."[27] Disturbingly, as biographer John Mack notes, "this was a time in which the leadership of the Western powers could still move men and countries around like pawns, and bargained and dealt in states and whole populations."[28]

Lawrence took on the responsibility of exercising leadership to get the British people to face reality and ensure that the government honored its promise. Given his wartime accomplishments, Lawrence was one of England's most well-known heroes and decided to use that fame as a platform to agitate on behalf of Arab independence. As a first step, he penned a series of provocative letters that were published in the *London Times*.[29] He explained to the people that "the Arabs did not risk their lives in battle to change masters, to become British subjects or French citizens."[30] He reinforced his message with a public speaking tour, appealing to the British sense of "fair play" and emphasizing what the Arabs had endured and achieved in their battle against the Turks. He told the public that his wartime contribution would be for naught if the government abandoned its promises. Such statements had a powerful effect on the many people who read his words or flocked to hear him speak.

While the public was coming around to Lawrence's point of view, the British foreign policy establishment had no regard for him. They were wary of his popularity and suspicious of his loyalties. They saw him as a brave but odd fellow and felt that he had "gone native." To them, the eccentric Lawrence was now the enemy of British interests.

Strategically Intervening to Expose the Contradiction in Values

An important aspect of leadership for an activist challenge is to intervene strategically to expose the contradiction of values. The task is to get sustained attention on the problem so that enough people are alerted to the concern and feel like they need to attend to it. Of course, Lawrence's letters and speeches helped, but he needed to do more. His chance came on October 30, 1918, when he made a very public and controversial intervention. He was invited to the royal court to receive his Distinguished Service Order (DSO) from King George V. Winston Churchill has given us a picture of what happened on that occasion:

> The long queue of recipients of honors was filing past the King. When Colonel Lawrence's turn came and the King took the decoration from the velvet cushion and prepared to hang it on the hook, which the officers in these circumstances had attached to their tunics, Lawrence stopped him and in a low voice stated with the utmost respect that it was impossible for him to receive any honor from His Majesty while Britain was about to dishonor the pledges he had made in His Majesty's name to the Arabs who had fought so bravely. The King was naturally surprised and displeased. The decoration, coveted by so many gallant men, was replaced upon its cushion. Lawrence bowed and passed on, and the ceremony proceeded.[31]

Later that year when Lawrence met Churchill in Paris, Churchill rebuked him for his rejection of the king's award. Churchill wrote:

> He accepted the rebuke with good humor. This was the only way in his power, he said, of rousing the highest authorities in the State to a realization of the fact that the honor of Great Britain was at stake in the faithful treatment of the Arabs, and their betrayal . . . would be an indelible blot in our history. The King himself should be made aware of what was being done in his name, and he knew no other way. I said that this was no defense at all for the method adopted.[32]

Yet even Churchill acknowledged that what Lawrence did actually succeeded in getting his attention and led him to examine the matter in more detail. "I must admit that this episode made me anxious to learn more about what actually happened in the desert war," Churchill wrote, "and opened my eyes to the passions which were seething in Arab bosoms. I called for reports and pondered them. I talked to the Prime Minister about it."[33] Lawrence's interventions were working.

Opening a Front When the Group Is Stalling You on Another

Even though he had offended the king, Lawrence's high profile and considerable knowledge of the Middle East were sufficient to get him invited to participate in the Peace Conference at Versailles that began on January 18, 1919. This was a meeting of all the Western powers and representatives of a few other invited countries to decide on the spoils of the "Great War." Enormous and formidable interests were at stake. The British wanted access to Middle Eastern oil and control of certain strategic areas. The French wanted to control Syria, where they had maintained a sphere of activity since the crusades. And the Americans wanted access to the region as well. They were in desperate need of oil, given that industry was burgeoning across the United States.

Lawrence was formally a delegate of the British team led by Winston Churchill but also acted as an adviser to Emir Feisal, who was there to ensure that Arab interests were given their due. To highlight whose side he was *really* on, he wore his Bedouin robes, much to the irritation of the British officials. This strategy provided him with considerable attention and the opportunity of influencing the negotiations in a way that few others could. Churchill was actually intrigued by Lawrence's style:

> He wore Arab robes, and the full magnificence of his countenance revealed itself. The gravity of his demeanor, the precision of his opinions, the range and quality of his conversation all seemed enhanced to a remarkable degree by the splendid Arab head-dress and garb. From amid the flowing draperies his noble features, his perfectly chiseled lips, and flashing eyes loaded with fire and comprehension shone forth. He looked what he was, one of nature's greatest princes.[34]

At Versailles, Lawrence concentrated on influencing the two leading power brokers, the British prime minister, David Lloyd George, and the French prime minister, Pierre Clemenceau. He was bold enough, given how busy and in demand both men were at the conference, to seek them out and ensure that they understood what was at stake for the Arabs.

Surprisingly, both prime ministers gave him considerable time and found the discussions engaging and fruitful. Churchill noted that although Lawrence "clashed with the French" and faced Clemenceau in many long controversies, "he was a foeman worthy of his steel."[35]

However, Lord Curzon, the foreign minister in the British government, was constantly frustrated by Lawrence's antics. After all, Lawrence was supposed to be a member of *his* delegation. Lawrence provoked, challenged, argued, and fought with Curzon repeatedly. At one meeting of the British delegation, Curzon tried to put Lawrence in his place with an introduction full of extravagant and patronizing praise for his wartime exploits and his knowledge of the Middle East. At the end of the introduction, Curzon asked Lawrence whether he had anything to say, to which Lawrence tersely replied, "Yes, let's get down to business. You people don't understand the hole you have put all of us into." Curzon suddenly burst into tears with "great drops running down his cheeks to an accompaniment of slow sobs." Lawrence said that the incident was like a medieval miracle or the wakening of the Buddha. He felt that Curzon was seeing the folly and the deceit of his position and that the emotional strain of the negotiation process had been too much for him.[36]

Although Versailles was not a victory for Lawrence or the Arabs, it was certainly not a loss. He was effective in securing the support of various key people for Feisal and the Arab cause. But Lawrence wanted more. He had fought so long and hard in the desert and in the negotiation rooms, and still there was no Arab state.

In 1920, the British had occupied Iraq, and the locals were agitating against them. The French were in Syria and claimed it as their long-lost territory. There were local uprisings in Damascus, and the mood in the region was very anti-French and anti-British. On August 8, 1920, Lawrence published another letter in the *London Observer*. It was a very harsh, sarcastic, and critical assessment of British and French policy. Some in the government were criticizing the French for their behavior, but Lawrence called attention to this duplicitous attitude.

> Yet we have really no competence in this matter to criticize the French. They have only followed in a very humble fashion, in their sphere in Syria, the example we have set in Mesopotamia. . . . It would show a lack of humor if we reproved them for a battle near Damascus . . . while we were fighting battles near Baghdad and trying to render the Mesopotamians incapable of self-government, by smashing every head that raised itself among them. . . . It is odd

that we do not use poison gas on these occasions. . . . By gas attacks the whole population of offending districts could be wiped out neatly; and as a method of government it would be no more immoral than the present system.[37]

Lawrence was becoming more provocative. As one writer noted, this was "Swiftian opposition to direct imperialism in the clearest and most public form possible."[38]

On August 22, 1920, in *The Sunday Times*, he continued his attack on British policy in Mesopotamia after another uprising by the local inhabitants.

> Our government is worse than the old Turkish system. They kept 14,000 local conscripts embodied, and killed a yearly average of 200 Arabs in maintaining peace. We keep ninety thousand men, with aeroplanes, armored cars, gunboats, and armored trains. We have killed about 10,000 Arabs in this rising this summer. We cannot hope to maintain this average. It is a poor country, sparsely peopled. We say we are in Mesopotamia to develop it for the rest of the world. . . . How long will we permit millions of pounds, thousands of Imperial troops, and tens of thousand of Arabs to be sacrificed on behalf of a form of colonial administration which can benefit nobody but its administrators?[39]

Lawrence's commitment to the Arabs during this immediate postwar period was perceived by some as being unreasonable and excessively stubborn. As one observer noted, "This stubbornness—let us call it by its true name, this absolute unwillingness to sell out—began to strike his British colleagues as unreasonable, an embarrassment to their diplomacy."[40] Unreasonable as he may have been, Lawrence's persistence did eventually pay off. In 1921, British sentiment began to shift, and the government began the process of moving toward the creation of independent Arab states. He had successfully exercised leadership in the context of a thorny and complicated activist challenge.

The Transition Challenge

Given that British policy had shifted and the government was now committed to creating an independent, or at least a semi-independent, Arab state, the leadership work next was to transition the Arabs to nationhood. In the transition challenge, the group must shift its values, habits, and mind-sets to deal with a changed condition and take advantage of the available opportunity. The British needed to use their power to create the conditions that would pave the way for a smooth transition, and the Arabs needed to build cohesion and alignment among themselves to ensure that internal squabbles did not lead the British to have second thoughts and renege on their promise.

In the spring of 1921, Churchill was sent to the Colonial Office to be responsible for Middle Eastern affairs and to pave the way for Arab independence. Churchill, sensing that Lawrence would be thrilled with the new policy, invited Lawrence to be a part of his team, even though some of Churchill's senior administrators, made up of traditional Foreign Service officers, were aghast with this invitation. One member stated to Churchill, "What! Wilt thou bridle the wild ass of the desert?"[41] Of course, Lawrence was not interested in being a petty bureaucrat but in getting people to face the real issues. But if Churchill wanted him to truly help create an Arab state, he would wear the bureaucratic bridle to the best of his ability.

Lawrence served as an adviser to Churchill for eighteen months. This was an unprecedented opportunity. His challenge, as he saw it, was to keep the real bureaucrats and politicians from wrecking the process. But since he had been given a position on the inside as a member of the Churchill team, he could no longer be the independent provocateur that he had been in the past. To everyone's surprise, Lawrence not only understood the changed situation but thrived in it. "Here is proof of the greatness of his character and versatility of his genius," Churchill later wrote. "He saw the hope of redeeming in a large measure the promises he had made to the Arab chiefs, and of reestablishing a tolerable measure of peace in those wide regions. In that cause he was capable of becoming—I hazard the word—a humdrum official. The effort was not in vain. His purposes prevailed."[42]

Crafting an Orienting Purpose

The Churchill team's first task was to organize a conference in Cairo for the purpose of thrashing out the issues and developing a plan for the transition. Held in March 1921, the conference lasted eighteen days. In attendance were the leading scholars and officials on Middle Eastern affairs. In preparing for the Cairo conference, Lawrence wrote, "We are making a most ambitious design for the Middle East: a new page in the loosening of the Empire tradition."[43] He was in his element.

It was a dynamic conference with real debate and exploration of alternatives. It is clear from the conference record that Lawrence was a major contributor in the drafting of the final policy that was approved by Churchill.[44] Captain Maxwell Coote, Churchill's aide during the Cairo Conference, said, "Lawrence, an unobtrusive figure, almost unobserved, influenced that Conference more than any other."[45] Lawrence knew that this was not a time for parading in Bedouin robes or provoking authority; on the contrary, this was a time for careful, reasoned argument and negotiation.

At the conference, it was agreed that Britain would repair the injury done to the Arabs and to the House of the Sherifs of Mecca by placing the Emir Feisal on the throne of Iraq as king and by entrusting his brother, the Emir Abdullah, with the government of Trans-Jordania. Second, Britain would remove practically all of its troops from Iraq, while providing nominal defense by the Royal Air Force. Third, Britain would support building a cooperative relationship between the Jews and Arabs in Palestine, which would serve as a foundation for the future development of the region.

The policies were not without significant opposition. The French opposed the placing of Feisal as head of Iraq, and the British War Office opposed removing its troops from Iraq. But the debates and negotiations carried on with Lawrence playing an essential role. Churchill noted:

> It required a year of most difficult and anxious administration to
> give effect to what had been so speedily decided. This was the
> phase in Lawrence's life when he was a civil servant. Everyone
> was astonished at his calm and tactful demeanor. His patience
> and readiness to work with others amazed those who knew him
> best. Tremendous confabulations must have taken place among
> these experts, and tension at times must have been extreme. But
> so far as I was concerned I received always united advice from
> two or three of the very best men it had ever been my fortune to
> work with.[46]

Indeed, Lawrence was very pleased with his contribution during this period. He later told his friend Robert Graves, "The work I did constructively in 1921 and 1922 seems to me, in retrospect, the best I ever did. It somewhat redresses to my mind the immoral and unwarrantable risks I took with the others' lives and happiness in 1917–1918."[47]

Getting People to Own the Transition

Churchill returned to London to prepare for the next challenge: defending his policy at home. He left Lawrence behind to pave the way for the transition with the Arab factions. It was tough, difficult work. A particularly frustrating hurdle was the petty jealousies and infighting among the Arabs themselves. Lawrence's colleague said of this problem:

> During his campaign he had worked and fought with Arabs who were men of action, willing to die for the cause, but now he found that the control of the various states in many cases was in the hands of a different type altogether—men who had been content to remain in the background while the campaign was in progress, but were now coming forth as leaders of the newly created governments. Owing to this were the private jealousies, old feuds and tribal hatreds stultifying the cause which was so clear to him and making an intricate situation more difficult of settlement.[48]

Lawrence went to Amman and began working with Prince Abdullah, Feisal's brother, to help stabilize Trans-Jordan. Prince Abdullah was quite agitated and felt that British policy for the region was impeding his plans of creating a pan-Arabic state. Some British officials wanted to get rid of Abdullah. They saw him as an inadequate leader who had too many radicals around him. Lawrence, however, was adamant that the British should honor the will of the Arabs themselves and that if the people wanted Abdullah, then Abdullah should be supported.[49]

Although the situation in 1921 had become a crisis challenge, Lawrence was able to exercise leadership and "dissipate the explosiveness of the predicament" and help the people get focused on the work of transition. John Philby noted that due to Lawrence's leadership, "The storm cleared with amazing suddenness," and he "gave the Emir a new lease of life."[50] Churchill, too, was amazed at what Lawrence was able to accomplish. He stated, "At last resort I sent him to Trans-Jordan, where sudden difficulties had arisen. He had plenary powers. He used them with his old vigor. He removed officers. . . . He restored complete tranquility. Everyone was delighted with the success of his mission."[51] Indeed, Lawrence did a remarkable job in precarious circumstances. Without his advice, Abdullah might never have kept his throne, and Jordan might never have become the successful state that it is today.

Toward the end of 1922, the situation began to improve. All the measures that Churchill, Lawrence, and the Cairo team had developed were implemented, one by one. The British army left Iraq, the Air Force was installed in a loop around the Euphrates, Baghdad acclaimed Feisal as king,[52] and Abdullah settled down comfortably in Trans-Jordan. Above all, Arab independence had been achieved.

Lawrence was pleased with his work and took pains to acknowledge Churchill, who had opened up the way for him to play a role in the transition process. "Powerful elements in the British Government were seeking to evade their war-time obligations to the Arabs," he later wrote. "That stage ended in March 1921, when Mr. Winston Churchill took charge of the Middle East. He set honesty before expediency in order to fulfill our promises in letter and in spirit."[53] This unlikely partnership with Lawrence as the provocateur and the idea generator, and Churchill as the political power broker, proved to be impressively effective.

The Next Development Challenge

There will come a point in a transition process when the leadership work is actually to let go of the reins and allow the people to fend for themselves. At that time, the people will face a development challenge and must then take responsibility for their predicament and learn their way forward through trial and error. They might succeed, or they might fail. Either way, so be it. The work is now *their* work.

The British authorities were very reluctant to relinquish power to the Arabs, arguing that they were too feudal and incompetent when it came to matters of governance. Lawrence's view was that the role of the British should be to train, support, and develop the managerial and leadership capacities of the Arabs. He recognized that developmental leadership required building bridges in many directions to ensure that relationships were established and communication channels were open, even if that meant partnering with and developing those who once opposed you. In his view, the activists, the agitators, and the revolutionaries could indeed be the future authorities and leaders of a country, and they should be aided and nurtured so that they could develop leadership capabilities with minimal disruption and maximum support. Lawrence knew that failure to connect with such people and groups and to include them in the developmental process could lead to further subversion and crisis.

We must be prepared to see them doing things by methods quite unlike our own, and less well, but on principle it is better that they half-do it than that we do it perfectly for them. In pursuing such courses, we will find our best helpers not in our former most obedient subjects, but among those now most active in agitating against us, for it will be the intellectual leaders of the people who will serve the purpose, and these are not the philosophers nor the rich, but the demagogues and the politicians.[54]

By 1927, due in part to the efforts of Lawrence, progress toward independence and stable government in Iraq and Jordan was coming along well. But Lawrence knew there was only so much he or anyone could do. The Arabs' challenge now was to take the reins. Lawrence commented on the developmental work:

All peoples . . . teach themselves to walk and to balance by dint of trying and falling down. Iraq did a good deal of falling between 1916 and 1921: and since 1921, under Feisal's guidance, has done much good trying and not falling. But I don't think it yet walks very well. Nor can any hand save it from making its messes: There is a point where coddling becomes wicked. . . . If they are to make good as a modern state then it must be by virtue of their own desire and excellence. . . . As for Iraq . . . well, some day they will be fit for self government and then they will not want a king; but whether 7 or 70 or 700 years hence, God knows. . . . Meanwhile Feisal is serving his race as no Arab has served it for many hundred years. He is my very great pride: and it has been my privilege to have helped him to supremacy.[55]

Feisal was made ruler of Iraq by the British, and his brother Abdullah was given the kingship of Trans-Jordan, which was separated from Palestine. Feisal remained on the throne of Iraq until his death in 1933, and Abdullah on the throne of Trans-Jordan until he was shot in 1951 by a Palestinian extremist. The current king of Jordan, Abdullah bin al-Hussein, is the great-grandson of Abdullah. Iraq stayed in the British orbit until 1958 when Nuri-al Said, who had fought with Lawrence in the desert and was the last important member of the Arab revolt to hold high office, was overthrown.[56] As the world knows, it has been chaotic in the region ever since. Indeed, Lawrence's prophetic comment that someday the Iraqis will be "fit for self-government . . . but whether 7 or 70 or 700 years hence, God knows" is a statement that we can all appreciate.

Lawrence Walks Away

Churchill asked Lawrence what he wanted to do now that their work was coming to an end. He felt that Lawrence could have a very rewarding career in the Foreign Office and invited him to continue working with him. Lawrence, however, felt otherwise. He responded, "All you will see of me is a small cloud of dust on the horizon."[57] Lawrence was tired and wanted to go home.

Lawrence never wanted to be a leader. "I hated responsibility," he once wrote, much preferring to be an administrator or academic. "All my life objects had been gladder to me than persons, and ideas than objects. So the duty of succeeding with men to any purpose would be doubly hard to me."[58] But in taking on the adaptive challenges of the Middle East, he assumed enormous responsibility and did succeed with men.

He clearly understood the distinction between self and role.[59] In order to exercise leadership and support the Arab cause, he had to assume a role that was appropriate to the context. That role allowed him to be an instrument, a tool, in the process of generating an Arab state. But he was not attached to the role, as many people are when they enjoy positions of authority, get caught up in a cause, or are the object of great acclaim. Because of his ability to distinguish between self and role, Lawrence could walk away. The work was done. There was nothing more that he could do. It would now be left to the Arabs themselves to see what they could make of their country.

Lawrence resigned from the Colonial Office and as a member of Churchill's team in July 1922, and he sought a life of obscurity. He entered the ranks of the Royal Air Force the following month under the assumed name John Hume Ross in order to avoid publicity. He did not want anyone to know him as the legendary "Lawrence of Arabia." He was discharged from the Air Force the following January due to a newspaper disclosing his identity. He then changed his name to T. E. Shaw and joined the Royal Tank Corps at the rank of private. When that no longer worked out, he rejoined the Royal Air Force as a mechanic.

While he sought to avoid fame and fortune, Lawrence did become a prolific writer. In 1926, he published the *Seven Pillars of Wisdom*, an epic tale that told of his experience in the Arab campaign. This was a cathartic exercise as he needed to take time to reflect on what really had happened in the desert—to himself and to the Bedouins whom he had led. Lawrence wrote a letter to a friend and provided some insight into how he thought about his activities in the Middle East and the purpose of the book:

I had been so much a free agent, repeatedly deciding what I (and others) should do: and I wasn't sure if my opportunity (or reality, as I called it) was really justified. Not morally justifiable. . . . By putting all the troubles and dilemmas on paper, I hoped to work out my path again, and satisfy myself how wrong, or how right, I had been. So the book is the self-argument of a man who couldn't see straight: and who now thinks that perhaps it did not matter: that seeing is only an illusion. We do these things in sheer vapidity of mind, not deliberately, not consciously even. To make out that we were reasoned cool minds, ruling our courses and contemporaries, is a vanity. Things happen, and we do our best to keep in the saddle. After the Arab business I rather foreswore saddles.[60]

Profound insights from an extraordinary man. Sadly, on May 19, 1935, Lawrence was killed in a motorcycle accident on a country road when he swerved to avoid two boys on bicycles. He was forty-six years old.

Lawrence's leadership prowess is an illustration in how to respond to demanding and shifting problematic realities. Admittedly, most of us will never be in a situation remotely similar to his. Nevertheless, the leadership principles of his actions are generalizable. His example highlights that (1) real leadership requires wisdom, courage, and creativity, (2) leadership can be exercised with or without authority, (3) one must be flexible to move between the various leadership challenges, and (4) a leader must be very sensitive to the context, group dynamics, and the threats and opportunities confronting the group to accurately figure out "what challenge do the people face?" and then respond accordingly.

CHAPTER 10

Odin, the Samurai, and You

Taking Responsibility for Yourself
as an Instrument of Power

The great Odin, even with all his wisdom, would occasionally allow his personal issues and natural tendencies to impede good judgment, acting out of greed, anger, the need to dominate, or the desire for revenge. In other words, even with the best intentions, at times he would *lose* it. Given his recognition of his foibles, Odin sought out the spirit of the sacred well of Mimir for advice on what he must do to increase in insight and understanding. The spirit told Odin that to gain such insight he would need to pluck out an eye and throw it into the well. Upon considering the consequences of permanent disfigurement and the loss of such a valuable asset, Odin did as the spirit suggested and plucked out his left eye and cast it into the water.[1] In doing so, he gained the knowledge that he needed.

But for those of us unwilling to part with an eye, Mimir might well give this advice: "You want insight? Begin by looking hard at yourself as an instrument of power. You are used to looking at *other* people. Yes, that is important, but you must now look at yourself and how you interact *with* other people to help them solve their problems. Your knowledge of yourself will come from what you see reflected back in the eyes, attitudes, and actions of others. But be careful, as that reflection is often distorted. To ensure that you are not deceived, turn one eye so that it gazes inward—so that you can observe how your deepest instincts and desires drive the choices you make with and for your people as they wrestle with their problematic realities. This will be hard, even painful—as painful as plucking out your own eye—but it is necessary if you are to succeed as a leader."

Real leadership, at times, *is* painful. It is painful to discover features of one's behavior and natural predilections that are not particularly helpful to the people in their problem-solving and opportunity-enhancing endeavors. Not only is it painful, but it is also a burden. It is a burden to be responsible for a group and to contend with their dysfunctions and damaging behavior, and to get them to shift their values, habits, practices, and priorities to meet the challenge confronting them. And it is a burden to be responsible for oneself as an instrument of power—to take responsibility for the blatant and subtle ways that one's power affects others. In being responsible, one must commit to the necessary personal discovery work to be able to fine-tune one's use of power, in the same way that a mountain climber taking on Everest must fine-tune his or her body to be able to cope in the thin air as the altitude increases. An ill-prepared person—physically, mentally, and knowledge-wise—will most likely perish on Mount Everest, as the hazards are significant.

Ronald Heifetz maintains that in exercising leadership for adaptive challenges you are often "walking on the razor's edge." Indeed, given that real leadership is about intervening into people's values and belief systems, it will, at times, be risky and dangerous work. Therefore, in the face of the demands and dangers of leading, you must take responsibility for yourself as an instrument of power and discover the ways you allow your personal issues to reduce your effectiveness, limit your options, or even hurt the group. These personal issues are what I call your *personal case.*

All of us have a personal case. It includes your factional loyalties, stylistic orientation, natural predilections, unconscious motives, blind spots, and habitual ways of operating that shape your approach to leadership. The task is to appreciate how your personal case can help or hinder the group's capacity to face the reality of their condition, tackle their challenges, and advance. It can be an asset or a liability. To illustrate this point, consider the personal case of Theng Bunma.

A few years ago I was an adviser to Cambodia's state-owned airline, Royal Air Cambodge. Cambodia at that time was struggling to rebuild its economy, which had been devastated from many years of war. Theng Bunma, head of the Cambodian Chamber of Commerce, was charged with the responsibility of representing the needs of the business community and helping build a climate that encouraged investment and entrepreneurship. Given Cambodia's terrible economic condition, Theng Bunma faced a demanding development challenge that required real leadership. But Theng had a major problem. He had a bad temper and took offense easily.

Over the years, Theng had had many disputes with Royal Air Cambodge over the quality of their service. One day, as he was checking in for a flight, he was charged a fee for his overweight baggage. Feeling insulted, he took the gun of one of his bodyguards, walked onto the tarmac, and shot out the tire of the Boeing 737 that was supposed to fly him to his next destination.[2] The passengers, the crew, and eventually the nation, when they heard about his behavior, were terrified, embarrassed, and appalled. Clearly Theng Bunma's use of his power was unwise and irresponsible, undermining the very objectives he was supposed to be using his power to champion. He allowed his personal case—his offense and anger—to impair his judgment at a crucial moment.

Your personal case is wrapped up in your history, values, preferences, and identity. It gets manifest in the choices that you make and the actions that you take, particularly under pressure. To exercise real leadership, you need the wisdom to discern in real time when your personal case is an asset in helping the group or a liability and impeding the group. For example, as Theng Bunma could *not* do, you should be able to keep yourself from expressing anger (even if you feel angry), if expressing anger would detract from the group's ability to attend to its immediate concern. Or, when you feel an urge to take control of the situation and "run the show," it might be better to hold still and give the people more time to remain in a fluid state of uncertainty and negotiation. If your personal case includes the need to be admired and adored, you must be able to resist the seductive pull of the group for you to be heroic and single-handedly solve the people's problems.

T. E. Lawrence, as described in the previous chapter, took responsibility for himself as an instrument of power and was able to diagnose features of his personal case. In seeing these inclinations in himself, he was able to manage them, to some degree at least.

> I was very conscious of the bundled powers and entities within me; it was their character which I hid. There was my craving to be liked—so strong and nervous that never could I open myself friendly to another. The terror of failure in an effort so important made me shrink from trying. . . . There was a craving to be famous; and a horror of being known to like being known. Contempt for my passion for distinction made me refuse every offered honor.[3]

Lawrence had the capacity to understand his personal case better than most people. Seeing these aspects of himself generated occasional bouts of emotional turmoil, even depression. But given his commitment to explore his inner mental world and understand the driving forces behind his actions, he was not held hostage to these sentiments but could face them and ensure that they did not spill needlessly onto the group's problem solving and adaptive work.

Your Personal Case and the Six Leadership Challenges

Each of the six challenges poses a different set of problems in which the leader's personal case can get in the way. Knowing the triggers that cause you to put too much of the negative features of your personal case into the problem-solving process is essential if you are to reduce the danger of a false set of tasks being put before the group.

In the *activist challenge*, the leader must get the people to face the reality of a contradiction in values and consider information that they are reluctant to consider. The people are generally defensive when initially provoked or challenged by the leader's interventions. Given the defensiveness and resistance, the leader's personal case can easily get in the way. Common ways a leader's personal case can get in the way include (1) becoming self-righteous about the cause and adopting the tactics of an unrelenting and unthinking crusader who tries to force change and (2) believing that it is all about the leader. In other words, the leader believes that he or she has to do everything, fight every battle, be the spokesperson on every issue, and run the entire show. When that happens, it becomes difficult for leaders to separate the cause from their own personality and role. They become the issue, and the issue becomes them—and the *real* issue gets buried under layers of heroism and self-sacrifice.

In a *development challenge*, the leadership work is to develop the latent capabilities of the people over the long term. The people need a lot of space, time, support, and encouragement. I have observed two common ways that people allow their personal case to get in the way in the face of a development challenge: (1) A leader might have a great need to get results at a rapid rate and fail to build an adequate holding environment and provide the support and encouragement needed for people to learn and develop; or (2) the leader might become excessively frustrated, disappointed, and even punitive when people make errors and do not develop in a way that is consistent with the leader's expectations. When that happens, the leader diminishes the motivation of the people and their propensity to take risks in their pursuit of learning.

In the *transition challenge*, the work of leadership is to shift the values and attitudes of the group to another set of values and attitudes. It includes the process of culture change. The people in a state of transition are generally anxious and afraid as they must give up their old ways of living, working, or operating and embrace new ways of living, working, or operating. The ways in which a leader's personal case might get in the way for a transition challenge include (1) the leader being insensitive to what the people have to give up and therefore pushing the people so hard that they become rebellious or (2), the leader, given his or her "achievement needs," getting too far out in front of the group and failing to bring the people along.[4]

In a *maintenance challenge*, the leadership work is to preserve and maintain essential resources of the group. The group is under threat from dysfunctional internal practices or an external enemy or forces in the environment. The ways a leader's personal case can get in the way include (1) succumbing to depression because the leader feels overwhelmed by the current condition; (2) being in denial and refusing to acknowledge the reality that the group or enterprise is in a state of decay; or (3) when noticing the threat or decay, adopting an excessively positive, upbeat attitude in the hope that the people can bypass the reality of their condition, because it is too painful to examine. In doing so, the leader ignores the work of maintenance in the same way that an unhealthy person ignores exercise and eating nutritious food.

In a *creative challenge*, the leadership work is to get the people to do something that has never been done before. The people must create or invent a new product, come up with a new idea, or discover a pathway forward that leads to a new opportunity or greater benefit. The ways that leaders can allow their personal case to get in the way include (1) trying to dominate the group and stifle dissent and (2) being unwilling to tolerate the messiness and chaos of the creative process. The creative process is both fickle and fragile, and therefore difficult to sustain. Leaders must manage their power very sensitively so that they do not impose too much of their opinion on the group or control the process, and thereby thwart the people in their exploratory and imaginative pursuits.

In a *crisis challenge*, the group is confronted with an explosive situation. The leadership work is to restore order, reduce the danger of further conflagration, and ascertain the underlying challenge of which the crisis is a symptom. The ways that a leader's personal case can get in the way include (1) taking the crisis personally and becoming angry, being offended, and then lashing out at others, even starting a fight; (2) being terribly afraid of conflict and retreating, thus allowing the crisis to persist or get worse; or (3) giving the people an easy solution to make them feel better and temporarily relieve the pain of the crisis. The strong inclination to give an easy answer will likely keep the people from having to sacrifice something that they value highly in order to deal realistically with the crisis and make genuine progress on the underlying adaptive challenge.

The primary task of real leadership is to get the people to wrestle with reality and take responsibility for their condition. It is precarious work, and anything can happen. The former prime minister of the Philippines, Fidel Ramos, told me that being the leader of a country is like walking a tightrope while juggling. The slightest misjudgment or moment of distraction could spell disaster. What's more, he said, many in the crowd aren't cheering for you, but want you to fall.[5] Given this precarious activity, it is very easy to allow one's personal case to distort one's thinking and limits one's options. It is easy to get distracted, and it is easy to cause distractions. Thus, when leaders allow too much of their personal case to get in the way, the adaptive work of progress is made messier and prolonged.

Case of the Lost Samurai

To illustrate the demands of leadership in helping the people face reality, and to appreciate how easy it is for one's personal case to distort the capacity to see with clarity what the real problem is and what should be done, consider the case of Saigo Takamori, immortalized by Hollywood as *The Last Samurai*. I prefer to call Saigo the *lost* samurai. Saigo lost sight of what the real work of progress was and allowed his personal case to get in the way. There was a time that he did provide leadership, but later he used his power to put counterfeit issues—a civil war—before the people.

Saigo first rose to prominence in Japan when he led the forces that overthrew the weak and ineffectual Tokugawa shogunate in 1868. His actions paved the way for the Meiji Restoration, as discussed in chapter 5 on the transition challenge. He was appointed by the new emperor as a member of the cabinet and was to play a key role in shaping many of the reform policies of the government. Saigo, however, eventually had second thoughts about what was happening in his country. In his mind,

Japan was blindly copying the West and modernizing too fast. Many of the country's best traditions and practices were being discarded in the name of progress.

After a few years in government, Saigo resigned in protest and returned to his home in the remote region of Satsuma. He was content to read philosophy, practice meditation, and attend to his farm. But Satsuma was a caldron of discontent. The lord of Satsuma, whose position was actually abolished by the new Tokyo government, refused to give up his power and continued as the resident authority figure. Lord Shimazu had nothing but contempt for the Tokyo government and therefore never obeyed any of its decrees. His region was the only region in the country where the samurai still wore their swords and kept their hair in the traditional manner.

For the people of Satsuma, having Saigo back home was an honor. He was a national hero and adored by the people. Rather relax and farm, he was called upon to teach young people the art of *busihido*—the ethics and code of a samurai. His lessons became so popular that hundreds of schools sprang up across the Satsuma district.

Given the general state of restlessness in Satsuma, the young samurai pleaded with the old master to lead them into battle and restore righteousness and integrity to the government. And this Saigo did. With forty thousand men, he launched a six-month struggle to take control of the national government. Unfortunately for him, none of the other regions joined in the fight, and he and his fellow Satsuma samurai were left to fend for themselves. They were no match for the new Japanese military with their Western advisers and sophisticated weaponry, and the rebellion eventually petered out. Saigo, in the true spirit of *bushido*, rather than surrender, committed *seppuku*—ritual suicide.[6]

* * *

The Saigo story is a gripping tragedy that illustrates how one's personal case can get in the way of responsible leadership and doing the adaptive work that is in the interest of the whole. This was a man who was venerated by all the people of Japan. He had a tremendous amount of informal authority and the potential to make a significant contribution. But he opted for war. And most of his countrymen were shocked that he would turn against his own government in such a violent fashion. The *Tokyo Times* in 1877 said of Saigo:

> It was incredible that the man whose whole existence had been a record of unswerving loyalty and of a devotion which lifted him to an eminence which few other of his countrymen have attained,

should without warning, without visible cause, turn in a moment to a course which must rob him of all his fame, and change the brightness of his past life to a deathless shame.[7]

Initially, when the people heard that Saigo was leading the rebellion, they did not want to believe it. When the evidence was irrefutable, the nation was in shock and very angry. "If we all had known at the beginning the treason that was in his heart," one journalist wrote, "instead of loving Saigo so greatly we should have hated him enough to have eaten all the flesh off his bones."[8]

This case raises many questions for those of us interested in the study of power and leadership. Why did Saigo use his power to rebel against the government that he had helped create? Could he not see that his war against the government would be futile? Why couldn't he envisage other more creative ways to exercise leadership to help his countrymen responsibly face the challenges of a difficult transition?

As the samurai's sword is a weapon that can be used for good or ill and must be mastered through years of practice and personal work, so must leaders think about the use, mastery, and consequences of their power as they seek to help the people face real problems and take advantage of opportunities before them. We know that Saigo did a considerable amount of personal work as a young man in preparation to be a samurai. He studied the Chinese classics and practiced Zen meditation. But even in what work he did, it was still insufficient in helping him distinguish the best mode of leadership intervention that would aid his people to progress. Furthermore, it did not help him in detecting how his personal case was getting in the way and impeding his capacity to see with clarity what the adaptive challenge was.

The Detective Work of Real Leadership

This process of learning about one's personal case is what I call *detective work*. We often talk about "reflection" as being an important part of leadership. And it is. However, the notion of "detection" is the essential skill that leaders must develop if they are to be effective with what power they have. In the context of real leadership, you are trying not only to reflect on what you did but to detect how your actions and strategies coordinate and integrate with others to nudge them closer to the problem and get them engaged in productive problem-solving work.

This is an ongoing process of looking for clues in the system that indicate how the people are reacting to your interventions. Do your interventions—your comments, presence, and tactics—contribute to getting people to face reality and consider the tough issues, or cause them to flee from reality and avoid the tough issues?

To help ensure your personal case is an asset and not a liability, I recommend that you do the following detective work: (1) Use partners to detect what you are missing due to your blind spots; (2) detect when you are doing too much crusading and not enough leading; (3) detect how your factional loyalties pull you away from the real work; (4) detect the people's reality by regularly wandering among them; and (5) detect when it is time to move aside and allow somebody else to lead or assume authority.

Use partners to detect what's missing due to your blind spots

Good detective work requires trusted partners to help you see what you cannot see—just as the master detective Sherlock Holmes had Dr. Watson. A partner helps the leader become more aware of his or her blind spots. All of us have blind spots and cannot know all that there is to know about the context and the factional dynamics in order to be effective all the time. Errors of judgment will produce errors of intervention. And errors of intervention will allow problems to persist. Therefore, the need for ongoing detective work through partnering to discover what it is that the leader might be missing.

In chapter 1, I described the debacle of Enron. This was one of the world's biggest and most prosperous companies, but it collapsed almost overnight due to counterfeit leadership. For either CEO Kenneth Lay or manager Sherron Watkins to have exercised real leadership at Enron, they would have needed to learn how to look past their personal case— their fears and preferences—so that they might appreciate the foreseeable consequences of their actions and explore other options for intervention. Simply said, their fears and personal preferences would not guide them in the right direction to bring positive resolution to the Enron problem. To succeed in getting their company to solve its real problems, they both would have needed insight into the group mechanics that, in all sorts of organizations and all sorts of circumstances, make it difficult for people to face up to harsh, often threatening realities. (Enron was not unique in having an aggressive, self-reinforcing corporate ideology that dismissed alternative worldviews.)

Enron's senior management likely had great attachment to values and priorities that blinded their capacity to deal with important aspects of reality. At Enron, real leadership would have consisted not only in diagnosing the real problem but in knowing the corrective actions that the company would need to take, and knowing how to intervene to produce the necessary shift in values and priorities that would allow people to take these actions. Given the size of the company and the blind spots of its management, and given the fact that Enron's entire corporate identity was bound up in an aggressive and greedy ideology that allowed the blind spots to persist, the amount of leadership wisdom required to save the company would have had to be truly prodigious.

Perhaps Kenneth Lay's blind spot was his unwillingness and inability even to consider the enormous implications of the company's finances resting on deception and accounting tricks; maybe the problem was simply too large and widespread to contemplate. Possibly, he would have responded differently if the problem had involved only a minor part of Enron. Certainly he could have used Sherron Watkins as a partner to help him catch a timely glimpse of his blind spot, but he clearly couldn't bear to look at what she was prepared to show him. Like a deer caught in the headlights, he froze.

Perhaps Watkins's blind spot was her naive assumption that Lay wanted the knowledge she offered and would be willing to act on it. When Lay froze up and denied the problem, Watkins's next challenge might have been to ask, "How can I present this knowledge in terms that will help him become more realistic and receptive? What shared values can I tap into to motivate him into taking action to tackle the organization's real problems?" Through a more active discerning process, she might have found clues to management's fears that they could not succeed with a realistic business model. Perhaps she would have found data in the areas in which some in Enron management knew themselves to be "in over their heads" but pretended otherwise.

It is likely that no one individual at Enron could have possessed all of the necessary insight to fix the problem: those in nominal authority (especially Kenneth Lay) possessed very little. In most organizations and in most situations, the discerning capacity rarely resides in one individual. Typically, leaders need to work cooperatively with a group of allies and partners at various levels in order to make a useful analysis of the shared dilemmas and underlying reasons for persistent problems, and to ascertain what kind of interventions are needed to get people facing the issues.

By way of analogy, think of the way that mirrors help you see into what would otherwise be perilous blind spots when you are driving a car. The combination of your natural path of vision and the columns of metal blocking your view in the two back corners of the vehicle create areas that are almost impossible to see without some sort of aid. If you do not take extra care, something coming from your blind spot likely will cause you great harm. To avoid potentially disastrous collisions, we need a well-placed mirror or two to help us see what is hidden in these vulnerable areas. Similarly, you can help yourself and others exercise leadership by developing a network of "mirrors" that reveal what may be coming at you from outside your field of vision—and you can repay those who help you in this way by serving as their mirror in return.

In finding partners who can serve as mirrors and highlight your blind spots, you need people who are willing to talk straight and not ingratiate themselves by distorting or withholding information. It is often difficult to find partners who can speak honestly and forthrightly about problematic issues pertaining to the leader's behavior or strategies. It is also difficult for some leaders to accept such advice without getting excessively defensive. Developing the capacity to hold steady, listen, and then inquire to learn how people arrived at their positions is an important skill. After all, good partners can ensure that one's blind spots do not lead to ill-informed choices or disastrous consequences.

Detect when you are crusading versus leading

Passionate people sometimes forget the group. Their commitment turns into a crusade, and they cease to provide real leadership. Real leadership orchestrates a process of adaptive work, while crusading forces a solution on the group. Tough challenges are integrally connected to the values and priorities of the group and the people's relationship to the context—the threats and opportunities. Therefore, real leadership must orchestrate a process that generates learning and discovery as people tackle their challenges and try to discover what it is they really care about and what sacrifices they might have to make in order to improve the enterprise or have better lives. Adaptive work is often riddled with anxiety and friction. Sometimes leaders cannot cope with the anxiety and the messiness of the process and, out of frustration, resort to crusader-like tactics to get their way. Or, leaders can become so obsessed with their goal that they believe that the rightness of their cause is justification enough to forgo the exercise of real leadership.

Crusaders often engage in wasteful battles to get their way—do or die (and they usually die). They are inclined not to think about what they are doing but just act. They put themselves on auto-pilot. For the crusader, the thinking has been done; therefore, there is no need to reflect on motives, strategies, and goals anymore. In fact, thinking is a distraction, as it might produce doubt and confusion. Because of this orientation, crusaders are potentially hazardous—to themselves, to the people, and to anyone who stands in the way. Consider the story of a real crusader, Little Peter (also known as Peter the Hermit). In 1096, Little Peter was a common monk in France who believed in asceticism—living as a hermit in abject poverty. Inspired by the pope's call for a holy war, he decided to become a model warrior. He personally took on the work of driving the Turks from the Holy Land and to reclaim Jerusalem for Christianity. Little Peter told any peasant who would listen that he had been commissioned by God to lead them in this righteous battle. Hundreds of thousands of peasants throughout Europe got caught up in a frenzy and joined this itinerant monk in his fanatical quest to reclaim Jerusalem. On their journey to the Holy Land, they traveled through the Rhineland, and the powerful Count Emich of Leisengen was converted to Little Peter's crusade. The count burned a cross on his forehead as a sign of his commitment to the cause.

Over the year, with Count Emich's support, the peasant army wreaked havoc on the Jewish settlements of Europe, as they saw the Jews as an impediment to the goal of reclaiming the Holy Land. Besides, Little Peter reminded his peasants, "the Jews killed Christ." Believing that they were doing God's work, Little Peter, Count Emich, and the crusader peasants massacred thousands of Jews before they had even set foot in the Holy Land or seen a Turk.[9]

Usually in crusades, it is the blind leading the blind, although the people are inclined to operate under the fantasy that they can actually see with great clarity what needs to be done. Given the burst of group excitement, the people easily go into a delusional state and believe that they are able to accomplish something quite extraordinary if they can just eradicate the enemy or those who stand in their way.

Saigo, too, became a crusader. He was an extraordinarily committed man who was, I am sure, thinking about what was in the best interest of Japan. However, his commitment turned into unthinking fanaticism, distorted his perception, and led to disastrous consequences. He wanted to bring Japan back to his notion of a "golden era," which never really existed. And, the reality was, Japan could not go back. The people's adaptive work was to figure out how to transition forward in a respectful and responsible manner. If Saigo had not succumbed to the temptation of being a crusader, he might have exercised real leadership on two fronts:

(1) with the emperor and the government, and (2) with his own constituency, the samurai.

In regard to the government, rather than quit in a huff, Saigo might have stayed on and tried to help figure out the values and traditions that were precious in Japanese culture and needed to be maintained, and what was no longer useful and therefore expendable.[10] When one is the deviant voice, it is easy to become frustrated and irritated, and walk away. But patience and persistence are essential. Saigo, no doubt, had many legitimate grievances about the rate of change occurring and the hasty adoption of foreign practices. For many years, both in and out of government, he was a powerful voice of moderation, and might have continued to play that role in a more positive, constructive way. If the government was pushing the people to change too fast, and if traditional values were being discarded without due consideration, then Saigo might have considered other more evocative and provocative ways to get the authorities to engage the reality of their predicament and pace the process. He, more than anyone, was positioned to make such a contribution. But because he could not distinguish between crusading and leading, he ended up shedding a lot of blood, including his own.

With his own constituency, the samurai, he might have challenged them to modify their values, craft new identities, and become a strong contributing force in transitioning Japan. The samurai had a vested interest in being samurai. It was a noble role with honored traditions. But the world was changing. The Japanese could no longer live in a hermetically sealed island and needed to make adjustments in their values, thinking, and practices. Saigo, therefore, could have helped his samurai put aside their swords and reinvent a new role that could be of value for themselves and the country. In the schools that Saigo created, rather than perpetuate a bygone notion of bushido, Saigo might have inculcated new practices and helped channel the youthful energy and spirit of the young samurai into more creative endeavors, thereby enhancing their capacity to contribute to the immediate and future challenges of a nation facing a transition challenge.

Certainly, knowing what course of action is best and how one should lead when there are multiple factions pulling you in different directions is difficult work. Therefore, real leaders need to be guided by more than just their own hunches and intuitions to orient them in the periods of anxiety and bewilderment that accompany the facing of adaptive challenges. Saigo lost sight of what the real work of progress was for Japan, and he and his samurai became a major mechanism for distraction when they put a false set of tasks—a war—before the people.

Admittedly, there is often a fine line between committed action and crusading. During the Arabia campaign, T. E. Lawrence found himself on that line, even crossing it, on many occasions. He later reflected on the experience of being so devoted to his cause:

> We were a self-centered army without parade or gesture, devoted to freedom, the second of man's creeds, a purpose so ravenous that it devoured all our strength, a hope so transcendent that our earlier ambitions faded in its glare. As time went by our need to fight for the ideal increased to an unquestioning possession, riding with spur and rein over our doubts. Willy-nilly it became a faith. We had sold into its slavery, manacled ourselves together in its chain-gang, bowed ourselves to serve its holiness with all our good and ill content. The mentality of ordinary human slaves is terrible—they have lost the world—and we have surrendered, not body alone, but soul to the overmastering greed of victory. By our own act we were drained of morality, of volition, of responsibility, like dead leaves in the wind.[11]

Lawrence acknowledges, with refreshing honesty, how easy it is to lose one's soul, even when engaged in a noble pursuit. There is always the possibility that one stops thinking and becomes a slave to the cause and ends up like "dead leaves in the wind." Given his reflective disposition and his relentless need to understand his motives and behavior, he was able to temper his fanaticism and ensure that it did not get out of control.

In the realm of real leadership, one must hold onto one's doubts. Excessive certainty about the rightness or righteousness of one's cause, as with a crusader, might diminish one's curiosity, questioning, open-mindedness, and experimentation. Without curiosity, questioning, open-mindedness, and experimentation, real solutions to complex problems will be elusive. Committed action is important, but to be a blind adherent to a quest, irrespective of how noble it is, will diminish one's effectiveness in exercising leadership. Leaders must have a passion for wisdom and keep questioning their strategies to ensure that they and the people do not become doggedly attached to a particular plan, answer, or notion of the truth, and cease from thinking.

Detect when your factional loyalties are impeding the adaptive work

Leadership is about choices. But sometimes it is difficult to make the right choices given one's factional loyalties and group affiliations. All of us have loyalties to our various groups and factions that shape our identity—be it our family, work team, community, religion, ethnic group, socioeconomic group, or country.[12] The loyalties are not always obvious, but they are there. These loyalties are subtle but powerful determinants of one's personal case. They often lead to in-groups and out-groups. The *in-group* is the group you identify with, and the *out-group* is "the other"—those people on the "other side of the river" who do not share your goals, your values, or your territorial space.

In a corporate context where a company has just acquired another company, it will undoubtedly take some time to merge the cultures, values, and habits of the two groups as people's loyalties and habits keep them attached to the old ways. From my experience with mergers, even the dominant group—the company that conducted the merger or takeover—is inclined to treat the people in the acquired company as "the other," acting in ways that diminish the knowledge and contribution of the people in the acquired company. They are treated as the conquered.

I once consulted to a company to get the five key divisions working together on behalf of the corporate mission. Every general manager understood the mission and espoused a commitment to honoring the mission, but they acted in ways that undermined the mission by perpetuating organizational silos. They refused to share resources and collaborate on projects, and in subtle ways they disparaged the CEO and the other general managers. Their actions seemed to suggest that they considered the protection of their respective divisions to be more important than the values of collaboration on behalf of shared goals and objectives. Their silo mentality, with its accompanying loyalties and attachments, took some time to break down and refashion into a corporate mind-set that valued the sharing of resources, working across boundaries, and joint problem solving.

Even those who seek to provide responsible leadership can easily find themselves bewildered and confused in regard to the right course of action when their group loyalties cloud their capacity to think clearly about alternative strategies. I suggest this is what happened with Saigo. His loyalties to the samurai code, his feudal lord, and his clan in Satsuma strongly influenced his actions and led him to lose sight of the greater good.

In identifying first and foremost with his clan and region, Saigo was subject to being influenced by the forces, concerns, and longings of his group. The ability to transcend one's immediate faction is hard, particularly when the group has unresolved issues in its past. This was so for Saigo's group. In chapter 5 on the transition challenge, I discussed the incident in which Lord Hisamitsu's samurai killed some insolent Englishmen for refusing to bow as the lord and his entourage were traveling through the countryside. Hisamitsu was Saigo's master—his daimyo. The incident led the British navy to retaliate and attack Saigo's home city of Kagoshima, burning much of it to the ground.

Given the humiliation that the people of Kagoshima felt at the hands of the British, combined with the general feelings of anxiety surrounding Japan's transition, the anger simmered for more than a decade. It was never resolved. Into this explosive dynamic walked Saigo. Rather than quell the rage, he exacerbated it, as the people now felt that they had someone who could lead them into battle, and win, just as the great Saigo had done years earlier when he overthrew the mighty Tokugawa shogunate. The pressure was on Saigo to "lead the way," and, unfortunately, he succumbed to the people's pleas to take them into battle and right the wrongs of recent years. The people were in "fight mode" and needed a heroic warrior at the helm. Saigo was seduced to assume that role.

In the realm of leadership, one's loyalties and affiliations constrain the choices that one makes and the actions that one takes. In many ways loyalties are like a spider web that trap you and limit your options. If your faction is a part of the problem and the people need to shift their values, practices, and priorities, it is hard to challenge them to change as the people might think you are betraying them. Not only is it difficult to challenge your own group, but the temptation is often there to embody their concerns, defend their immediate interest at the expense of progress for the larger system, and take on the task of fighting their battles—as Saigo did. Of course, loyalties are not negative by any means, because they produce an identity and association with a team, community, or enterprise. The problem for leaders is when their loyalties impede their capacity to challenge their own faction, transcend group boundaries, and act for the collective good. The ability to detect the pull, even the seductive power, of one's loyalties and affiliations, can help leaders slow down and reorient themselves to the principal challenge and the real work of progress.

Detect the people's reality— stay grounded and wander

Leaders need to constantly examine to what degree their interventions—their actions, words, and presence—are useful in keeping the people focused on the principal challenge. To ascertain how the people were coping, Odin would regularly wander in disguise among the people, visit them in their homes, drink with them in their taverns, and observe them in their work. Likewise, leaders must regularly wander the community or enterprise to detect whether the people are making adjustments or avoiding reality and persisting in their old habits.

What the leader must do is seek to answer the questions "What is going on in the system that I did not see from my normal vantage point?" "Are there any tasks that are deficient or defective?" "How have I, from my lofty perch, misread what is going on?" And, "Since I last looked, how have things changed? Are there any new threats or opportunities? And, what realities are the people avoiding?"

In wandering in disguise, Odin was able to access information that would normally not be available when he was present with all the power and celebrity that came with being god of the gods. Likewise, when authority figures show up and expect the people to talk forthrightly and honestly about their concerns, given dominance–submission dynamics and the fear people have if they say the "wrong" thing, it is difficult to get an accurate read on what is happening and how people are responding. Leaders must, therefore, develop their own form of disguise to enable them to better access valid data. By *disguise*, I do not mean a wig and a false beard but a way to diminish the effect of one's role and power so that information coming from the people is not subject to distortion.

Part of the disguise process includes disguising one's power and authority so that it does not intimidate people. This includes relating to the people at their level and in their environment, thus allowing the leader to see the world through the vantage point of the people. For example, Beverly Hall, the superintendent of education in Atlanta, Georgia, goes into the home of a different family every month for a "fireside chat" about the problems and concerns families have about schools in Atlanta. She explained to me how in a recent visit she went into the home of a Vietnamese refugee family and was joined by four other families. These people had never been visited by a superintendent before and felt greatly honored to have her in their home. Essentially, her purpose in visiting families in the comfort of their homes is (1) to detect whether her interventions are having an effect on the education of children, as manifest by anecdotal comments by parents, and (2) to discover "what's missing" in the realm of her leadership that she now needs to start providing.

Although formal reports can provide data on events and developments in the field, as Hall found, there is no substitute to being in the homes of real parents, sensing real emotions, and hearing from their mouths their real fears and hopes regarding their children. Simply to experience the ambiance of the environments where the children come from is informative. Indeed, wandering, when done with purpose and with a degree of disguise, allows the leader to learn about the contextual nature of problems and the specifics of the environment, in a way that statistics and reports can never provide.

To ascertain the people's reality and to find out how they were coping, Gandhi crisscrossed all of India and visited with the peasants. Although everyone knew Gandhi, he disguised his power by wearing the loincloth of a peasant. Nehru wrote of Gandhi's wandering and his commitment to connect to the people and learn about the problems from their vantage point:

> He took each province by turn and visited every district and almost every town of any consequence, as well as remote rural areas. Everywhere he attracted enormous crowds. . . . In this manner he got to know every bit of the vast country from the north to the far south, from the eastern mountains to the western sea. I do not think any other human being has ever traveled about India as much as he had done. In the past there were great wanderers who were continually on the move, pilgrim souls with the wanderer lust. But their means of locomotion were slow, and a lifetime of wandering could hardly compete with a year by railway and motor car, but he did not confuse himself to them; he tramped also. In this way he gathered his unique knowledge of India and her people, and in this way also scores of millions saw him and came in personal touch with him.[13]

As Gandhi knew, the leader must be able to hear the conversations of ordinary people and appreciate their concerns and dreams. Without such an appreciation, leadership is reduced to salesmanship—the art of convincing others what is in their best interest—without even knowing what their interests really are.

It is particularly important for a leader to connect with the most disenfranchised of groups within the organization, community, or nation, and listen to those who are normally never listened to. It is easy for leaders to get preoccupied with attending to their most powerful or demanding constituents and neglect connecting to those whose voices are suppressed, ignored, or marginalized. Using the metaphor of the pebble tossed in a pond, if the ripples of your interventions are not reaching the people who really need your help and support, then you probably are failing in the exercise of real leadership.

For example, in the United States, and certainly in my country, Australia, a lot of people have failed to provide leadership that made a difference for indigenous communities, such as Native Americans or Aborigines. Few people have worked with them to help them face the maintenance challenge of preserving vital aspects of their culture and identity. And few people have supported them in the development challenge of fostering latent capabilities to deal with the complexities of the modern world. The wandering and listening work of leadership for marginalized groups and communities, sadly, is often neglected.

To his credit, in July 1999, President Bill Clinton made a historic trip to the Pine Ridge Indian reservation in South Dakota. This was the place where the massacre of three hundred Sioux Indians took place in 1876—specifically in an area known as Wounded Knee. Also, two FBI agents were killed there in 1973 during a three-month period of major social and political unrest. Pine Ridge is one of the most destitute places in the United States, and acts of violence are a regular occurrence. Clinton toured the area and met with local members of the community and heard about the plight of the people. What is disturbing is that he was the first U.S. president since Franklin Roosevelt in 1936 to visit an Indian reservation.

Of course, leadership is not just about wandering among the most marginalized, it also includes gathering data on what is going well. Accessing data on the people's gains and successes is just as important. For example, rather than foment a war, had Saigo wandered more among the people, the peasants and merchants in particular, he might have realized that many of them were thrilled with their new freedoms. They were no longer beholden to a feudal lord, nor did they have to worry about being beheaded by an insulted samurai. They could now go to schools, open businesses, and pursue careers that were formerly off-limits. Not all of Japan was suffering from the pangs of transition, and Saigo, therefore, needed to hear the voices of a broader spectrum of society.

Popular notions of leadership highlight the importance of vision as a motivating tool in moving people from A to B. Vision is important. As Solomon said, "When there is no vision, the people perish."[14] But, in the context of real leadership, the vision of a country or any enterprise must, at a profound level, be connected to the realities and aspirations of all the people and the various factions of the system. Sometimes the realities and the aspirations of the people shift, and sometimes people are left out, therefore modifications in vision and strategy need to be made. As Heifetz and Sinder aptly put it, "a vision has to have accuracy and not just imagination and appeal."[15] When no one is wandering, listening, and connecting, then it is difficult to ascertain who is progressing and who is being left behind, and to ensure that the vision has appeal to all.

Leadership in such a setting becomes a hit-or-miss activity—a game of luck. When the people believe that leadership is something that someone is doing *to* them, and not *with* them, then they will become suspicious and resentful. Those on the margins who feel invisible or neglected may become cynical and bitter. Invariably, in such situations that bitterness can be played out in violent behavior, as happened at Wounded Knee, or subtle forms of sabotage, as happens in corporations by marginalized employees every day. As the mythological Odin's lifelong quest for wisdom represents, given the constant threats, dangers, and opportunities that arise in all groups and enterprises, the leader can never do enough wandering, questioning, and listening to ascertain how the people are coping.

Detect when to move to the side

If you are honest and take responsibility for yourself as an instrument of power, a time may come when what is required to exercise real leadership is to get out of the way. In other words, you get to a point where you cannot do any more than what you have already done, and someone else must now step forward and assume responsibility. You may have exhausted your repertoire of leadership strategies, or, as often happens, your personal case may have become so rigid and inflexible that it now slows the group down considerably. When you feel like no more options are available or that your personal case has become an impediment, then it is probably time to move to the side, change your role, or retire to the farm.

Understandably, it is often hard to move aside and retire to the farm. Saigo, upon quitting his position as a cabinet member in the emperor's government, returned to his farm in Satsuma. He had already made a significant contribution to his country, and now he wanted to raise pigs and chickens. Unfortunately Saigo was not able to stay at home and simply farm. He had to launch a civil war. If he had stayed at home, he might actually have been a more powerful voice of constructive provocation to the government, and helped to ensure the process of the country's transition was paced at a rate the people could tolerate, particularly for the samurai. On the farm he would have had the time to think, write, and design occasional interventions, without the burden and limitations of being a formal authority figure.

In 1900, the great woman's right activist, Susan B. Anthony, retired honorably from her role as president of the National American Women Suffrage Association (NAWSA), the organization that she had started

with Elizabeth Cady Stanton more than three decades earlier for the purpose of getting American women the right to vote. She told her beloved
members and colleagues, "I am not retiring now because I feel unable,
mentally or physically, to do the necessary work, but because I wish to
see the organization in the hands of those who are to have its management in the future. I want to see you all at work, while I am alive, so I
can scold you if you do not do it well."[16]

Singapore's Lee Kuan Yew also knew the importance of moving to
the sidelines. He had been the prime minister of Singapore for thirty-one
years when he resigned at the age of sixty-seven in 1990. During my interview with Lee, he explained the dilemma he faced of staying on in
power or moving aside:

> My simple calculation was thus: Let me carry on for another five
> years. . . . What does it prove? That I'm vigorous? That I'm still
> agile? That I can still get things done? So what! . . . Or should I
> get out, allow the system to loosen up, get the new leader ap-
> proved, reconfigure the government, reconfigure the driving seat
> and help them so that there is no crashing of gears? [For the first
> choice,] I've only proved that I'm still healthy. [For the second
> choice,] I have done immense benefit to the country, to the gov-
> ernment, and to myself, that I've got a government in place that
> can do without me. [The new leaders] were dealing with a
> younger generation, a changing environment, and changing tech-
> nology. It has to be different. Let's say I had hung on for another
> ten years. It would have been a disaster.[17]

When Lee announced that he was resigning, there were no street
demonstrations calling for him to remain. And, certainly there had never
been any demonstrations demanding that he leave. It really was not a
surprise to the people that he was stepping to the side, because all along
he had indicated that he had no intention of being an old decrepit ruler
who could not let go of his power. Lee had done his work, and the people respected his decision to resign. He had nurtured capable, committed
men and women to provide leadership in all aspects of government operations. It was an extraordinarily smooth transition. Lee remained in
the background to further mentor and advise the new team when
needed. "I was able to help my successor get a grip on his job and succeed,"
Lee said, and "that would be my final contribution to Singapore."[18]

The people of the United States did not want their first president,
George Washington, to return to his farm. They wanted him to continue
in the role as president, with some wanting him to be their king. In order

not to promote an unhealthy dependency on himself, Washington refused to continue in office, and, as he finished up second term, he wrote a wonderful and provocative letter to the American people that became known as "Washington's Farewell Address." In the letter, he spoke to the values of the newly created United States and how those values and principles needed to be abided by and respected if the country was to survive. He urged "Northern and Southern, Atlantic and Western, to properly estimate the value of your national union." He shared with the people his insights and learnings born of ten years as a general in the War of Independence and eight years as the first president of the country. Clearly, he realized that the nation could be distracted by his retirement, as the people had known no other president besides him. He used this opportunity of moving aside to make a unique and important intervention that could put the "spotlight" on the ideals he stood for and not himself as a person.[19]

The lesson from Susan B. Anthony, Lee Kuan Yew, and George Washington is, rather than tenaciously hold onto power, to aid and support the development of leadership throughout the group or enterprise, a leader must be very careful not to perpetuate the myth that one is irreplaceable. When powerful people refuse to get out of the way, the group's capacity to face and resolve its problems is significantly diminished. And, when leaders do move aside, they need to do so graciously and ensure that their departure does not become a distraction for the group. If the group's dependency needs are so strong and the people are excessively anxious, the group might be reluctant to see their leader depart. They might clamor and scream for him or her to stay just a while longer. They might even fight to ensure that that happens. These longings of the group can be very seductive and trigger all sorts of sensations in their personal case. The wise and responsible leader steadily prepares the group for his or her eventual departure and is able to walk away even when the people are saying, "Please, don't leave us." Ideally, a leader should enter high office with an eye on his or her succession, even if they are at the peak of their performance.

The challenge, however, is to know *when* to move aside. I suggest that to make an informed choice (versus being pushed out), one needs to examine four critical factors: the context, one's personal capacity, one's passion, and the possibility of a new role.

In looking at the context, one needs to ascertain to what degree has the context shifted and a new challenge is before the group. One might not resonate with the group's interests and concerns as one did in the past. New leadership might be needed that can be more sensitive to the aspirations of the people and better connect to their reality.

Second, one needs to examine one's personal capacity—skills, abilities, and health—to ascertain if one "has what it takes" to continue to make the desired contribution. Each of the challenges presented in this book poses a capacity challenge for the one who seeks to lead. Leadership is demanding and tiring work, so when a leader begins to notice that he or she is "slipping up" and making too many errors in the realm of diagnosis and intervention, it is probably a signal that it might be time to move on.

Third, if one's passion for the work of leadership has waned, then it may not be in the best interest of the group to be hanging around—in a position of significant authority at least—even if the people adore you. The exercise of leadership is a not a trivial matter. If you start something but your interest and passion begin to peter out, then the adaptive problems for which leadership is needed might actually get worse. Passion is an important element in the realm of real leadership. If you are not passionate about making things better in your local school, enterprise, or community, then you should probably not seek to be the primary actor in the process of leadership and consider moving to the side.

Finally, a leader should realize that there is always the possibility of reconfiguring one's role. One can be a coach and mentor to others, and can speak out from the sidelines as appropriate to call attention to the dangers ahead. When the sprightly eighty-year-old Susan B. Anthony retired as head of the national women's organization she had built, she told the group, "I have constantly been saying to myself, 'Let go, let go, let go!' I am now going to let go of the machinery, but not the spiritual part. I expect to do more for woman suffrage in the next days than ever before."[20] Indeed, the "spiritual part," that part of the work that is connected to the higher purpose of improving the human condition, must be attended to by all of us—and we must welcome the contribution of those individuals, young and old, who are willing to stand and be counted and provide whatever they can in the way of real leadership to further the work of progress.

A Final Note

Thomas Carlyle once wrote, "The history of the world is but the biography of great men."[21] I think Carlyle should have said, "The history of the world is but the biography of foolish men." The history of the world is riddled with counterfeit leadership *and*, thank goodness, sporadic bouts of real leadership provided by ordinary but courageous men *and* women.

Real leadership is challenging. Anyone who tries to lead will inevitably falter, undoubtedly many times, as one must manage one's personal case (have one eye inward) and manage the adaptive work of the group (have one eye outward). Given the burden, demands, and opportunities of leadership, I have used the mythical Odin to serve as a metaphor throughout this book to remind us that even a god, with all his power and authority, needs to pursue wisdom to lessen the impact of his foolishness, reduce his mistakes, and increase his capacity to be effective in the face of complex and demanding challenges. To help in that process, I have presented a model for diagnosis (a way of seeing) and a model of intervention (a way of mobilizing) that will assist leaders to foster behavior and values that actually benefit organizations and society in the context of the six common challenges—activist, development, transition, maintenance, creative, and crisis.

Fundamentally, the exercise of real leadership begins with an existential declaration that one does care enough to be responsible for the well-being and success of the team, enterprise, or community, even though such work might be burdensome, confusing, and, at times, dangerous. But with wisdom, persistence, and the right tools, one can succeed. South Africa's first black president, Nelson Mandela, wrote of the spirit of being a real and responsible leader:

> I have walked that long road to freedom. I have tried not to falter; I have made missteps along the way. But I have discovered the secret that after climbing a great hill, one only finds that there are more hills to climb. I have taken a moment here to rest, to steal a view of the glorious vista that surrounds me, to look back on the distance I have come. But I can rest only for a moment, for with freedom comes responsibilities, and I dare not linger, for my long walk is not yet ended.[22]

I agree with Mandela—with freedom comes responsibilities. Without people taking responsibility for their predicament and providing the necessary leadership interventions, the enterprise or community is in danger from counterproductive dynamics from within—such as deceit, politics, and self-interest—or powerful forces from without—such as new and more nimble competitors, an unbridled free market, or blatantly hostile groups be they terrorists or invading armies. The key to progress on our shared adaptive challenges can be found in the recognition that leadership itself must become the perturbing force that prods people to face reality far more deliberately and efficiently than the "natural" forces of politics, environmental change, passive evolution, or even the "hidden hand" of the marketplace. While the practice of real leadership, at times, can be onerous, it can also be exhilarating and extremely rewarding.

REAL LEADERSHIP FOR TAKING RESPONSIBILITY FOR YOURSELF AS AN INSTRUMENT OF POWER

- Use partners to detect what's missing due to your blind spots.
- Detect when you are crusading versus leading.
- Detect when your factional loyalties are impeding the adaptive work.
- Detect the people's reality—stay grounded and wander.
- Detect when to move to the side.

Notes

Introduction

1. See John Lukacs, *Five Days in London, May 1940* (New Haven, CT: Yale University Press, 1999). This is an excellent account of the brilliant leadership of Churchill at the beginning of World War II.
2. See Victor Wallace Germains, *The Tragedy of Winston Churchill* (London: Hurt & Blackett, 1931); and Geoffrey Penn, *Fisher, Churchill and the Dardanelles* (London: Cooper, 1999).
3. Charles Lucier, Rob Schuyt, and Eric Spiegel, "CEO Succession 2002: Deliver or Depart," *Strategy & Business* (Summer 2003).
4. Lucier et al., "CEO Succession 2002."
5. Rakesh Khurana, *Searching for a Corporate Savior: The Irrational Quest for Charismatic CEOs* (Princeton, NJ: Princeton University Press, 2002).
6. V. H. Vroom and A. G. Jago, *Leadership and Decision Making* (Pittsburgh, PA: University of Pittsburgh Press, 1973).
7. Ronald Heifetz and Riley Sinder, "Political Leadership: Managing the Public's Problem Solving," in *The Power of Public Ideas*, ed. Robert Reich (Cambridge, MA: Harvard University Press, 1990), 179–203. For a more detailed presentation of this model, see Ronald Heifetz, *Leadership without Easy Answers* (Cambridge, MA: Belknap Press of Harvard University Press, 1994).

Chapter 1: Odin, Enron, and the Apes

1. See Carlos Ghosn, *Shift: Inside Nissan's Historical Revival* (New York: Currency Doubleday, 2005).
2. Ghosn, *Shift*, 97.
3. Riley Sinder and Dean Williams, "Employee Needs," in *Clinical Laboratory Management in the 21st Century*, ed. Lynne S. Garcia (Washington, D.C.: ASM Press, 2004), 211–224.
4. Andy Orchard, *Dictionary of Norse Myth and Legend* (London: Cassell, 1997).
5. Victor Rydberg, *Teutonic Mythology* (London: Schonenschein, 1891), 491.
6. Patricia Terry, trans., *Poems of the Elder Edda* (Philadelphia: University of Pennsylvania Press, 1990).
7. Richard E. Neustadt, *Presidential Power: The Politics of Leadership* (New York: Wiley, 1960), 9.
8. Robert Sternberg, *Wisdom, Intelligence, and Creativity Synthesized* (Cambridge: Cambridge University Press, 2003), 152.
9. Robert Sternberg and Victor Vroom, "The Person versus the Situation in Leadership," *Leadership Quarterly* 13 (2002): 306.
10. *Webster's New World College Dictionary,* 4th ed. (California: IDG Books Worldwide, 2000).

11. *American Heritage College Dictionary*, 4th ed. (New York: Delta, 2001).
12. Jacob Grimm, *German Mythology*, trans. Vivian Bird (Washington: Scott-Townsend, 1997).
13. Leon Goldensohn, *The Nuremberg Interviews*, ed. Robert Gellately (New York: Knopf, 2004).
14. George B. Schaller, *The Mountain Gorilla: Ecology and Behavior* (Chicago: University of Chicago Press, 1963), 241.
15. Frans de Waal, "Conflict as Negotiation in Great Ape Societies," in *Great Ape Societies*, ed. William McGrew, Linda Marchant, and Toshida Nishida (Cambridge: Cambridge University Press, 1996), 166.
16. Jane Goodall, *The Chimpanzees of Gombe: Patterns of Behavior* (Cambridge, MA: Belknap Press of Harvard University Press, 1986).
17. See Diane McGuinness, ed., *Dominance, Aggression and War* (New York: Paragon House, 1988).
18. Felicia Pratto, Jim Sidanius, Lisa M. Stallworth, and Bertram F. Malle, "Social Dominance Orientation: A Personality Variable Predicting Social and Political Attitudes," *Journal of Personality and Social Psychology* 67, no. 4 (October 1994): 741–763; see also Jim Sidanius, Felicia Pratto, and Lawrence Bobo, "Social Dominance Orientation and the Political Psychology of Gender: A Case of Invariance?" *Journal of Personality and Social Psychology* 67, no. 6 (December 1994): 998–1011.
19. David C. McClelland, *Power: The Inner Experience* (New York: Irvington, 1975).
20. For the story of David Hornbeck, see "The Toughest Job in America," *The Merrow Report* (PBS Television, April 2000), available at www.pbs.org/merrow/tv/transcripts/tough.pdf (accessed April 2, 2005).
21. *The Merrow Report*, "School Crusade: A Tale of Urban School Reform" (PBS Television, September 1997). For program transcript, go to www.pbs.org/merrow/tv/transcripts/sc_dream.pdf (accessed April 2, 2005).
22. "School Crusade."
23. "School Crusade."
24. Jolley Bruce Christman and Amy Rhodes, *Civic Engagement and Urban School Improvement* (Philadelphia: Consortium for Policy Research in Education, University of Pennsylvania, 2002), 57.
25. Tom Corcoran and Jolley Bruce Christman, *The Limitations and Contradictions of Systemic Reform: The Philadelphia Story* (Philadelphia: Consortium for Policy Research in Education, University of Pennsylvania, 2002), 22.
26. Corcoran and Christman, *The Limitations and Contradictions of Systemic Reform*, 22.
27. Corcoran and Christman, *The Limitations and Contradictions of Systemic Reform*, 33.
28. Cole Maxwell, *The Journey of Burke and Wills* (Sydney: Hamlyn, 1977), 9.
29. Maxwell, *The Journey of Burke and Wills*, 73.
30. Maxwell, *The Journey of Burke and Wills*, 73.
31. Maxwell, *The Journey of Burke and Wills*, 73.
32. See National Library of Australia archive at www.nla.gov.au/epubs/wills/pages/intro02.html (accessed May 13, 2005).

33. For an interesting presentation of the ignorance, arrogance, and insensitivity of Burke and his team in their relationship with the Aborigines, see Sarah Murgatroyd, *The Dig Tree: The Story of Burke and Wills* (Melbourne: Text, 2002).
34. For a description of life during the Cultural Revolution, see Feng Jicai, *Ten Years of Madness: Oral Histories of China's Cultural Revolution* (San Francisco: China Books and Periodicals, 1997).

Chapter 2: Diagnostic Work

1. Louis V. Gerstner, *Who Says Elephants Can't Dance? Inside IBM's Historic Turnaround* (New York: HarperBusiness, 2002).
2. Arthur Hawkey, *Bligh's Other Mutiny* (London: Angus & Robertson, 1975), 74.
3. Hawkey, *Bligh's Other Mutiny*, 75.
4. Hawkey, *Bligh's Other Mutiny*, 76.
5. H. V. Evatt, *Rum Rebellion: A Study of the Overthrow of Governor Bligh by John Macarthur and the New South Wales Corps* (Sydney: Angus & Robertson, 1955).
6. Hawkey, *Bligh's Other Mutiny*, 112.
7. Hawkey, *Bligh's Other Mutiny*, 112.
8. Robert McNamara and James G. Blight, *Wilson's Ghost: Reducing the Risk of Conflict, Killing, and Catastrophe in the 21st Century* (New York: Public Affairs, 2001), 67.
9. McNamara and Blight, *Wilson's Ghost*, 70.
10. Gerstner, *Who Says Elephants Can't Dance?* 69.
11. Gerstner, *Who Says Elephants Can't Dance?* 71.
12. Gerstner, *Who Says Elephants Can't Dance?* 190–191.
13. Ronald Heifetz, *Leadership without Easy Answers* (Cambridge, MA: Belknap Press of Harvard University Press, 1994), 88–100.

Chapter 3: The Activist Challenge

1. Chris Argyris calls the process of learning about underlying assumptions "double loop learning." He presents an excellent model on how to raise difficult issues and get people to confront problematic concerns. See Chris Argyris, *Knowledge for Action: A Guide to Overcoming Barriers to Organizational Change* (San Francisco: Jossey-Bass, 1993).
2. Linda Ford, *The Suffragette Militancy of the National Woman's Party, 1912–1920* (Lanham, MD: University Press of America, 1991), 137.
3. Ford, *The Suffragette Militancy*, 158.
4. Ford, *The Suffragette Militancy*, 243.
5. *New York Times*, March 15, 1920.
6. Martin Luther King, *I Have a Dream—40th Anniversary Edition: Writings and Speeches That Changed the World*, ed. James M. Washington (San Francisco: HarperCollins, 1992). For a discussion of the impact that the speech had on people, see Drew D. Hansen, *The Dream: Martin Luther King, Jr., and the Speech That Inspired the Nation* (New York: Ecco, 2003).

7. Margaret Rioch, "All We Like Sheep," in *Group Relations Reader*, ed. Arthur D. Colman and W. Harold Bexton (Sausalito, CA: GREX, 1975).

8. S. R. Bakshi, *Gandhi and the Salt Satyagraha* (Malayattor, Keralla: Vishwa-vidya, 1981), 40.

9. Bakshi, *Gandhi*, 50.

10. Bakshi, *Gandhi*, 43.

11. Bakshi, *Gandhi*, 47.

12. Bakshi, *Gandhi*, 49.

13. Ford, *The Suffragette Militancy*, 240.

14. Yuri Orlov, *Dangerous Thoughts: Memoirs of a Russian Life* (New York: Morrow, 1991), 164.

15. Riley M. Sinder, Ronald Heifetz, Hugh O'Doherty, Dean Williams, and Sousan Abadian, "The Empirical Evidence for the Distinction between Leadership and Authority," unpublished manuscript, 2004.

16. For the story of Meena and RAWA, see Moldy Ermachild Chavis, *Meena, the Hero of Afghanistan: The Martyr Who Founded RAWA* (New York: St. Martin's, 1973).

17. Anne Brodsky, *With All Our Strength: The Revolutionary Association of the Women of Afghanistan* (New York: Routledge, 2003).

18. Ronald A. Heifetz and Marty Linsky, *Leadership on the Line: Staying Alive through the Dangers of Leading* (Boston: Harvard Business School Press, 2002).

19. Interview with Jose Ramos-Horta by Dean Williams and David Gergen, Center for Public Leadership, February 28, 2001.

20. Interview with Ramos-Horta.

21. For a presentation on the importance of partners to help you "stay alive," see Heifetz and Linsky, *Leadership on the Line*.

22. B. R. Nanda, P. C. Joshi, and Raj Krishna, *Gandhi and Nehru* (Delhi: Oxford University Press, 1979), 2.

23. Nanda et al., *Gandhi and Nehru*, 2.

24. Nanda et al., *Gandhi and Nehru*, 29.

25. Nanda et al., *Gandhi and Nehru*, 5.

26. Nanda et al., *Gandhi and Nehru*, 7.

27. Stanley Wolpert, *Gandhi's Passion: The Life and Legacy of Mahatma Gandhi* (New York: Oxford University Press), 181.

28. Erik Erikson, *Gandhi's Truth: On the Origins of Militant Nonviolence* (New York: Norton, 1969), 265.

Chapter 4: The Development Challenge

1. Stephen Jay Gould, *The Structure of Evolutionary Theory* (Cambridge, MA: Belknap Press of Harvard University Press, 2002).

2. "A. T. Kearny Globalization Index," *Foreign Policy* (May–June 2005).

3. Lee Kuan Yew, *The Singapore Story: Memoirs of Lee Kuan Yew* (New York: Prentice Hall, 1998), 306.

4. Speech given by Lee Kuan Yew at Singapore management conference, December 8, 1963.

5. For a discussion on the concept of the holding environment as it pertains to leadership, see Ronald A. Heifetz, *Leadership without Easy Answers* (Cambridge, MA: Belknap Press of Harvard University Press, 1994).

6. For example, this value of the common good could be found in the Confucian heritage of the Singapore Chinese.
7. In social psychology, what I call the "mantle of the ideal" is similar to *prototypicality*. The most prototypical member of the group is the one who is assigned the role of the chief authority figure because he or she best represents the norms of the group. See M. A. Hogg and D. van Knippenberg, "Social Identity and Leadership Processes in Groups," in *Advances in Experimental Social Psychology*, ed. M. P. Zanna (San Diego, CA: Academic Press, 2003), vol. 35: 1–52.
8. Lee Kuan Yew, *From Third World to First: The Singapore Story 1965–2000* (New York: Prentice Hall, 2000), 158.
9. Yew, *From Third World to First*, 158.
10. Yew, *From Third World to First*, 170.
11. Yew, *From Third World to First*, 166.
12. Tom Corcoran and Jolley Bruce Christman, *The Limitations and Contradictions of Systemic Reform: The Philadelphia Story* (Philadelphia: Consortium for Policy Research in Education, University of Pennsylvania, 2002), 22.
13. Thomas Corcoran and Ellen Foley, "The Promise and Challenge of School Reform," in *Research Perspectives on School Reform: Lessons from the Annenberg Challenge* (Providence, RI: Annenberg Institute, 2003), 116.
14. Corcoran and Foley, "The Promise and Challenge of School Reform," 114.
15. Lee, *From Third World to First*, 146.
16. Lee, *From Third World to First*, 147–148.
17. Interview with Malcolm Fraser, conducted by Dean Williams and Ronald Heifetz, Center for Public Leadership, Kennedy School of Government, Harvard University, April 6, 2001.
18. Interview with Fraser.
19. Malcolm Fraser, Rerum Novarum Lecture, given to the Catholic Commission for Justice, Development and Peace, July 17, 2001.
20. Fraser, Rerum Novarum Lecture.
21. Fraser, Rerum Novarum Lecture.
22. *Fortune*, February 7, 2005.
23. Interview with Willem Roelandts by Patrick Murphy, director of the Institute for Ethical Business Worldwide, University of Notre Dame, spring 2003.
24. Lee, *From Third World to First*, 96.
25. Lee, *From Third World to First*, 106.
26. Lee, *From Third World to First*, 104.
27. Lee, *From Third World to First*, 96–97.
28. Lee, *From Third World to First*, 105.
29. Lee, *From Third World to First*, 102.
30. Lee, *From Third World to First*, 106.

Chapter 5: The Transition Challenge

1. *American Heritage Dictionary*, 4th ed. (Boston: Houghton Mifflin, 2002).
2. Yukichi Fukuzawa, *The Autobiography of Yukichi Fukuzawa*, trans. Eiichi Kiyooka (New York: Colombia University Press, 1966), 131.
3. Louis V. Gerstner, *Who Says Elephants Can't Dance? Inside IBM's Historic Turnaround* (New York: HarperBusiness, 2002), 78.

4. Gerstner, *Who Says Elephants Can't Dance?* 205.

5. Gerstner, *Who Says Elephants Can't Dance?* 205.

6. Gerstner, *Who Says Elephants Can't Dance?* 207.

7. Donald Keene, *Emperor of Japan: Meiji and His World, 1852–1912* (New York: Columbia University Press, 2002), 141.

8. Keene, *Emperor of Japan.*

9. This counterproductive behavior has been researched and written about by Chris Argyris. See Chris Argyris, *On Organizational Learning* (San Francisco: Jossey-Bass, 1992). For a discussion on work avoidance mechanisms in society, see Ronald A. Heifetz, *Leadership without Easy Answers* (Cambridge, MA: Belknap Press of Harvard University Press, 1994).

10. Keene, *Emperor of Japan*, 200.

11. Keene, *Emperor of Japan*, 279.

12. Gerstner, *Who Says Elephants Can't Dance?* 206.

13. Li Zhisui, *The Private Life of Chairman Mao: The Memoirs of Mao's Personal Physician*, trans. Tai Hung-Chao (New York: Random House, 1994), 277.

14. Li, *The Private Life of Chairman Mao*, 278.

15. Li, *The Private Life of Chairman Mao*, 279.

16. Li, *The Private Life of Chairman Mao*, 279.

17. For further elaboration on this point, see Ronald Heifetz and Marty Linsky, *Leadership on the Line: Staying Alive through the Dangers of Leading* (Boston: Harvard Business School Press, 2004).

18. Gerstner, *Who Says Elephants Can't Dance?* 214.

19. Kenneth B. Pyle, *The New Generation in Meiji Japan: Problems of Cultural Identity, 1885–1895* (Stanford, CA: Stanford University Press, 1969), 20.

20. Pyle, *The New Generation in Meiji Japan*, 7.

21. Pyle, *The New Generation in Meiji Japan*, 174.

22. Pyle, *The New Generation in Meiji Japan*, 193.

23. Pyle, *The New Generation in Meiji Japan*, 198.

24. Pyle, *The New Generation in Meiji Japan*, 198.

25. Old Testament, Exodus chapter 32, verse 1: "When the people saw that Moses delayed to come down from the mountain, the people gathered themselves together to Aaron, and said to him, 'Make us gods who shall go before us; as for this Moses, the man who brought us up out of Egypt, we do not know what has become of him.'"

26. Pyle, *The New Generation in Meiji Japan*, 215.

27. Gerstner, *Who Says Elephants Can't Dance?* 188.

Chapter 6: The Maintenance Challenge

1. Words of Willem Roelandts, CEO of Xilinx, in Harvard Business School Case, "Xilinx, Inc.," 2003.

2. Wayne Cascio and Peg Wynn, "Managing a Downsizing Process," *Human Resource Management* (Winter 2004): 425–436.

3. Lee Hsien Loong, speech at National Day Rally, Singapore, August 22, 2004.

4. Weary Dunlop, *The War Diaries of Weary Dunlop*, foreword by Laurens van der Post (Melbourne: Nelson, 1986), viii.

5. Dunlop, *The War Diaries of Weary Dunlop*, x.
6. Margaret Geddes, *Remembering Weary* (Ringwood: Viking, 1996), 125.
7. Geddes, *Remembering Weary*, 86.
8. Moses Maimonides, *Epistles of Maimonides: Crisis and Leadership*, trans. Abraham Halkin (Philadelphia: Jewish Publication Society, 1993).
9. *Boston Globe*, June 15, 2002, A11.
10. *Columbia Accident Investigation Board Report*, August 2003, vol. 1: 195; available at www.caib.us (accessed May 10, 2005).
11. *Columbia*, 180.
12. *Columbia*, 187.
13. *Columbia*, 187.
14. Geddes, *Remembering Weary*, 103.
15. Matt Dickinson, *Everest: Triumph and Tragedy in the World's Highest Peak* (New York: HarperCollins, 2002), 26.
16. "Testimony of John Werner before the Senate Judiciary Committee," July 18, 2001, available at www.fas.org/irp/congress/2001_hr/071801_werner.html (accessed April 22, 2005).
17. Deb Reichmann, "FBI Haunted by Blunders in Big Cases," *Time*, July 2, 2002.
18. "Statement of Colleen M. Rowley, FBI Special Agent and Minneapolis Chief Division Counsel before the Senate Committee on the Judiciary, Oversight Hearing on Counterterrorism," June 6, 2002, available at www.fas.org/irp/congress/2002_hr/060602rowley.html (accessed April 22, 2005).
19. Geddes, *Remembering Weary*, 108.

Chapter 7: The Creative Challenge

1. Rollo May, *Courage to Create* (New York: Bantam Books, 1975), 22. May got the term from George Bernard Shaw, who used it in a letter to the great violinist Jascha Heifetz.
2. Rasmus Anderson, *Norse Mythology* (Chicago: Griggs, 1879), 222.
3. Anderson, *Norse Mythology*, 222.
4. See James Madison, *Notes of Debates in the Federal Convention of 1787* (Athens: Ohio State University Press, 1966); and Jeffrey St. John, *Constitutional Journal: A Correspondent's Report from the Convention of 1787* (Ottawa, IL: Jameson, 1987).
5. Washington to John Jay, August 1, 1786, in *The Writings of George Washington from the Original Manuscript Sources, 1745–1791*, ed. John C. Fitzpatrick (Washington, D.C.: U.S. Government Printing Office, 1931–1944).
6. William Carr, *The Oldest Delegate: Franklin in the Constitutional Convention* (Newark: University of Delaware Press, 1990), 20.
7. St. John, *Constitutional Journal*, 21.
8. St. John, *Constitutional Journal*, 20.
9. Madison, *Notes*, 210.
10. Madison, *Notes*, 209–211.
11. Madison, *Notes*, 226–228.
12. Madison, *Notes*, 659.

13. James Madison to Thomas Jefferson, October 24, 1787, in *The Papers of James Madison*, ed. William T. Hutchinson et al., vol. 1, chap. 17, document 22 (Chicago: University of Chicago Press, 1962).
14. Madison to Jefferson, 56.
15. Kurt Lewin, *A Dynamic Theory of Personality* (New York: McGraw-Hill, 1935).
16. Stanley J. Linden, ed., *The Alchemy Reader: From Hermes Trimestigus to Isaac Newton* (Cambridge: Cambridge University Press, 2003).
17. Carr, *The Oldest Delegate*, 67.
18. Carr, *The Oldest Delegate*, 58.
19. Carr, *The Oldest Delegate*, 160.
20. For a description of Argyris's dialogue methodology, see Chris Argyris, *Reasoning, Learning and Action* (San Francisco: Jossey-Bass, 1984).
21. Charles Murray and Catherine Bly Cox, *Apollo: Race to the Moon* (New York: Simon & Schuster, 1989), prologue.
22. Murray and Cox, *Apollo*, 100.
23. Murray and Cox, *Apollo*, 105.
24. Carr, *The Oldest Delegate,* 71.
25. This comment was relayed to the author in an interview with the manager.
26. Carr, *The Oldest Delegate*, 49.
27. Carr, *The Oldest Delegate*, 160.
28. Training and development journal, July 1998.

Chapter 8: The Crisis Challenge

1. The details of this case are taken from Linda Hill and Suzy Wetlaufer, "Leadership When There Is No One to Ask: An Interview with Eni's Franco Bernabe," in *Harvard Business Review on Crisis Management* (Boston: Harvard Business School Press, 2000).
2. David Usburne, *The Independent* (London), September 12, 1999.
3. Interview with Alexander, recorded in Don Greenless and Robert Garran, *Deliverance: The Inside Story of East Timor's Fight for Freedom* (Sydney: Allen & Unwin, 2002), 245.
4. Greenlees and Garren, *Deliverance,* 246.
5. President Bill Clinton, "Statement on East Timor," September 9, 1999.
6. Nicholas J. Wheeler and Tim Dunne, "East Timor and the New Humanitarian Interventionism," *International Affairs* 77, no. 4 (2001): 805–827.
7. Greenlees and Garran, *Deliverance*, 151.
8. See Greenlees and Garran, *Deliverance*, 153.
9. Hill and Wetlaufer, "Leadership When There Is No One to Ask," 191.
10. Hill and Wetlaufer, "Leadership When There Is No One to Ask," 175.
11. Arthur M. Schlesinger, *Coming of the New Deal* (Boston: Houghton Mifflin, 1958), 3.
12. Schlesinger, *Coming of the New Deal*, 1.
13. Schlesinger, *Coming of the New Deal*, 2.
14. Schlesinger, *Coming of the New Deal*, 6.
15. Schlesinger, *Coming of the New Deal*, 5.

16. Schlesinger, *Coming of the New Deal*, 13.
17. Schlesinger, *Coming of the New Deal*, 12.
18. Schlesinger, *Coming of the New Deal*, 13.
19. Schlesinger, *Coming of the New Deal*, 13.
20. Hill and Wetlaufer, "Leadership When There Is No One to Ask."
21. The speech is presented in Nelson Mandela, *Nelson Mandela Speaks: Forging a Democratic, Nonracial South Africa*, ed. Steve Clark (New York: Pathfinder, 1993).
22. Geoffrey Penn, *Fisher, Churchill and the Dardenelles* (London: Cooper, 1999), 170.
23. Penn, *Fisher*, 170.
24. Winston Churchill, *The World Crisis, 1911–1915* (New York: Scribner's, n.d.), 273.
25. Presentation at the fortieth anniversary of the Cuban Missile Crisis, John F. Kennedy School of Government, Harvard University, October 18, 2002.
26. Robert McNamara and James Blight, *Wilson's Ghost: Reducing the Risk of Conflict, Killing, and Catastrophe in the 21st Century* (New York: Public Affairs, 2001), 72.

Chapter 9: Leading in Multiple Challenges

1. T. E. Lawrence, *Seven Pillars of Wisdom* (London: Book Club Associates, 1974), 23.
2. Lawrence, *Seven Pillars of Wisdom*, 114.
3. Lawrence, *Seven Pillars of Wisdom*, 98.
4. Lawrence, *Seven Pillars of Wisdom*, 102.
5. John Mack, *Prince of Our Disorder: The Life of T. E. Lawrence* (Boston: Little, Brown, 1976), 198.
6. Mack, *Prince of Our Disorder*, 206.
7. Mack, *Prince of Our Disorder*, 207.
8. See Mack, *Prince of Our Disorder*, 202. Mack quotes from Pierce Joyce, transcript of BBC broadcast of July 14, 1941.
9. T. E. Lawrence, "Letter to V. W. Richards, July 15, 1918," in *The Letters of T. E. Lawrence*, ed. David Garnett (London: Cape, 1938), 244.
10. Lowell Thomas, *With Lawrence in Arabia* (New York: Century, 1924), 245.
11. Mack, *Prince of Our Disorder*, 207.
12. B. H. Liddell Hart, in *T. E. Lawrence by His Friends*, ed. A. W. Lawrence (London: Cape, 1937), 183.
13. W. F. Stirling, in *T. E. Lawrence by His Friends*, 155.
14. Stirling, in *T. E. Lawrence by His Friends*, 155.
15. Wavell, in *T. E. Lawrence by His Friends*, 149.
16. W. H. Brooks, in *T. E. Lawrence by His Friends*, 167.
17. Irving Howe, *A World More Attractive* (New York: Horizon, 1963), 11.
18. Hart, in *T. E. Lawrence by His Friends*, 183.
19. T. E. Lawrence, "June 26, 1923," in *The Letters of T. E. Lawrence*.
20. S. C. Rolls, in *T. E. Lawrence by His Friends*, 169.
21. Lawrence, *Seven Pillars of Wisdom*, 253.
22. Lawrence, *Seven Pillars of Wisdom*, 254.
23. Lawrence, *Seven Pillars of Wisdom*, 255.

24. Lawrence, *Seven Pillars of Wisdom*, 256.
25. Lawrence, *Seven Pillars of Wisdom*, 181.
26. Lawrence, *Seven Pillars of Wisdom*, 181.
27. Lawrence, *Seven Pillars of Wisdom*, 23.
28. Mack, *Prince of Our Disorder*, 245.
29. Between September 11, 1919, and October 1920, he published twelve articles in the *London Times* and other newspapers.
30. *London Times*, July 22, 1920.
31. Churchill, in *T. E. Lawrence by His Friends*, 193.
32. Churchill, in *T. E. Lawrence by His Friends*, 194.
33. Churchill, in *T. E. Lawrence by His Friends*, 195.
34. Churchill, in *T. E. Lawrence by His Friends*, 195.
35. Churchill, in *T. E. Lawrence by His Friends*, 195.
36. Letter to Robert Graves, 1927, in T. E. Lawrence Collection, Houghton Library, Harvard University.
37. *The Observer*, August 8, 1920; see *Letters of T. E. Lawrence*, 11.
38. Stephen E. Tabachnick and Christopher Matheson, *Images of Lawrence* (London: Cape, 1988), 137.
39. *The Sunday Times*, August 22, 1920; see *Letters of T. E. Lawrence*, 315.
40. Mack, *Prince of Our Disorder*, 249.
41. Churchill, in *T. E. Lawrence by His Friends*, 197.
42. Churchill, in *T. E. Lawrence by His Friends*, 198.
43. T. E. Lawrence, *Lawrence to His Biographers, Robert Graves and Liddell Hart* (London: Cassell, 1963), 12.
44. Aaron Kleiman, "Lawrence as Bureaucrat," in *The T. E. Lawrence Puzzle*, ed. Stephen E. Tabachnick (Athens: University of Georgia Press, 1984), 243–268.
45. Maxwell Coote, in *T. E. Lawrence by His Friends*, 233.
46. Churchill, in *T. E. Lawrence by His Friends*, 198.
47. Lawrence, *Lawrence to His Biographers*, 15.
48. C. S. Jarvis, *Arab Command: The Biography of Lieutenant Colonel F. G. Peake Pasha* (London: Hutchinson, 1942), 85.
49. Aaron Kleiman, "Lawrence as Bureaucrat," in *The T. E. Lawrence Puzzle*, 259.
50. St. John Philby, *Arabian Days: An Autobiography* (London: Hale, 1948).
51. Churchill, in *T. E. Lawrence by His Friends*, 199.
52. A constitution and Feisal, as constitutional monarch, were put to a referendum in Iraq. Millions of Iraqis voted for the first time in their lives and approved the constitution and elected Feisal as king. Feisal became king August 23, 1921.
53. Lawrence, *The Letters of T. E. Lawrence*, 334.
54. Mack, *Prince of Our Disorder*, 250.
55. Letter from Lawrence to Charlotte Shaw, October 18, 1927, cited in Mack, *Prince of Our Disorders*, 302.
56. Tabachnick and Matheson, *Images of Lawrence*, 134.
57. Churchill, in *T. E. Lawrence by His Friends*, 199.
58. Lawrence, *Seven Pillars of Wisdom*, 114.
59. For an explanation of this concept, see Ronald Heifetz and Marty Linsky, *Leadership on the Line: Staying Alive through the Dangers of Leading* (Cambridge, MA: Harvard University Press, 2002).
60. *The Letters of T. E. Lawrence*, 691.

Chapter 10: Odin, the Samurai, and You

1. Rasmus B. Anderson, *Norse Mythology* (Chicago: S.C. Griggs, 1879).
2. *Fortune*, June 9, 1997.
3. T. E. Lawrence, *Seven Pillars of Wisdom*, 580.
4. For a discussion of the need for achievement, the need for power, and the need for affiliation as they pertain to management, see the classic *Harvard Business Review* article by McClelland: David McClelland and David Burnham, "Power Is the Great Motivator," *Harvard Business Review* (January–February 1995).
5. Fidel Ramos, interview with Dean Williams at Center for Public Leadership, Kennedy School of Government, Harvard University, April 26, 2001.
6. For information on Saigo Takamori, see Augustus Mounsey, *The Satsuma Rebellion: An Episode of Modern Japanese History* (London: Murray, 1879), 45; *Mark Ravina: The Life and Battles of Saigo Takamori* (Hoboken, NJ: Wiley, 2004).
7. *Tokyo Times*, March 3, 1877.
8. *Nichi Nichi Shibun*, February 26, 1877, and reported in English in the *Tokio Times*, March 3, 1877.
9. August Kreys, *The First Crusade: The Accounts of Eye Witnesses and Participants* (Gloucester, MA: Smith, 1958).
10. For a more detailed discussion of the notion "what's precious and what's expendable," see Ronald Heifetz and Marty Linsky, *Leadership on the Line: Staying Alive through the Dangers of Leading* (Cambridge, MA: Harvard University Press, 2002).
11. T. E. Lawrence, *Seven Pillars of Wisdom* (London: Book Club Associates, 1974), 29.
12. For more discussion on loyalties, see Heifetz and Linsky, *Leadership on the Line.*
13. Jawaharlal Nehru, *An Autobiography* (London: Lane), 142.
14. Proverbs 29: 18.
15. Ronald Heifetz and Riley Sinder, "Political Leadership: Managing the Public's Problem Solving," in *The Power of Public Ideas*, ed. Robert Reich (Cambridge, MA: Harvard University Press, 1990).
16. Lynn Sherr, *Failure Is Impossible: Susan B. Anthony in Her Own Words* (New York: Times Books, 1999), 319.
17. Interview with Lee Kuan Yew, conducted by Dean Williams, Ronald Heifetz, David Gergen, and John Thomas at the Center for Public Leadership, Kennedy School of Government, Harvard University, October 17, 2000.
18. Lee Kuan Yew, *From Third World to First: The Singapore Story 1965–2000* (New York: Prentice Hall, 2000), 672.
19. George Washington, *Washington's Farewell Address to the People of the United States* (Washington, D.C.: U.S. Government Printing Office, 2004).
20. Sherr, *Failure Is Impossible,* 320.
21. Thomas Carlyle, *On Heroes, Hero Worship and the Heroic in History* (London: Ward, Lock, 1900).
22. Nelson Mandela, *Long Walk to Freedom* (New York: Little, Brown, 1994), 625.

Index

About the Author

Dean Williams was born and raised in Geelong, Australia. He is on the faculty of Harvard University's Kennedy School of Government, and is located at the Center for Public Leadership. He earned his doctorate and master's degrees from Harvard University, where he studied organizational change and leadership development. As a young man, he was an auto-worker on the factory floor of Ford Motor Company in Australia.

Williams has consulted to governments and businesses around the world on leadership and change. His interests in the study of organizations, leadership, human development, and social change have taken him into some of the leading companies in Japan, the United States, Southeast Asia, Europe, and Australia, as well as into the jungles of Borneo to study indigenous tribal peoples.

He was formerly a senior consultant in the Singapore government's National Productivity Board, an adviser to the Sultanate of Brunei on civil service reform, the head of organizational development for Suncorp, Australia, and the adviser to the Queensland Department of Education on reforming the state educational system. At Harvard, he has been the co-director of the Superintendents Leadership Program, a two-year leadership development initiative for superintendents of education from large urban districts in the United States. He has also worked extensively with business, political, and community leaders in Barranqvilla, Colombia in developing a strong civil society through the exercise of real leadership. At Harvard's Center for Public Leadership, he directs the World Leaders Archive Project, which entails interviewing presidents and prime ministers (past and present) about the leadership challenges they have faced.

Williams has partnered with the World Bank on various projects and initiatives. He has provided training, coaching, and support to the leadership of East Timor, before and after independence, and is currently an adviser to the president of Madagascar and working with his cabinet to generate rapid development. Some of the companies he has consulted to include the New York Times, M&T Bank, Dun and Bradstreet, Energex Australia, Royal Air Cambodge, the National Computer Board of Singapore, and Raychem Asia.

He is president of the Great You Yang Leadership Society. He can be reached at dean_williams@harvard.edu.

About Berrett-Koehler Publishers

Berrett-Koehler is an independent publisher dedicated to an ambitious mission: Creating a World that Works for All.

We believe that to truly create a better world, action is needed at all levels—individual, organizational, and societal. At the individual level, our publications help people align their lives and work with their deepest values. At the organizational level, our publications promote progressive leadership and management practices, socially responsible approaches to business, and humane and effective organizations. At the societal level, our publications advance social and economic justice, shared prosperity, sustainable development, and new solutions to national and global issues.

We publish groundbreaking books focused on each of these levels. To further advance our commitment to positive change at the societal level, we have recently expanded our line of books in this area and are calling this expanded line "BK Currents."

A major theme of our publications is "Opening Up New Space." They challenge conventional thinking, introduce new points of view, and offer new alternatives for change. Their common quest is changing the underlying beliefs, mindsets, institutions, and structures that keep generating the same cycles of problems, no matter who our leaders are or what improvement programs we adopt.

We strive to practice what we preach—to operate our publishing company in line with the ideas in our books. At the core of our approach is *stewardship*, which we define as a deep sense of responsibility to administer the company for the benefit of all of our "stakeholder" groups: authors, customers, employees, investors, service providers, and the communities and environment around us. We seek to establish a partnering relationship with each stakeholder that is open, equitable, and collaborative.

We are gratified that thousands of readers, authors, and other friends of the company consider themselves to be part of the "BK Community." We hope that you, too, will join our community and connect with us through the ways described on our website at www.bkconnection.com.

Be Connected

Visit Our Website

Go to www.bkconnection.com to read exclusive previews and excerpts of new books, find detailed information on all Berrett-Koehler titles and authors, browse subject-area libraries of books, and get special discounts.

Subscribe to Our Free E-Newsletter

Be the first to hear about new publications, special discount offers, exclusive articles, news about bestsellers, and more! Get on the list for our free e-newsletter by going to www.bkconnection.com.

Participate in the Discussion

To see what others are saying about our books and post your own thoughts, check out our blogs at www.bkblogs.com.

Get Quantity Discounts

Berrett-Koehler books are available at quantity discounts for orders of ten or more copies. Please call us toll-free at (800) 929-2929 or email us at bkp.orders@aidcvt.com.

Host a Reading Group

For tips on how to form and carry on a book reading group in your workplace or community, see our website at www.bkconnection.com.

Join the BK Community

Thousands of readers of our books have become part of the "BK Community" by participating in events featuring our authors, reviewing draft manuscripts of forthcoming books, spreading the word about their favorite books, and supporting our publishing program in other ways. If you would like to join the BK Community, please contact us at bkcommunity@bkpub.com.